THE FATHERS OF THE CHURCH

A NEW TRANSLATION

VOLUME 98

THE FATHERS OF THE CHURCH

A NEW TRANSLATION

EDITORIAL BOARD

Thomas P. Halton
The Catholic University of America
Editorial Director

Elizabeth Clark
Duke University

Robert D. Sider
Dickinson College

Joseph T. Lienhard, S.J.
Fordham University

Michael Slusser
Duquesne University

Frank A.C. Mantello
The Catholic University of America

Cynthia White
The University of Arizona

Kathleen McVey
Princeton Theological Seminary

Robin Darling Young
The Catholic University of America

David J. McGonagle
Director
The Catholic University of America Press

FORMER EDITORIAL DIRECTORS

Ludwig Schopp, Roy J. Deferrari, Bernard M. Peebles,
Hermigild Dressler, O.F.M.

Edward Strickland
Cornelia Horn
Staff Editors

ST. GREGORY THAUMATURGUS
LIFE AND WORKS

Translated by
MICHAEL SLUSSER
Duquesne University

THE CATHOLIC UNIVERSITY OF AMERICA PRESS
Washington, D.C.

Copyright © 1998
THE CATHOLIC UNIVERSITY OF AMERICA PRESS
All rights reserved
Printed in the United States of America

The paper used in this publication meets the minimum requirements of the
American National Standards for Information Science—
Permanence of Paper for Printed Library Materials, ANSI Z39.48–1984.
∞

LIBRARY OF CONGRESS CATALOGING-IN-PUBLICATION DATA
Gregory, Thaumaturgus, Saint, ca. 213–ca. 270.
[Works, English, 1998]
Works of St. Gregory Thaumaturgus / St. Gregory Thaumaturgus,
Life of Gregory the Wonderworker / St. Gregory of Nyssa : translated
by Michael Slusser.
p.   cm. — (The Fathers of the Church : v. 98)
Translated from the Greek and Syriac.
Includes bibliographical references and index.
I. Slusser, Michael, 1940–   . II. Gregory of Nyssa, Saint, ca.
335–ca. 394. De vita Gregorii Thaumaturgi. English. III. Title.
IV. Title: Life of Gregory the Wonderworker. V. Series.
BR60.F3G74   1998
[BR60.A62]
270 s—dc21
[270.1]
97-49907
ISBN 0-8132-0098-9 (alk. paper)
ISBN 978-0-8132-2765-8 (pbk.)

To Sebastian Brock, Maurice Wiles, and Henri Crouzel
in gratitude for their example and encouragement

CONTENTS

Acknowledgments	ix
Abbreviations	xi
Bibliography	xiii
Introduction	1

ST. GREGORY OF NYSSA

Life of Gregory the Wonderworker	41

ST. GREGORY THAUMATURGUS

Address of Thanksgiving to Origen	91
Metaphrase on the Ecclesiastes of Solomon	127
Canonical Epistle	147
To Theopompus, on the Impassibility and Passibility of God	152
To Philagrius [Evagrius], on Consubstantiality	174

ASSOCIATED WORKS

To Tatian, on the Soul	181
Glossary on Ezekiel	187
Letter of Origen to Gregory	190

INDICES

General Index	195
Index of Holy Scripture	198

ACKNOWLEDGMENTS

It was an article by Henri Crouzel, S.J., which first directed my attention to St. Gregory Thaumaturgus. Fascinated by Gregory's *To Theopompus on the Impassibility and Passibility of God*, I wrote my doctoral dissertation under the supervision of Professor Maurice F. Wiles on the second-century precedents for Gregory's startling assertions about the suffering of God. Sebastian Brock recommended me to write the article on Gregory for the *Theologische Realenzyklopädie*, a task which led me to undertake the present volume. All three scholars continued to encourage me in my scholarly work and in my studies of Gregory in particular. Without Sebastian Brock's assistance on the translation of *To Theopompus*, I doubt if I would have had the courage to publish the rest of these translations.

In addition, Michel Van Esbroeck, of the Société des Bollandistes, gave me a valuable preview of some of his unpublished studies of the complex literary materials which have Gregory at their center. Raymond Van Dam, of the Department of History at the University of Michigan, helped my study of St. Gregory of Nyssa's *Life of Gregory the Wonderworker* not only by his own penetrating study of that text but by reviewing my translation of it and making a number of valuable suggestions.

Finally, I wish to express my thanks to my colleagues at Duquesne University for their support, and to the university for a Presidential Scholarship Grant to facilitate completion of this project.

ABBREVIATIONS

CPG Clavis Patrum Graecorum. Vol. 1. Edited by M. Geerard. Turnhout: Brepols, 1974.

GCS Die griechischen christlichen Schriftsteller der ersten drei Jahrhunderte. Leipzig, 1897–.

LXX Septuagint

PG   Patrologiae cursus completus: Series graeca. 161 volumes. Edited by J.-P. Migne. Paris, 1857–66.

PL   Patrologiae cursus completus: Series latina. 221 volumes. Edited by J.-P. Migne. Paris, 1878–90.

PWS Paulys Real-encyclopädie der classischen Altertumswissenschaft. Edited by August Friedrich von Pauly and Georg Wissowa. Stuttgart : A. Druckenmüller, 1893–1963.

SC   Sources chrétiennes. Edited by H. de Lubac and J. Daniélou. Paris, 1942–.

Abbreviations of Classical and Patristic texts follow H. G. Liddell, R. Scott, and H. S. Jones, eds., *A Greek-English Lexicon* (Oxford, 1940) and G. W. H. Lampe, ed., *A Patristic Greek Lexicon* (Oxford, 1961).

BIBLIOGRAPHY

Texts and Translations of Gregory Thaumaturgus

Gregory Thaumaturgus. *Discorso a Origene: Una pagina di pedagogia cristiana.* Edited and translated by Eugenio Marotta. Rome: Città Nuova Editrice, 1983.
———. *Oratio prosphonetica ac panegyrica in Origenem. Dankrede an Origenes.* Translated by Peter Guyot, introduced by Richard Klein. Fontes Christiani, vol. 24. Freiburg: Herder, 1996.
———. *Remerciement à Origène, suivi de la Lettre d'Origène à Grégoire.* Edited and translated by Henri Crouzel. Sources chrétiennes, vol. 148. Paris: Cerf, 1969.
Holl, Karl. *Fragmente vornicänischer Kirchenväter aus der Sacra Parallela.* Texte und Untersuchungen, vol. 20.2, 156–60, nos. 396–408. Leipzig: Hinrichs, 1899.
Koetschau, Paul. *Des Gregorios Thaumaturgos Dankrede an Origenes.* Sammlung ausgewählter kirchen- und dogmengeschichtlicher Quellenschriften, vol. 9. Freiburg-im-Breisgau/Leipzig: J. C. B. Mohr (Paul Siebeck), 1894.
Lagarde, Paul de. *Analecta syriaca.* Leipzig: G. B. Teubner, 1858.
Metcalfe, W. *Gregory Thaumaturgus. Address to Origen.* Translations of Christian Literature, Series 1. London: Society for Promoting Christian Knowledge, 1920.
Pitra, Johannes Baptista. *Analecta sacra spicilegio Solesmensi,* vol. 4, 100–20, 360–76. Paris: Ex publico Galliarum typographeo, 1883.
———. *Iuris ecclesiastici graecorum historia et monumenta,* vol. 1. Rome: Typis Collegii Urbani, 1864.
Salmond, S. D. F. trans., *The Works of Gregory Thaumaturgus, Dionysius of Alexandria, and Archelaus,* Ante-Nicene Christian Library 20 (Edinburgh: T. & T. Clark, 1871).

Texts and Translations of Gregory of Nyssa's *Vita*

Aitzetmüller, R. *Mihanovic Homiliar.* Graz: Akademische Druck- und Verlagsanstalt, 1957.
Gregory of Nyssa. *De Vita Gregorii Thaumaturgi.* Edited by Gunther Heil. *Gregorii Nysseni Sermones,* pt. 2. Gregorii Nysseni Opera, vol. 10.1. Leiden: E. J. Brill, 1990.

Scholarship Related to the
Life and Works of Gregory Thaumaturgus

Abramowski, Luise. "Das Bekenntnis des Gregor Thaumaturgus bei Gregor von Nyssa und das Problem seiner Echtheit." *Zeitschrift für Kirchengeschichte* 87 (1976): 145–66.

———. "Die Schrift Gregors des Lehrers 'Ad Theopompum' und Philoxenus von Mabbug." *Zeitschrift für Kirchengeschichte* 89 (1978): 273–90.

Aranda, Antonio. "El Espíritu Santo en la 'Esposición de Fe' de S. Gregorio Taumaturgo." *Scripta Theologica* 10 (1978): 373–407.

Baethgen, Friedrich. Review of *Gregorius Thaumaturgus* by Victor Ryssel. *Göttingische gelehrte Anzeigen*, pt. 44 (1880): 1389–408.

Bernardi, Jean. *La prédication des Pères Cappadociens*. Paris: Presses Universitaires de France, 1968.

Bonwetsch, Nathaniel. "Gregor der Wunderthäter." *Reallexikon für protestantische Theologie und Kirche* 7 (1899): 155–59.

Brock, Sebastian. "Clavis Patrum Graecorum III, 7717." *Journal of Theological Studies*, n.s. 32 (1981): 176–78.

Brinkmann, August. "Gregor des Thaumaturgen Panegyricus auf Origenes." *Rheinisches Museum für Philologie* 3, ser. 56 (1901): 55–76.

Caro, Roberto. *La Homilética Mariana Griega en el Siglo V*, vol. 2. Dayton: Marian Library Studies (n.s. 4), 1972.

Caspari, C. P. *Alte und neue Quellen zur Geschichte des Taufsymbols und der Glaubensregel*. Christiania: Malling, 1879.

———. "Nogle nye kirkehistoriske Anecdota II: Et Gregorius Thaumaturgus tillagt Fragment met Begyndelsen: 'Af det, der finder Sted hos os, kan man erkjende det, der er over os.'" *Theologiske Tidsskrift for den evangelisk-lutherske Kirche i Norge*, ser. 2.8 (1882): 53–59.

Cavallera, Ferdinand. "Origène éducateur." *Bulletin de littérature ecclésiastique* 44 (1943): 61–75.

Chadwick, Henry. *The Sentences of Sextus. A Contribution to the History of Early Christian Ethics*. Cambridge: University Press, 1959.

Crouzel, Henri. "La cristologia in Gregorio Taumaturgo." *Gregorianum* 61 (1980): 745–55.

———. "L'École d'Origène à Césarée. Postscriptum à une édition de Grégoire le Thaumaturge." *Bulletin de littérature ecclésiastique* 71 (1970): 15–27.

———. "Faut-il voir trois personnages en Grégoire le Thaumaturge?" *Gregorianum* 60 (1979): 287–319.

———. "Grégoire le Thaumaturge et le Dialogue avec Élien." *Recherches de science religieuse* 51 (1963): 422–31.

———. "Grégoire le Thaumaturge (saint)." *Dictionnaire de spiritualité ascétique et mystique* 6 (1967): 1014–20.

——— (with Heinzgerd Brakmann). "Gregor I (Gregor der Wunder-

täter)." *Reallexikon für Antike und Christentum* 12 (1983): 779-83.
———. "La Passion de l'Impassible: un essai apologétique et polémique du IIIᵉ siècle." In *L'homme devant Dieu: Mélanges offerts au Père Henri de Lubac*, vol. 1, 269-79. Paris: Aubier, 1963.
———. "Le 'Remerciement à Origène' de saint Grégoire le Thaumaturge. Son contenu doctrinal." *Sciences ecclésiastiques* 16 (1964): 59-91.
Dölger, Franz Joseph. "Sonnenscheibe und Sonnenstrahl in der Logos- und Geisttheologie des Gregorios Thaumaturgos." *Antike und Christentum* 6.1 (1940): 74-75.
Dräseke, Johannes. "Adnotatiuncula Laodicena." *Zeitschrift für wissenschaftliche Theologie* 39 (1896): 436-42.
———. "Der Brief des Origenes an Gregorios von Neocäsarea." *Jahrbücher für protestantische Theologie* 7 (1881): 102-26.
———. *Gesammelte patristische Untersuchungen*. Altona and Leipzig: A. C. Reher, 1889.
———. "Johannes Zonaras' Commentar zum kanonischen Brief des Gregorios von Neocäsarea." *Zeitschrift für wissenschaftliche Theologie* 37 (1894): 246-60.
———. "Der kanonische Brief des Gregorios von Neocäsarea." *Jahrbücher für protestantische Theologie* 7 (1881): 724-56.
———. "Über den Verfasser der Schrift Πρὸς Εὐάγριον μόναχον περὶ θεότητος." *Jahrbücher für protestantische Theologie* 8 (1882): 343-84, 553-68.
———. "Über die dem Gregorios Thaumaturgos zugeschriebenen vier Homilien und den ΧΡΙΣΤΟΣ ΠΑΣΧΩΝ." *Jahrbücher für protestantische Theologie* 10 (1884): 657-704.
———. "Zu Euagrios Pontikos." *Zeitschrift für wissenschaftliche Theologie* 37 (1894): 125-37.
———. "Zu Gregorios Thaumaturgos." *Zeitschrift für wissenschaftliche Theologie* 39 (1896): 166-69.
———. "Zu Gregorios' von Neocäsarea Schrift 'Über die Seele.'" *Zeitschrift für wissenschaftliche Theologie* 44 (1901): 87-100.
———. "Zu Victor Ryssel's 'Gregorius Thaumaturgus.'" *Jahrbücher für protestantische Theologie* 9 (1883): 634-40.
———. "Zu Victor Ryssel's Schrift." *Jahrbücher für protestantische Theologie* 7 (1881): 379-84.
Einarson, B. "On a Supposed Pseudo-Aristotelian Treatise on the Soul." *Classical Philology* 28 (1933): 129-30.
Esbroeck, Michel van. "The *Credo* of Gregory the Wonderworker and its Influence through Three Centuries." In *Studia Patristica* 19, edited by Elizabeth A. Livingstone, 255-66. Leuven: Peeters, 1989.
———. "Fragments sahidiques du Panégyrique de Grégoire le Thaumaturge par Grégoire de Nysse." *Orientalia Lovaniensia Periodica* 6-7 (1975-76): 555-68.
———. "Sur quatre traités attribuées à Grégoire, et leur contexte mar-

cellien (CPG 3222, 1781 et 1787)." In *Studien zu Gregor von Nyssa und der christlichen Spätantike*, edited by Hubertus R. Drobner and Christoph Klock, 3–15. Leiden: E. J. Brill, 1990.

———. "Témoignages littéraires sur les sépultures de saint Grégoire l'Illuminateur." *Analecta Bollandiana* 89 (1971): 387–417.

Fouskas, Konstantinos M. Γρηγόριος ὁ Νεοκαισαρείας 'Επίσκοπος ὁ θαυματουργός *(Ca. 211/3–270/5)*. Athens: University of Athens Press, 1969.

Froidevaux, Léon. "Le Symbole de saint Grégoire le Thaumaturge." *Recherches de science religieuse* 19 (1929): 193–247.

Gätje, H. *Studien zur Überlieferung der aristotelischen Psychologie im Islam.* Heidelberg: C. Winter, 1971.

Godet, P. "Grégoire de Néocésarée, ou Le Thaumaturge." *Dictionnaire de Théologie Catholique* 6 (1920): 1844–47.

Graf, G. "Zwei dogmatische Florilegien der Kopten." *Orientalia Christiana Periodica* 3 (1937): 49–77, 345–402.

Haidacher, Sebastian. "Zu den Homilien des Gregorius von Antiocheia und des Gregorius Thaumaturgus." *Zeitschrift für katholische Theologie* 25 (1901): 367–69.

Halkin, François. "La prétendu Passion inédite de s. Alexandre de Thessalonique." *La nouvelle Clio* 6 (1954): 70–72.

Heather, Peter, and John Matthews. *The Goths in the Fourth Century.* Liverpool: Liverpool University Press, 1991.

Hilgenfeld, Adolph. Review of *Des Gregorios Thaumaturgos Dankrede an Origenes* by Paul Koetschau. *Berliner philologische Wochenschrift* 15 (1895): 808–10.

Hilgenfeld, Heinrich. "Die Vita Gregor's des Wunderthäters und die syrischen Acta Martyrum et Sanctorum." *Zeitschrift für wissenschaftliche Theologie* 41 (1898): 452–56.

Janim, Raymond. "Gregorio Taumaturgo." *Bibliotheca Sanctorum*, vol. 7, 214–17. Rome: Città Nuova Editrice, 1966.

Jarick, John. *Gregory Thaumaturgos' Paraphrase of Ecclesiastes.* Septuagint and Cognate Studies, vol. 29. Atlanta: Scholars Press 1990.

Jouassard, G. "Marie à travers la patristique." In *Maria: Études sur la sainte vierge*, vol. 1. Paris: Beauchesne, 1949.

Jugie, Martin. "Les homélies mariales attribuées à saint Grégoire le Thaumaturge." *Analecta Bollandiana* 43 (1925): 86–95.

Junod, Eric. "Particularités de la Philocalie." In *Origeniana*, edited by Henri Crouzel, Gennaro Lomiento, and Josep Rius-Camps, 186–87. Bari: Istituto di Letteratura Cristiana Antica, 1975.

Knauber, Adolf. "Das Anliegen der Schule des Origenes zu Cäsarea." *Münchener theologische Zeitschrift* 19 (1968): 182–203.

Knorr, U. W. "Gregor der Wundertäter als Missionar." *Evangelisches Missionsmagazin* 110 (1966): 70–84.

Koetschau, Paul. "Zur Lebensgeschichte Gregors des Wunderthäters." *Zeitschrift für wissenschaftliche Theologie* 41 (1898): 211–50.

Lane Fox, Robin. *Pagans and Christians.* San Francisco: Harper and Row, 1988.
Lebreton, Jules. "Le traité de l'âme de saint Grégoire le Thaumaturge." *Bulletin de littérature ecclésiastique* 8 (1906): 73–83.
MacMullen, Ramsay. *Christianizing the Roman Empire* (A.D. *100–400*). New Haven: Yale University Press, 1984.
Marotta, Eugenio. "A proposito di due passi dell' 'Orazione panegirica' di Gregorio il Taumaturgo (16,187; 18,203. Koetschau)." *Vetera Christianorum* 13 (1976): 81–86.
———. "I neologismi nell'orazione ad Origene di Gregorio il Taumaturgo." *Vetera Christianorum* 8 (1971): 241–56.
———. "I reflessi biblici nell'orazione ad Origene di Gregorio il Taumaturgo." *Vetera Christianorum* 10 (1973): 59–77.
———. Review of *Remerciement à Origène* edited by Henri Crouzel. *Vetera Christianorum* 8 (1971): 309–17.
Martin, Ch. "Note sur deux homélies attribuées à saint Grégoire le Thaumaturge." *Revue d'histoire ecclésiastique* 24 (1928): 364–73.
Mateo-Seco, Lucas F. "El cristiano ante la vida y ante la muerte: Estudio del Panegirico de Gregorio de Nisa sobre Gregorio Taumaturgo." In *The Biographical Works of Gregory of Nyssa*, edited by Andreas Spira, 197–219. Cambridge: Philadelphia Patristic Foundation, 1984.
Merino, Marcelo. "Teología y filosofía en S. Gregorio el Taumaturgo: Aspectos conceptuales en el Discurso de Agradecimiento a Orígenes." *Scripta Theologica* 17 (1985): 227–43.
Modrzejewski, Joseph. "Grégoire le Thaumaturge et le droit romain. À propos d'une édition récente." *Revue historique de droit français et étranger* 49 (1971): 313–24.
Nautin, Pierre. "Grégoire le Thaumaturge." *Dictionnaire d'histoire et de géographie ecclésiastique* 22 (1988): 39–42.
———. *Lettres et écrivains chrétiens des IIe et IIIe siècles.* Paris: Cerf, 1961.
———. *Origène, sa vie et son oeuvre.* Paris: Beauchesne, 1977.
Nestle, Eberhard. Review of *Gregorius Thaumaturgus* by Victor Ryssel. *Zeitschrift der deutschen morgenländischen Gesellschaft* 35 (1881): 784–86.
Noakes, Kenneth W. "The Metaphrase on Ecclesiastes of Gregory Thaumaturgus." *Studia Patristica* 15.1 (1984): 196–99.
Noret, J. "Fragments hagiographiques, patristiques et liturgiques de la collection Moravcsik à Budapest." *Analecta Bollandiana* 92 (1974): 349–51.
Papadopoulos, K. N. "Λειτουργικὰ σημειώματα." *Kleronomia* 12 (1980): 3–18.
Pasquali, Georgius. *Gregorii Nysseni epistulae.* Gregorii Nysseni Opera, vol. 8.2. Berlin: Apud Weidmannos, 1925.
Poncelet, Albert. "La Vie Latine de saint Grégoire le Thaumaturge." *Recherches de science religieuse* 1 (1910): 132–60, 567–69.
Refoulé, François. "La date de la lettre à Évagre." *Recherches de science religieuse* 49 (1961): 520–48.

Riedinger, Rudolf. "Das Bekenntnis des Gregor Thaumaturgus bei Sophronius von Jerusalem und Macarius von Antiocheia." *Zeitschrift für Kirchengeschichte* 92 (1981): 311–14.

Riggi, Calogero. "Elementi costitutivi della paideia nel Panegyrico del Taumaturgo." In *Crescità dell'uomo nella catechesi dei Padri (età prenicena)*, edited by Sergio Felici, 211–27. Rome: Libreria Ateneo Salesiano, 1987.

Ritter, A. M. "Gregor der Wundertäter (Thaumaturgos)." *Lexikon der christlichen Ikonographie*, edited by Wolfgang Braunfels, vol. 6, 453–54. Rome: Herder, 1974.

Ryssel, Victor. *Gregorius Thaumaturgus, Sein Leben und seine Schriften.* Leipzig: L. Fernau, 1880.

———. "Zu Gregorius Thaumaturgus." *Jahrbücher für protestantische Theologie* 7 (1881): 565–73.

———. "Eine syrische Lebensgeschichte des Gregorius Thaumaturgus." *Theologische Zeitschrift aus der Schweiz* 11 (1894): 228–54.

———. "Zwei neu aufgefundene Schriften der graeco-syrischen Literatur." *Rheinisches Museum für Philologie* 3, ser. 51 (1896): 1–20, 318–20.

Sauget, Joseph-Marie. "Deux Homéliaires Syriaques de la Bibliothèque Vaticane." *Orientalia Christiana Periodica* 27 (1961): 387–424.

Schönfeld, Moritz. "Goti." *Pauly-Wissowa Supplementband* 3, 797–845.

Simonetti, Manlio. "Gregorio Nazianzeno o Gregorio Taumaturgo?" *Rendiconti, Istituto Lombardo di scienze e lettere, Classe di lettere e scienze morali e storiche* 86 (1953): 101–17.

———. "Una nuova ipotesi su Gregorio il Taumaturgo." *Rivista di storia e letteratura religiosa* 24 (1988): 17–41.

Sinko, Thaddeus. *De traditione orationum Gregorii Nazianzeni*, pt. 1. Meletemata Patristica, vol. 2. Cracow: G. Gebethner, 1917.

Slusser, Michael. "Gregor der Wundertäter." In *Theologische Realenzyklopädie*, vol. 14, 188–91. Berlin: Walter de Gruyter, 1985.

———. "The Main Ethical Emphases in the Writings of Gregory Thaumaturgus." In *Studia Patristica*, edited by Elizabeth A. Livingstone, 357–62. Leuven: Peeters, 1997.

———. "The 'To Philagrius on Consubstantiality' of Gregory Thaumaturgus." In *Studia Patristica*, edited by Elizabeth A. Livingstone, vol. 19, 230–35. Leuven: Peeters, 1989.

Soloviev, Alexandre. "Saint Grégoire, patron de Bosnie." *Byzantion* 19 (1949): 263–79.

Telfer, William. "The Latin *Life* of St. Gregory Thaumaturgus." *Journal of Theological Studies* 31 (1930): 142–55.

———. "The Cultus of St. Gregory Thaumaturgus." *Harvard Theological Review* 29 (1936): 225–344.

Vailhé, S. "Amasea." *Dictionnaire d'histoire et de géographie ecclésiastiques*, vol. 2, 964–70. Paris: Letouzey et Ané, 1912.

Valantasis, Richard. *Spiritual Guides of the Third Century: A Semiotic Study*

of the Guide-Disciple Relationship in Christianity, Neoplatonism, Hermetism, and Gnosticism. Minneapolis: Fortress Press, 1991.
Van Dam, Raymond. "Hagiography and History: The Life of Gregory Thaumaturgus." *Classical Antiquity* 1 (1982): 272–308.
Vinel, Françoise. "La Metaphrasis in Ecclesiasten de Grégoire le Thaumaturge: entre traduction et interprétation, une explication du texte." *Lectures anciennes de la Bible.* Cahiers de Biblia Patristica, vol. 1, 191–216. Strasbourg: Centre d'Analyse et de Documentation Patristiques, 1987.
Weijenborg, Reinoldus. "De authenticitate et sensu quarundam epistularum s. Basilio Magno et Apollinario Laodiceno adscriptarum." *Antonianum* 33 (1958): 197–240, 371–414; 34 (1959): 245–98.
Weischer, Bernd Manuel. "Die Glaubenssymbole des Epiphanios von Salamis und des Gregorios Thaumaturgos im Qērellos." *Oriens Christianus* 61 (1977): 20–40.
Weymann, Carl. "Beiträge zur Geschichte der altchristlichen Literatur." *Philologus* 55 (n.s. 8) (1895): 462–73.
Whealey, A. "'To Tatian on the Soul': A Treatise from the Circle of Tatian the Syrian and Justin Martyr?" *Recherches de théologie ancienne et médiévale* 63 (1996): 136–45.
Winfield, David. "The Northern Routes across Anatolia." *Anatolian Studies* 27 (1977): 151–66.

INTRODUCTION

INTRODUCTION

St. Gregory Thaumaturgus, "the Wonderworker"

(1) The man whose life and works are the subject of this volume was a bishop in the third century. Until the early fourth century, he was known as "Gregory the Great" or (in Gregory of Nyssa's *Life* of him) "the Teacher."[1] His see was the city of Neocaesarea (modern Niksar) in the interior of Pontus, the area south of the Black Sea. Of his life not much is known, and the data which are available are the subject of some controversy, but the following brief outline is probably reasonably accurate. More details will be found in the discussion of his individual works.

(2) Born of pagan parents in Cappadocian Pontus[2] about A.D. 210–15, Gregory had a sister, whose name we do not know, and (according to Eusebius)[3] a brother named Athenodorus, who also became a bishop in Pontus. When Gregory was fourteen, his father died, but family resources enabled him to continue his education in rhetoric and also in the Latin language, the language of Roman law. When his sister went to join her husband in Palestine, Gregory accompanied her with a view to studying law at

---

1. Michel van Esbroeck, "The *Credo* of Gregory the Wonderworker and its Influence through Three Centuries," in *Studia Patristica*, volume 19, ed. Elizabeth A. Livingstone (Leuven: Peeters, 1989), 262, says, "The nickname Thaumaturgos only begins with many quotations found in the *Refutation of Chalcedon* of Timothy Aelouros before 477." Konstantinos M. Fouskas, Γρηγόριος ὁ Νεοκαισαρείας Ἐπίσκοπος ὁ θαυματουργός *(Ca. 211/3–270/5)* (Athens: University of Athens Press, 1969), 44, 105, points out that Sozomen's *Historia ecclesiastica* 7.27, says that he believed that a certain miracle (the "minor incident about the road" which starts in 940C) τεθαυματουργῆσθαι Γρηγορίῳ τῷ θαυμασίῳ, which is very close to calling him "Thaumaturgus," and Sozomen was writing before 450.

2. From the time of Trajan (107–13) until Diocletian, Pontus was administratively a part of the province of Cappadocia; see the *Oxford Classical Dictionary* under "Cappadocia" and "Pontus."

3. Eusebius, *h.e.* 6.30; see also 7.14, 28.

Berytus[4] (modern Beirut). Whether he managed to begin those studies or not, he came under the influence of the Christian theologian and philosopher Origen, and spent five years (probably 233–38) as part of his circle of students in Caesarea.[5]

(3) If he had not been baptized a Christian earlier,[6] he seems to have become one by the time he returned to Pontus and to the city of Neocaesarea. There he continued, with a few companions, to lead a retiring life, until he was pressed into service as the bishop of the Christian community at the insistence of Phaidimos, bishop of the metropolis of Cappadocian Pontus, Amaseia (modern Amasya).[7] He maintained that leadership through the persecution of Decius in 250–51 (during which he, like St. Cyprian of Carthage and St. Dionysius of Alexandria, evaded the authorities) and the incursions of Goths into the region in 257.[8] Eusebius reports his presence at a synod in Antioch in 264 to help

4. Berytus and its surrounding region were a "unique island of Roman culture in the Near East," thanks to the settlement there of demobilized Latin-speaking legionaries, starting in 15 B.C., according to Fergus Millar. He adds, "We know nothing of the formal structure of teaching there, and are hardly entitled to speak of a 'Law School.' Rather it was the wider, 'Roman' cultural setting and the possibility of finding instruction in Roman law in different 'schools' (*auditoria*) which attracted them." Fergus Millar, *The Roman Near East, 31 BC–AD 337* (Cambridge: Harvard University Press, 1993), 279–80.

5. This description of Origen's "school" is deliberately cautious; for discussion, see Adolf Knauber, "Das Anliegen der Schule des Origenes zu Cäsarea," *Münchener theologische Zeitschrift* 19 (1968): 182–203, and the reply by Henri Crouzel, "L'École d'Origène à Césarée. Postscriptum à une édition de Grégoire le Thaumaturge," *Bulletin de littérature ecclésiastique* 71 (1970): 15–27.

6. Henri Crouzel, *Origen* (San Francisco: Harper and Row, 1989), 25: "Gregory's first contact with Christianity occurred at the age of fourteen, but it is possible that he was not yet baptised when he came to Caesarea." Richard Klein, *Oratio Prosphonetica ac panegyrica in Origenem. Dankrede an Origenes*, trans. Peter Guyot, Fontes Christiani, vol. 24 (Freiburg: Herder, 1996), 8, thinks that Gregory was baptized at the end of his stay with Origen; he extends his analysis on 30–44. Fouskas, Γρηγόριος, 69–70, takes *Address* 5 to mean that Gregory was baptized at fourteen. I see no compelling reason for that conclusion, but if Gregory was baptized while in Caesarea, the fact that he does not mention it in the *Address* would suggest that the rite was considerably less significant to him than was the change in his thinking.

7. Gregory of Nyssa, in the *Life* (909BC), says that the ordination was originally carried out at a distance, and the ceremonies were supplied later.

8. The movements of the Goths into Asia in the 250's are difficult to reconstruct; here I accept the date suggested for the activity in the Pontic area by Moritz Schönfeld, "Goti," PWS, 3:804. Johannes Dräseke, "Der kanonische Brief des Gregorios von Neocäsarea," *Jahrbücher für protestantische Theologie* 7 (1881): 739–48, argues for the summer of 254.

deal with the case of Paul of Samosata,[9] but the attempts to place him at the second synod convened for the same purpose in 268 are probably mistaken.[10] The traditional date of his death is during the reign of Aurelian (270-75).[11] Gregory of Nyssa tells us that he left explicit instructions to keep his grave secret,[12] which shows at least[13] that his tomb was not a focal point of devotion in Neocaesarea.[14] An interesting and plausible expansion of the above skeletal narrative is offered by Robin Lane Fox.[15]

(4) In ancient times the fame of Gregory was spread not only by Gregory of Nyssa's Greek *Life* of him, which is translated into English in this volume, but also by translations of that *Life* into several oriental languages, and other *Lives* in Latin, Syriac, and Armenian which draw on essentially the same material as Gregory of Nyssa did. Likewise Rufinus, in his translation of Eusebius's *Historia ecclesiastica*, inserts a selection of the stories about Gregory at the end of Book 7, chapter 28.[16] There is sufficient

9. *h. e.* 7.28.1.

10. Gustave Bardy, *Paul de Samosate: Étude historique*, 2nd ed. (Louvain: Spicilegium Sacrum Lovaniense, 1929), 299, explains that if Gregory had been present at the synod of 268, he would have deserved prominent mention among the signatories to its letter (Eusebius, *h. e.* 7.30.2). Henri Crouzel, "Gregor I (Gregor der Wundertäter)," in *Reallexikon für Antike und Christentum* 12 (1983): 782, speculates that in 268 he must have been bed-ridden or already dead, but earlier, *idem*, ed., *Remerciement à Origène, suivi de la Lettre d'Origène à Grégoire*. Sources chrétiennes, vol. 148 (Paris: Cerf, 1969), 26, he accepted the traditional 270-75 estimate for the date of Gregory's death.

11. Fouskas, Γρηγόριος, 102-3 gives the references from the *Menologion* of Basil (PG 117.165AB) and Balsamon (PG 137.1237AB), and authors as early as Gerard De Vos have corrected the text of the Suidas lexikon from the impossible "Julian" to Aurelian.

12. *Life* 956A.

13. It is hard not to wonder if Nyssa, who regarded Gregory as a kind of new Moses (see *Life* 908C), was not influenced in this detail of his account by Deut 34.6: "... but no man knows the place of his [Moses'] burial to this day."

14. William Telfer, "The Cultus of St. Gregory Thaumaturgus," *Harvard Theological Review* 29 (1936): 232, makes this point, and adds that in northern Pontus "[t]he practice was already general at the beginning of the Christian era, not to bury in earth, but to cut slots or *loculi* in the horizontal (sometimes in the vertical) face of the rock, each large enough to take a human body and allow for the superposition of a stone slab, and to lay the dead in these." After a period these *loculi* were re-used for other dead (*ibid.*, 234).

15. Robin Lane Fox, *Pagans and Christians* (San Francisco: Harper and Row, 1988), 516-42.

16. The text is in the GCS *Eusebius Werke*, vol. 2, pt. 2, ed. Eduard Schwartz (Leipzig: J. C. Hinrichs, 1908), 953-56. Rufinus gives stories about the two brothers who quarreled about a lake (see the Life 925B-29A); how Gregory

4   INTRODUCTION

variation among these *Lives*[17] to discourage attempts to identify
one of them as the source of all the others, even though Gregory
of Nyssa's seems to be earliest in date. The preferred explanation nowadays is that popular traditions about Gregory in the
local church of Neocaesarea were at the basis of them all.[18] Gregory of Nyssa's family was in a position to know these traditions,
as his brother St. Basil claimed kinship with the Neocaesareans
through their grandmother St. Macrina,[19] knew the bishop of
Neocaesarea, Musonius,[20] and knew some of the same stories as
his brother, along with some ethical maxims which he attributes
to our Gregory.[21] There is consequently some chance that elements of the *Life* are based upon genuine memories handed
down in circles familiar to Gregory of Nyssa and Basil.[22]

(5) Gregory is known in modern times less for his occasional
appearances on the scene of history than for his writings, both
those which are authentic and those which have been placed

---

cleared enough ground to build a church (no exact parallel in the Life, but possibly a version of the account Gregory of Nyssa adds at its end, 956B–58C); the
stilling of the oracle (see the Life 916A–17A; but in Rufinus, this takes place in
the snowy Alps!), followed by the conversion of its priest (who later, according to
Rufinus, succeeds Gregory as bishop, while Gregory of Nyssa [948A] describes
him as having become his deacon); there is mention of the Metaphrase on Ecclesiastes and a quotation of the Creed in Latin translation.

17. Fouskas, Γρηγόριος, 60–61, provides an illuminating table of comparison.

18. This is the view of Paul Koetschau, "Zur Lebensgeschichte Gregors des
Wunderthäter," *Zeitschrift für wissenschaftliche Theologie* 41 (1898): 238, 244–48,
who notes also the mention of one Musonius by name (at 921B), and the connection between Basil and Gregory of Nyssa's family with the area and the Wonderworker himself. Fouskas, Γρηγόριος, 57, agrees with that estimate.

19. Basil, *epist.* 204.6; see earlier in the same letter, where he speaks of αἱ
σωματικαὶ οἰκειότητες ... ἡμῖν ... πρὸς ὑμᾶς.

20. Basil, *epist.* 28 and 210.

21. Basil, *de spiritu sancto* 74, and *epist.* 207.4.

22. Paul Koetschau, *Des Gregorios Thaumaturgos Dankrede an Origenes.* Sammlung ausgewählter kirchen- und dogmengeschichtlicher Quellenschriften, vol. 9
(Freiburg-im-Breisgau/Leipzig: J. C. B. Mohr (Paul Siebeck), 1894), v–vi, treats
the following items as historical: that Gregory knew Firmilian of Caesarea and
like him studied with Origen; that Gregory returned to his native country; that
he was ordained by Phaidimos of Amaseia; that he built a church which survived
an earthquake; and that he made Alexander bishop of the nearby city of Comana. Crouzel, "Gregor I," 781, takes only ordination by Phaidimos, the ordination of Alexander, Gregory's hiding during the Decian persecution, and the institution of martyr-feasts after the end of the persecution as historical events.

under his name in the hope that they might get a better hearing. The controversies surrounding issues of authenticity are complex and passionately argued, and the reader should be aware that in this volume I have taken what may be termed a "maximalist" position with regard to Gregory's writings, ascribing to him as genuine not only the *Metaphrase on Ecclesiastes* (henceforth referred to as the *Metaphrase*) and the *Canonical Epistle*, but also the *Address of Thanksgiving to Origen* (henceforth the *Address*), *To Theopompus*, and *To Philagrius*, for reasons which I shall give below. As doubtful or spurious I have included *To Tatian*, a *Glossary on Ezekiel*, and the famous *Creed*, which appears in Gregory of Nyssa's oratorical *Life* of Gregory Thaumaturgus.[23] For comparison, here are the lists of works accepted as genuine by two other modern students of Gregory: Henri Crouzel, in the introduction to his edition of the *Address*, accepts the *Address*, *Creed*, *Canonical Epistle*, *Metaphrase*, and *To Theopompus*, and questions *To Philagrius*, *To Tatian*, and the lost dialogue cited by Basil of Caesarea, *ep*. 210.[24] Constantinos Fouskas agrees with Crouzel on the first five items, but he would add *To Philagrius* to the genuine works.[25]

(6) How should the works be arranged chronologically? The *Address* should be placed at the time when Gregory left Caesarea to return to his homeland (thus in 238), and the *Canonical Epistle* after the incursion of the Goths into Pontus in 257. The other writings cannot be dated.[26]

---

23. Thus I differ from the *Clavis Patrum Graecorum* which accepts the *Creed* (with qualification) and lists *To Philagrius* among the *spuria* (CPG 1774); in addition, it leaves the *Glossary on Ezekiel* among the *spuria* of Gregory Nazianzen (CPG 3060).

24. Crouzel, *Remerciement*, 27–31; he repeats that judgment in his later article in *idem*, "Gregor I," 782–91.

25. Fouskas, Γρηγόριος, 155, 162–63, 169, 175–76, 181–82; for *To Philagrius*, see his extensive review of the question on 193–96.

26. Earlier scholars have also attempted to estimate the dates of Gregory's life. Here are a few of their chronologies: Victor Ryssel, *Gregorius Thaumaturgus, Sein Leben und seine Schriften* (Leipzig: L. Fernau, 1880): Gregory's stay with Origen in Caesarea (231–35); *Address* (239); selection as bishop (240); *Canonical Epistle* (258); death (270). Fouskas, Γρηγόριος, 120: born (211/13), came to Christianity at the death of his father (225/27), studied with Origen (231–35), *Address* and return to Neocaesarea (235), selected and ordained as bishop (237), *Canonical Epistle* (254/55), death (270/75). Fouskas also ventures dates for the other works which he recognizes as genuine: *To Theopompus* (248–50), *Metaphrase on*

(7) It is not possible here to list all the later works of other writers which were placed under Gregory's name. References to most of them can be found in the *Clavis Patrum Graecorum* 1775-94, but manuscript attributions to Gregory Thaumaturgus appear in many other places.[27] The most illuminating observations on this phenomenon have been made by Michel van Esbroeck, who shows that Gregory of Neocaesarea was adopted as a patron first by the Apollinarians at the end of the fourth century and beginning of the fifth, and then by the supporters of Zeno's *Henotikon*.[28]

(8) No manuscript collection of Gregory's writings was made in antiquity;[29] this fact has hindered the recovery and study of their text. The series *Griechische-christliche Schriftsteller der ersten Jahrhunderte*, the main corpus of critical editions of the Greek Fathers of the first three centuries, passed over Gregory (and Dionysius of Alexandria as well). Because of the complexity of the manuscript tradition, it is unlikely that a complete critical edition of Gregory's writings will be produced in the foreseeable future.

(9) Under the circumstances, we are fortunate that an attempt at a complete collection of Gregory's works was printed as early as 1604.[30] Our benefactor was Gerard De Vos, the provost

---

Ecclesiastes (256-60), *To Philagrius* (260-64), *Creed* (264-65). Crouzel in *Remerciement* estimates: birth (210/13), stay with Origen in Caesarea (231/33-38), became bishop several years before 250, died (270/75).

27. See for example those listed by J. Muyldermans, "Répertoire de pièces patristiques d'après le catalogue arménien de Venise," *Le Muséon* 47 (1934): 279, and the spells described by Heinzgerd Brakmann in the section "Gebetsliteratur" at the end of Crouzel's article "Gregor I," 791-93.

28. Michel van Esbroeck, "The *Credo* of Gregory the Wonderworker and its Influence through Three Centuries," *Studia Patristica* 19 (1989): 261-66.

29. The small group of works usually found together in the manuscripts of Gregory Nazianzen may constitute a partial exception; see the discussions below concerning *To Philagrius* and *Glossary on Ezekiel*.

30. Sancti Gregorii Episcopi Neocæsariensis, cognomento Thaumaturgi, *Opera Omnia*, quotquot in insignioribus, praecipuè Romanis Bibliothecis reperiri potuerunt; Una cum eiusdem Authoris Vita, græcè et latinè. Interprete, et scholiaste Reverendo D. Doct. Gerardo Vossio Borchlonio, Germ. Prep. Tungrensi. Moguntiae [Mainz]: Apud Balthasarum Lippium, sumptibus Antonii Hierat., M.DC.IV [1604]. De Vos published at the same time a second volume of works by other authors, not only to make them available but also to fatten the edition of Gregory ("ut Tomus Thaumaturgi in iustius Volumen excrescat").

INTRODUCTION

of Tongeren,[31] who died in 1609. De Vos is perhaps most famous for publishing an *opera omnia* of Ephrem Syrus (Rome, 1589).[32] In the *editio princeps*, De Vos published the *Creed*; "another profession of faith," the so-called κατὰ μέρος πίστις which is now recognized as an Apollinarian composition;[33] the "Twelve Chapters on Faith" (CPG 1772); four homilies, three of them on the Annunciation (CPG 1775, 1776, and 4519) and one on the Theophany at the baptism of Jesus (CPG 7385); the *Canonical Epistle* (CPG 1765); *To Tatian on the Soul* (CPG 1773); the *Metaphrase on Ecclesiastes* (CPG 1766);[34] the *Address of Thanksgiving to Origen* (CPG 1763); and the *Life* by Gregory of Nyssa (CPG 3184). He seldom speaks of his manuscript sources.[35] At Cologne in 1618, these works were included in the third volume of a larger patristic collection.[36]

(10) A second publication of Gregory's *opera omnia* was produced by Fronton Du Duc (Ducaeus), *SS. PP., Gregorii, Neocaesar. Episc., cognomento Thaumaturgi, Macarii Aegyptii et Basilii, Seleuciae Isauriae Episc. Opera Omnia, quae reperiri potuerunt.* Nunc primum

---

31. Tongeren or Tongres is a market town north of Liège. De Vos himself tells us in the introduction to his book that as of 1603 he is 56 years old and in his thirtieth year of residence in Rome ("urbicae mansionis").

32. Further information can be found in the article by J.-J. Thonissen, "De Vos (Gérard)," *Biographie Nationale* 5 (1875): 850–51.

33. De Vos gives only a Latin translation of this work, without explaining why. For the best edition of the Greek text, see Hans Lietzmann, *Apollinaris von Laodicea und seine Schule* (Tübingen: J. C. B. Mohr, 1904), 167–85.

34. De Vos provides only the Latin translation by Jacobus Billius, just as it is still to be read in the Latin column of Migne's *Patrologia Graeco-Latina* 10.988–1017.

35. A surprising exception is in his notes to *To Tatian on the Soul*, where he mentions several manuscripts, but names them only in quite general terms.

36. *Magna Bibliotheca veterum Patrum & antiquorum Scriptorum ecclesiasticorum*: primo quidem a Margarino de la Bigne Sorbonico in Academia Parisiensi Theologo collecta, & tertio in Lucem edita; Nunc vero plus quam centum Auctoribus, & opusculis plurimis locupletata, historica methodo per singula secula, quibus Scriptores quique vixerunt, disposita, & in XIV. Tomos distributa; opera & studio doctissimorum in Alma Universitate Colon. Agripp. Theologorum ac Professorum. Coloniae Agrippinae, sumptibus Antonii Hierati, sub signo Gryphi. Anno M.DC.XVII. Antonius Hieratus had also put up the capital for De Vos's edition. This information comes from Thomas Ittig, *De Bibliothecis et Catenis Patrum . . . Tractatus* (Leipzig, 1707), 420–24, who also tells us (*ibid.*, 43) that of the works translated here the 1575 edition of the de la Bigne collection contained only *To Tatian on the Soul*; the 1589 edition added the *Metaphrase* and the *Canonical Epistle* (*ibid.*, 56). Ittig does not report on the third (1609) and fourth (1624) editions.

gr. et lat. coniunctim edita. Parisiis, 1621. Du Duc adds his own annotations in this edition, but otherwise simply reproduces De Vos.[37]

(11) A third publication was in the third volume of the *Bibliotheca veterum Patrum, antiquorumque Scriptorum ecclesiasticorum, postrema Lugdunensi longe locupletior atque accuratior*, edited by Andreas Galland (Venice, 1767).[38] Galland promises many improvements to the texts in his collection, and he certainly did have access to some better editions which had appeared since Du Duc. It is Galland's edition which was taken over and reprinted in J.-P. Migne, *Patrologia Graeco-Latina*, volume 10.

Gregory's Theology

(12) Henri Crouzel's introduction to his edition of the *Address of Thanksgiving* gives an overall description of Gregory's theology.[39] Crouzel's portrayal of Gregory's ideas is affected by two factors about which I would disagree: Crouzel's acceptance of the so-called "Creed" of Gregory from the *Life* as genuine, rather than a forgery by Gregory of Nyssa, and his willingness to transfer onto Gregory many of the virtues of Origen's fully worked out theology, despite the lack of evidence for those qualities in Gregory's own works. I believe that Luise Abramowski has made a persuasive case[40] that the "Creed" was constructed by Gregory of Nyssa as part of his attempt to bring the Christians of Neocaesarea into agreement with the rest of the Church after the Council of Constantinople in 381, when the emperors made him a standard of orthodoxy for Pontus.[41] As for the independence of

---

37. Likewise, for the fifty homilies of Macarius he reproduces "Io. Picus," for Basil of Seleucia, "Cl. Dausqueius," and for Zonaras' explication of the canonical letters (including Gregory's which reappears here), "Antonio Salmatia."

38. The first volume of the set is dated 1765.

39. Crouzel, *Remerciement*, 46–78.

40. Luise Abramowski, "Das Bekenntnis des Gregor Thaumaturgus bei Gregor von Nyssa und das Problem seiner Echtheit," *Zeitschrift für Kirchengeschichte* 87 (1976): 145–66.

41. Cod. Theod. 16.1.3; *The Theodosian Code*, translated with commentary by Clyde Pharr (New York: Greenwood Press, 1969), 440: "... in the Diocese of Pontus, with Helladius, bishop of Caesarea, and with Otreius, bishop of Melitene, and with Gregorius, bishop of Nyssa ... Those bishops who are of the communion and fellowship of such acceptable priests must be permitted to obtain the Catholic churches." The date is July 30, 381.

Origen's pupils from their teacher, we need look no farther than his other famous student, Dionysius of Alexandria, who seems not to have rehabilitated Origen after becoming bishop of Alexandria, and whose theology is apparently less like Origen's than was once assumed.[42]

(13) As I indicated above, I have taken what may be considered a "maximalist" position in regard to the genuineness of Gregory's works. That is, where a work could be by Gregory and is attributed to him in some ancient source, I have tended to include it in his corpus. This could have the disadvantage of requiring the reader to make sense of materials which seem disparate; somewhat to my surprise, the differences among the works are not particularly great. Even if they had been, however, to divide them up among various authors on the grounds of those differences would have been to beg the question. With a writer from such a distant time and place as Gregory, difficulties are to be expected, and should not be solved by the simple expedient of inventing hypothetical figures. With that said, let us consider some characteristics of Gregory's theology as it appears in the present body of works.

(14) As I have noted at various points in discussion of the individual works, Gregory's references to Jesus Christ and to the Holy Spirit are sparser than one would expect from a pupil of Origen. There are several unmistakable references to the Incarnation of the divine Savior, and from the *Address* in particular it is apparent that Gregory is familiar with the gospels as well as the rest of Scripture, but he seems to think of Christ more as the divine Logos than as the human Jesus. This bias is not docetistic, since the *To Theopompus* is a ringing affirmation of the reality of God's suffering and death. Rather, Gregory seems to find our converse in heaven, even while we are on earth, and the object of our love and contemplation in God above. In this sense the Incarnation seems more instrumental than the mystery in its own right which much Christian thought has emphasized.

(15) The Holy Spirit appears but once each in the *Address of Thanksgiving* and the *Canonical Letter*, and not at all in the *Metaphrase on Ecclesiastes* or *To Theopompus*. In *To Philagrius* the Holy

---

42. Wolfgang Bienert, *Dionysius von Alexandrien: Zur Frage des Origenismus im dritten Jahrhundert* (Berlin: Walter de Gruyter, 1978).

Spirit comes up in the formal setting of a trinitarian credal affirmation, and not in a functional role; that formal character itself is one of the reasons I am willing to accept *To Philagrius* as a genuine work of Gregory. As I suggest in a note to the mystagogical vision in the *Life*, where Gregory of Nyssa attributes quite a detailed creed to Gregory Thaumaturgus and says that it is still to be seen in the church in Neocaesarea written in the saint's own hand, a trinitarian formula of a simple coordinate kind may be the occasion for Nyssa's development of the trinitarian theme.

(16) In short, there is little dogmatic development in the genuine works of Gregory—even *To Philagrius*—that would tax the credulity of a non-Christian who was slightly acquainted with the particularities of Christian belief. There are three possible explanations of this phenomenon: (1) Gregory's Christianity was rudimentary, and reflects the kind of simplification that can be expected when a religious faith is transplanted from a cultural setting where many corollary beliefs and practices support it to the stony soil of a new territory and population; (2) the works we have are exoteric, addressed precisely to outsiders, and present quite a different theological vision from the one which would have been the theme of Gregory's preaching within Christian circles; (3) the works we have, apart from the *Canonical Epistle*, were produced by Gregory in his early enthusiasm for Christianity as a student under Origen, and document the process by which he was absorbing Christian ideas, rather than the developed vision of his later years as a bishop. The third suggestion has in its favor the fact that Gregory's writings were preserved in Palestine and Syria, where he had been a student; the second, the avoidance of argument from Scripture (and in the case of the *Metaphrase*, its protreptic character); the first, the evidence that a century later Neocaesarea was still something of a theological backwater whose simplistic views taxed the patience of both Gregory of Nyssa and his brother Basil. While all three explanations are defensible, I tend to think that the sophistication of Gregory's arguments speaks against the theory that these are all works of his early years as a Christian.

(17) Whatever the answer to that question, we are better informed about Gregory's moral teaching than about his dogmatic

vision.⁴³ For Gregory, the goal of the moral life is "to come to God and remain in him, having been made like him by a clean mind." This is primarily the work of true piety, εὐσέβεια, which he calls "the mother of the virtues ... the beginning and the culmination of all the virtues."⁴⁴ In the *Metaphrase*, he says that "for those people who remain upon the earth there is one salvation, if their souls would recognize and attach themselves to the one who gave them birth,"⁴⁵ a formulation which matches closely the *Address*'s statement of the goal of the moral life.

(18) This true piety, in Gregory's view, calls for leading a philosophic life, and both the *Address* and the *Metaphrase* describe the urgent need for conversion to philosophy. In the *Metaphrase* he uses the experience of the futility of the unreflective life to break down the reader's resistance to philosophy, as Origen broke down Gregory's own resistance through the process so eloquently described in the *Address* 6.73–92. Driven to the recognition of how futile other pursuits are, he concludes, "I saw clearly the goods which lie before a human being, the γνῶσις of wisdom and the possession of virtue," accompanied by a desire for peace and quiet (ἡσυχία).⁴⁶ Here are signs not only of philosophic *otium* but also of monastic ἀναχώρησις.

(19) Gregory's vision of the philosophic life places a high value on personal relationships. That comes through repeatedly in the *Address*, for example, in the famous passage where he compares the drawing power of Origen's friendship to David's attraction for Jonathan (6.81–92), and in his appreciative remarks about the other men who form the circle around Origen (1.3–4,⁴⁷ 16.189⁴⁸ and 196). We see the same preference for relationship

43. A more extended treatment can be found in Michael Slusser, "The Main Ethical Emphases in the Writings of Gregory Thaumaturgus," in *Studia Patristica*, Proceedings of the Twelfth International Conference on Patristic Studies, Oxford, August 21–26, 1995 (Leuven, Belgium: Peeters Publishers, 1997), 357–62.
44. *Address* 12.149; see also *Address* 14.165, where he calls "the knowledge of the divine and true piety" "the greatest and most necessary of all."
45. PG 10.1017A5–7; see also PG 10.1005C1: "The greatest good is to lay hold of God."
46. *Metaphrase*, PG 10.993C; compare *Address* 16.185: "How profitable I learned it is to live in quietness ... !" (ἡσυχίαν ἄγειν).
47. "... these wonderful men who have embraced the good philosophy."
48. Gregory compares life in Origen's company to paradise: "... the good

over the solitary life in the way in which the *Metaphrase* develops Ecclesiastes' reflections on the isolation of the miser.[49] This passage lends some credibility to the way Gregory of Nyssa later portrayed the Wonderworker as always accompanied by associates, and may foreshadow the Cappadocians' own experiments with a spiritual community.

(20) The path of virtue to which true piety summons us includes of course the cardinal virtues so well known from earlier Greek tradition.[50] The language Gregory uses, "mastery and understanding of the impulses themselves" (*Address* 11.137), is characteristic of the period and would fit well in a Stoic context,[51] as would the emphasis on doing "what really belongs to us," rather than focusing on what others do (*Address* 11.138–39). Gregory places particular emphasis on temperance (σωφροσύνη) and detachment from worldly possessions. While the biblical Qoheleth says that wisdom protects a person like money (Eccles 7.12), Gregory says, "Real life, for a human being, comes not from the precarious possession of wealth, but from wisdom" (PG 10.1005B). The strength of Gregory's feeling on this issue may be reflected in the way that the *Canonical Epistle* devotes canons 2–5 and 8–10 to harsh censure of those who have taken advantage of the chaos

---

land, where I obtained the homeland I never knew of before, and relatives, whom I finally began to know when I had them as soul mates, and what is truly our father's house, where the father stays and is nobly honored and celebrated by his true sons who wish to remain there."

49. PG 10.997CD–1000A, based on Eccles 4.7–12.

50. *Address* 9.122–25. These virtues are presented in the usual way, but there is nothing wrong with that, despite the rather contemptuous characterization which Pierre Nautin gives in *Origène, Sa vie et son œuvre* (Paris: Beauchesne, 1977), 185.

51. See also *Address* 9.115, where virtue produces "the calm and steady condition of the soul's impulses." The absence of any mention of ὁρμαί in the *Enchiridion Sexti* is one of the indications that the latter reflects a somewhat different view of the moral life than Gregory's. Cf. Henry Chadwick, *The Sentences of Sextus* (Cambridge: Cambridge University Press, 1959), 184–92, for an index of the Greek words in Sextus. Although Crouzel, *Remerciement*, 147, n. 4, says that the "most recent" philosophers in *Address* 9.124, whom Gregory derides, were Stoics, I am not convinced; nor can we be sure that Gregory divided philosophers into the same groupings which historians use today. As Crouzel notes, (*ibid.*, 62), one of the derided "modern" doctrines in *Address* 9.124 reappears in 11.142, this time assigned to the ancients, and with commendation.

left behind by the Goths to enrich themselves at their neighbors' expense.[52]

(21) Gregory introduces the notion of reward and punishment after death into his *Metaphrase* of Ecclesiastes, making it a significant ethical factor in his exhortation to take up the life of wisdom and goodness. In the *Address of Thanksgiving*, however, no such destiny after death is discussed. True, Origen is described as a man who "has already completed most of the preparation for the re-ascent to the divine world" (*Address* 2.10), whose "inner being connaturally touches God, though it is for the moment enclosed in what is visible and mortal" (*Address* 2.13). It is hard to know whether this represents a conventional type of praise, or whether Gregory himself thought in those terms. But in the *Address*, true piety is its own reward, and God's paradise for us today is the life of philosophy led in union with God. At the root of our capacity to lead such a life, Gregory sees "the leader of our souls and our Savior, [God's] first-begotten Word" who "is the truth and the wisdom and the power of the Father of the universe himself, and is also with and in him and united to him completely" (*Address* 4.35-36)—exactly the description which Gregory gives of the life of εὐσέβεια itself. The *To Theopompos*, however, ascribes such a role not to "the Word" but explicitly to Jesus.[53]

Gregory of Nyssa's Life of Gregory the Wonderworker

(22) The oration of Gregory of Nyssa which goes under the title of *The Life of Gregory the Wonderworker* is, as was noted above in the general discussion of Gregory's life, thought to be the closest of our many written accounts to the oral traditions in Neo-

52. These passages from the *Canonical Epistle* are especially moving to read when one realizes that Gregory Thaumaturgus is the patron saint of the Christians of Bosnia; see Alexandre Soloviev, "Saint Grégoire, patron de Bosnie," *Byzantion* 19 (1949): 263-79.

53. *To Theopompus* 17.32: "He came therefore, O happy one, Jesus came, who is king over all things, that he might heal the difficult passions of human beings, being the most blessed and generous one. . . . He came therefore, he came in haste, to make people blessed and rich in good things, immortals instead of mortals, and has renewed and recreated them blessed and forever."

caesarea about their founding saint. However difficult it may be to rely on this *Life* for historical data on Gregory Thaumaturgus himself, it has recently been used as a valuable resource for understanding what Christian missionary work in the Roman Empire was like.[54] It is an important component of the dossier on Gregory.

(23) The most remarkable trait of this *Life* is that Gregory of Nyssa shows no evidence of knowing any of the written works of Gregory Thaumaturgus.[55] Nonetheless, he knows that Gregory had studied with Origen, and returned to his own country equipped with extensive knowledge of philosophy. If he learned about the study with Origen from Eusebius's brief mention in the *Historia ecclesiastica*, he passes over in silence Eusebius's mention of a brother Athenodorus, and of the participation of both Gregory and Athenodorus in the first synod called to deal with Paul of Samosata.[56] Since Nyssa also names Firmilian of Caesarea in Cappadocia as an important influence on the Wonderworker, and in fact as the one who sent him to Origen, Nyssa may be depending on Cappadocian sources entirely, and not on Eusebius.

(24) One implication of this is that Gregory's works would have been transmitted only outside Cappadocia. In the case of the *Address of Thanksgiving* and perhaps the *Metaphrase on Ecclesiastes*, which Jerome knew, that might not surprise us, but the *Canonical Epistle* presumes an audience in Pontus and Cappadocia. Still, too much should not be made of Nyssa's silence about Gregory's writings; hagiographical homilies often reflect little of our other sources about the persons they praise.[57]

(25) A second remarkable characteristic of the *Life*, at least in contrast to modern expectations, is the sparsity of references to

---

54. Ramsay MacMullen, *Christianizing the Roman Empire (A.D. 100–400)* (New Haven: Yale University Press, 1984), 59–61; Lane Fox, *Pagans*, devotes most of chapter 10 to Gregory's episcopal career, with heavy dependence on Nyssa's *Life*.

55. Raymond Van Dam, "Hagiography and History: The Life of Gregory Thaumaturgus," *Classical Antiquity* 1 (1982): 281–82, discusses this issue at some length. Jean Bernardi, *La prédication des Pères Cappadociens* ([Paris]: Presses universitaires de France, [1968]), 310, states the fact bluntly.

56. Eusebius, *h. e.* 6.30 (cf. 7.14, 7.28.1).

57. Gregory Nazianzen's panegyric on Athanasius of Alexandria, for example, gives scant attention to his writings.

INTRODUCTION   15

Jesus Christ. Nyssa portrays Gregory as centered on God, believing in the Trinity, and instituting an ecclesial and sacramental Christian life in Pontus, but the references to the Incarnation are exceedingly rare. The temple custodian doubted that "the Divine had appeared to human beings in the flesh," and Gregory assured him that this had been confirmed by wonders;[58] and this same custodian, having become Gregory's deacon, called on the name of Christ and made "the Sign upon himself" (presumably the sign of the cross) when he found himself in mortal danger.[59] Even the famous "Creed"[60] prescinds from any mention of the Incarnation; and the name of Jesus is not to be found in the entire oration. Whatever Nyssa's reasons for constructing the *Life* in this way, the theocentric narrative harmonizes with Gregory's works as we have them and as they are translated here. Perhaps Gregory's comparative silence on Jesus as the Word incarnate is more typical of that time and place than modern Christians would care to think.

(26) Scholars have made various attempts to identify the circumstances under which the *Life* was composed. Raymond Van Dam summarizes scholarly opinion with the probable year being 380, the date perhaps Gregory's feastday, November 17, and the location probably Neocaesarea itself.[61] W. Telfer places it early in Nyssa's career, "in some Pontic church ... not St. Gregory's own church of Neocaesarea,"[62] while Luise Abramowski believes that it was delivered after 381, after Gregory of Nyssa had been thrust into prominence by his designation as one of the standards of doctrinal orthodoxy by the emperor Theodosius.[63] While the text itself begins in a fashion which fits the picture of an oral delivery

58. PG 46.917AB.
59. PG 46.952BC.
60. PG 46.912D–13A.
61. Van Dam, "Hagiography and History," 277. He draws the year from Bernardi, *La prédication*, 308; Bernardi selects 380 because it was an "année où Grégoire voyagea beaucoup."
62. Telfer, "The Cultus," 229. He continues, "It would appear to have looked up to the church of Amasea and to have been near the sea. It may have been Ibora, the little town near which was the country mansion where Aemilia lived, the widowed mother of Basil and Gregory Nyssen." This is a curious suggestion, since Ibora, on the Iris River, is farther from the sea than Neocaesarea.
63. Abramowski, "Das Bekenntnis," 162.

before an audience, the last few pages (from 956A13 = H54.17 on; in this translation the addendum begins at p. 84) appear to be a written addition. We may assume that Gregory of Nyssa added such improvements as he wished before letting the oration circulate more widely.

(27) The translation printed here was made from the text printed in the *Patrologia Graeco-Latina* 46.893–958. In the meantime, the long-awaited critical edition by Gunther Heil has appeared in the Leiden corpus of the works of Gregory of Nyssa,[64] and I have attempted to reflect in my translation some of the improved readings offered by Heil. Neither Heil's text nor the older text reprinted in Migne's *Patrologia* is divided into chapters, which makes reference to the text of the oration very awkward. To alleviate that problem, I have included in brackets in my translation the column references to Migne and the page references to Migne.[65] At the risk of hubris, I have also divided the text into "chapters," in a somewhat simpler version of the division proposed by Constantinos Fouskas,[66] and added my own brief headings to help the reader use the text more easily.

Address of Thanksgiving to Origen

(28) The *Address of Thanksgiving*[67] is the most famous of the works attributed to our Gregory. Its fame is due to the fact that it gives us the most extensive contemporary description of Origen. While a challenge was recently mounted against the genuineness of the traditional attribution,[68] it has been staunchly (and to my mind adequately) defended.[69] I find nothing in the *Address*

---

64. Gregory of Nyssa, *De Vita Gregorii Thaumaturgi*, ed. Gunther Heil, in *Gregorii Nysseni Sermones, Pars II*, ed. Friedhelm Mann, *Gregorii Nysseni Opera*, 10.1 (Leiden: E.J. Brill, 1990), 3–57.
65. I owe this suggestion to Professor Raymond Van Dam.
66. Fouskas, Γρηγόριος, 31–35, proposes 27 chapters.
67. Sometimes called the "Panegyric," a term which is not quite appropriate to its form and content, and which risks confusion with Gregory of Nyssa's *Life* of Gregory Thaumaturgus, which is also widely referred to as a "panegyric."
68. Nautin, *Origène*, 81–86, claims that the *Address* was the work of another student of Origen in Caesarea named "Theodore," and that Eusebius conflated him with the famous bishop of Pontus.
69. Henri Crouzel, "Faut-il voir trois personnages en Grégoire le Thauma-

INTRODUCTION   17

which is inconsistent with its being an authentic work of Gregory the Wonderworker.

(29) We apparently owe the preservation of the *Address* to the manuscript tradition of Origen's *Contra Celsum*, which is prefaced in the manuscript transmission by the *Address*.[70] Consequently, since Koetschau in his edition of the *Contra Celsum* established that the other five manuscripts of the latter work all derived from a single archetype still in our possession, Codex Vaticanus gr. 386 (13th century), he quite reasonably used that manuscript as the basis of his *editio minor* of the Greek text of the *Address*. That is likewise the text which, with a few emendations suggested over the years, Henri Crouzel has printed in his edition for the *Sources chrétiennes*, and which is translated here.

(30) On the basis of internal evidence, the *Address* was to be delivered publicly on the occasion of Gregory's departure from Caesarea to return to his native land. There are references to others of Origen's company presumably in attendance, and to the speaker's imminent departure. A more difficult issue in the text is the alternation between "I" and "we," which I have tried to reflect exactly in my translation: commentators on this text have proposed that the plural is inclusive of Gregory's brother Athenodorus,[71] who is referred to by Eusebius in his *historia ecclesiastica* 6.30:

---

turge?" *Gregorianum* 60 (1979): 287–320. Klein, *Oratio prosphonetica*, 47–63, reviews all the arguments and inclines to the traditional view of a single Gregory.

70. Koetschau, in his introduction to *Dankrede*, XXX–XXXI, points this out and adds that it was natural for Origen to publish copies of the address with his own writings; Gregory did not publish it himself, but intended it solely for Origen. That seems to me a reasonable hypothesis, but nothing more. There are, incidentally, other manuscripts of the *Address* besides those noted by Koetschau, but they are generally quite late: (a) Cod. Vat. gr. 1902 (s. xv–xvi), f. 107–108v, contains the beginning and excerpts of the *Address*, and notes connecting it with Cardinal Sirleto, Gerard De Vos's patron (Canart, 1:604); (b) Cod. Milan. Bibl. Ambros. gr. 1056, I 91 inf. olim N 351, f. 84–102 (Martini-Bassi, 2:1128); (c) Cod. Vindob. Phil. gr. 181 (s. xvi), f. 20v–30v (Hunger, 1:289); (d) Cod. Athos Mon. Iviron gr. 4508 (388), f. 562ff. (Lampros, 2:131).

71. Crouzel, *Remerciement*, 14–15, acknowledges that "le *Remerciement* ne le mentionne pas explicitement, mais le mélange continuel des 'je' et des 'nous,' parfois dans la même phrase, ne peut s'expliquer dans bien des cas que par sa présence: tantôt Grégoire parle de lui seul, tantôt des deux; tantôt en son seul nom, tantôt au nom des deux. S'il s'agissait seulement des 'nous' oratoires, cette

[Origen's] services were in constant demand not only by the local people but also by innumerable foreign students who had left their own countries. The most distinguished names known to me are those of Theodore—who was none other than that illustrious bishop of my own day, Gregory—and his brother Athenodore. They were passionately devoted to Greek and Roman studies, but he implanted in them a love of true philosophy and induced them to exchange their old enthusiasm for a theological training. Five whole years they spent with him, making such remarkable progress in theology that while still young both were chosen to be bishops of the churches in Pontus.[72]

But it seems unnecessary to connect the frequent use of the first person plural in the *Address* with Eusebius's assertion that Athenodorus, a brother of Gregory, also studied with Origen, and to make them mutually dependent on each other.[73] "We" in the *Address* occurs where a brother can hardly be meant,[74] and the singular sometimes appears where one would expect a brother to be explicitly included, had one been present.[75] Since Firmilian of Caesarea in Cappadocia studied with Origen, brought Origen to Caesarea for a visit, and knew Gregory,[76] and Caesarea,

---

variété manifesterait une négligence peu compréhensible dans un texte si composé."

72. The translation used here is that of G. A. Williamson, Eusebius, *A History of the Church from Christ to Constantine* (Minneapolis: Augsburg, 1975), 268.

73. This is so even if one rejects Nautin's argument based on other passages where "I" and "we" are mingled; see Nautin, *Origène*, 447–48. Both passages show Origen himself mixing first person singulars and plurals in the same fashion as Gregory in the *Address*. Incidentally, the second passage is from Eusebius, *h. e.* 6.19.12–13, not 6.14 as Nautin cites it.

74. E.g., *Address* 2.18, 18.203. Richard Valantasis, *Spiritual Guides of the Third Century* (Minneapolis: Fortress Press, 1991), 16, suggests that "it could be the speaker's brother (V.69), or fellow students, or the audience at the presumed presentation of the speech, or a combination of these. The result, however, is that the speech includes in its expression a narrative voice beyond the speaker, a voice which indicates a speaker and a more inclusive voice. This 'we' is the point at which the audience at the speech-giving and 'we,' the historical reader, enter the text. This includes both audiences, not as an objectified 'you' to whom information is given as to people excluded from the discourse, but as (albeit passive) participants in the event."

75. E.g., *Address* 5.55, "the remarkable dispensation by which I came to this man"; 5.56, "my mother . . . my parents"; 5.62, "I became a student of these very laws"; 5.65, "my sister's husband"; 16.185–89.

76. Eusebius, *h. e.* 6.27, tells us that Firmilian brought Origen to Caesarea,

as the capital of the province of Cappadocia, would have been in relatively frequent contact with Pontus,[77] there is no reason to suppose that Gregory's studies would have offered the only opportunity for Athenodorus to make Origen's acquaintance.

(31) The *Address* gives us our fullest contemporary account of Origen's teaching methods. It would be tempting to try to find in this account the description of a church center for catechesis, a place where Christians alone, whether catechumens or baptized, were formed in the faith.[78] Even if that was the case when Origen taught as a layman in Alexandria, it cannot be presumed that his setting was the same in Caesarea. Working from the data provided by Gregory in the *Address*, Adolf Knauber arrived at a significantly different picture: the students were not Christians or even catechumens in any regular sense, but typical young pagan seekers after wisdom, and the "school" may not even have been connected with the Church. According to Knauber, "The school of Origen . . . was an essentially propagandistic—more exactly philosophical/missionary—endeavor . . . It neither arose from a speculative-theological demand within the faith nor filled in any direct way practical sacramental and pastoral tasks for the

---

and himself traveled to Judaea to spend time with Origen; and in 7.28 says that they both (with Athenodorus) attended the Council of 264 against Paul of Samosata.

77. It should be remembered that Basil of Caesarea's and Gregory of Nyssa's grandmother Macrina knew Gregory Thaumaturgus (Basil, *ep.* 204.6), and their family's country estate (and later monastic retreat) of Annesi was not far from Neocaesarea, on the Iris River. It would be unsound to restrict our view of social contacts among figures in that area to those which our fragmentary evidence mentions directly.

78. The classic description by Charles Bigg, *The Christian Platonists of Alexandria* (Oxford: Clarendon Press, 1913), 69–70, is an example of this: "Hence the catechetical instruction, which in most other communities continued to be given in an unsystematic way by Bishop or Priest, had in Alexandria developed about the middle of the century into a regular institution."

"This was the famous Catechetical School. It still continued to provide instruction for those desirous of admission into the Church, but with this humble routine it combined a higher and more ambitious function. It was partly a propaganda, partly we may regard it as a denominational college by the side of a secular university."

For the prehistory of this view, see Alain Le Boulluec, "L'École d'Alexandrie: De quelques aventures d'un concept historiographique," in ΑΛΕΞΑΝΔΡΙΝΑ: *Mélanges offerts au P. Claude Mondésert* (Paris: Cerf, 1987), 403–17.

community." It was a participation by a Christian philosopher and teacher in the public market of ideas addressed to young men.[79]

(32) Henri Crouzel was at first cautious about Knauber's portrayal,[80] but grants its basic outlines:

> It is not correct to describe Origen's school at Caesarea as a "catechetical school," still less as a faculty of theology.... Following A. Knauber we think that the school of Caesarea was more a kind of missionary school, aimed at young pagans who were showing an interest in Christianity but were not ready, necessarily, to ask for baptism: Origen was thus introducing these to Christian doctrine through a course in philosophy, mainly inspired by Middle Platonism, of which he offered them a Christian version. If his students later asked to become Christians, they had then to receive catechetical teaching in the strict sense.
>
> But the *didascaleion* [school] of Caesarea is above all a school of the inner life: all its teaching leads to spirituality.[81]

(33) In our time, when not only elementary but higher education of young people has been formalized to an extent unimaginable in the third century, we may have difficulty seeing Origen in direct competition to the other philosophers who were competing for their attention and allegiance. Yet that is what he was apparently doing in Caesarea, and that is what the serious young law student came to hear. We should remember that not only "mainstream" philosophers engaged in this competition, but also Gnostic teachers.[82]

(34) What was necessary to succeed was a combination of the ability to convince young people in terms of what they already knew from their studies in rhetoric; a way of presenting (or at

---

79. Knauber, "Das Anliegen," 182–203, especially 196 and 201–2.
80. Henri Crouzel, "L'École d'Origène à Césarée: Postscriptum à une édition de Grégoire le Thaumaturge," *Bulletin de littérature ecclésiastique* 71 (1970): 15–27. Crouzel especially contested Knauber's view that Gregory was unbaptized at the time of his studies with Origen, and contended that there would have been Christian students in the group, training to do missionary work.
81. Crouzel, *Origen*, 27–28.
82. On this, a perusal of Alexander Böhlig, "Die griechische Schule und die Bibliothek von Nag Hammadi," in Alexander Böhlig and Frederik Wisse, *Zum Hellenismus in den Schriften von Nag Hammadi* (Wiesbaden: Otto Harrassowitz, 1975), 9–53, especially 32–34, is instructive. See also the extended treatment "Die frühe Kirche und die heidnische Bildung," in Klein and Guyot, *Oratio prosphonetica*, 83–116.

least dealing with) those texts to which authority was attributed; and less tangible factors of a social, psychological, and intellectual nature. Both Gnostics and Christians drew on special texts which claimed authority even though their authors were, from a Greek point of view, "barbarian." In the third century, such claims were not necessarily a handicap, since oracles, hermetic texts, and Pythagoreans such as Numenius of Apamaea were enjoying a vogue. It should not surprise us that Origen makes great claims for Solomon as a most ancient and most knowledgeable authority. It is possible that Origen's Alexandrian teaching also had this open-ended, scarcely "Christian" character, and thus competed more openly and directly with Gnostic teachers than his superiors in Alexandria were willing to countenance.[83]

(35) Nonetheless, Gregory's *Address* testifies to an unmistakably Christian culture. He employs scriptural imagery frequently and accurately.[84] Although he never employs the name "Jesus" or the title "Christ," he speaks of God's divine Word in ways which reflect a Christian perspective.[85] Particularly striking is what he says after his evocation of the parable of the Good Samaritan: "But why am I grieving this way? There is the Word, the Savior of all, who protects and heals all those half-dead and robbed, the unsleeping guardian of all human beings" (17.200). As Origen himself says, there was already a long tradition of identifying the Samaritan in the parable with Christ.[86] While we may be surprised at the lack of any explicit mention of the Incarnation, the Passion, or the Resurrection, the explanation must fall within, not outside, third-century Christianity.[87]

83. Their disapproval seems to be reflected in Eusebius, *h. e.* 6.19; see Nautin, *Origène*, 53–55, and the longer discussion in *idem, Lettres et écrivains chrétiens des II*[e] *et III*[e] *siècles* (Paris: Cerf, 1961).

84. E.g., *Address* 3.28, 4.36, 4.41–42, 6.85–92, 7.93–94, 7.96, 7.108, 15.173–74, 15.180, 15.183, 16.185–91, 16.193–97, 16.199–202, 17.200–202.

85. See the extended treatment by Crouzel, *Remerciement*, 47–53, who underlines the parallels between the doctrine of the *Address* and the teachings of Origen.

86. Origen, *Homilies on Luke* 34.3; see Origen, *Homélies sur Luc*, ed. and trans. Henri Crouzel, François Fournier, and Pierre Périchon (Paris: Cerf, 1962), 402–3, where the lengthy note 1 documents that widespread interpretation.

87. One explanation which is *not* feasible would be the suggestion that these were not significant factors in Origen's own exposition of Christianity; for detailed evidence to the contrary, see Manlio Simonetti, "La morte di Gesù in Ori-

Metaphrase on Ecclesiastes

(36) This is the best attested work of Gregory Thaumaturgus. Jerome, in *de viris inlustribus* 65,[88] and Rufinus, in his appendix to Eusebius's *historia ecclesiastica* 7.28,[89] both mention it, and Jerome very explicitly quotes it in his own commentary on Ecclesiastes.[90] Other quotations show up in Procopius of Gaza's *Catena in Ecclesiasten*.[91] This early and multiple attestation notwithstanding, it is among the manuscripts of the works of Gregory Nazianzen that we find the *Metaphrase*. It is part of a characteristic extension of a briefer manuscript corpus of Nazianzen's writings. In a search of manuscript catalogs which I made fifteen years ago, I identified 48 manuscripts containing the *Metaphrase*; all of them were devoted to works of Gregory Nazianzen except two late (15th-16th century) miscellanies. What was especially striking to me was the fact that it usually occurred next to or in close proximity to Nazianzen's "letter 243" (the *To Philagrius*) and the *Glossary on Ezekiel*. I shall return to this coincidence when I discuss those two documents below.

(37) The translation contained in this volume has been made from the Greek text printed in Migne, PG 10.988–1017, with consultation of the Maurist edition of the works of Gregory Nazianzen, volume 1.

(38) Various attempts have been made in recent years to

---

gene," *Rivista di storia e letteratura religiosa* 8 (1972): 3–41, reprinted in *idem, Studi sulla cristologia del II e III secolo* (Roma: Institutum Patristicum Augustinianum, 1993), 145–82.

88. "Scripsit et μετάφρασιν in Ecclesiasten brevem quidem, sed valde utilem."

89. ". . . in Ecclesiasten namque metafrasin idem Gregorius magnificentissime scripsit . . ."

90. "Vir sanctus Gregorius, Ponti episcopus, Origenis auditor, in Metaphrasi Ecclesiastae ita hunc locum intellexit: Ego vero praefero . . ." The passage is from PG 10.1000A.

91. The passage (from PG 10.993A) is quoted with minor additions: see Procopius Gazaeus, *Catena in Ecclesiasten, necnon Pseudochrysostomi Commentarius in eundem Ecclesiasten*, ed. Sandro Leanza, Corpus Christianorum Series Graeca 4 (Turnhout: Brepols, 1978), 18. The passage is ascribed simply to "Gregory," but Leanza points out that quotations from Gregory of Nyssa are ascribed simply to "Nyssa," xi, n. 19. He says that a longer version appears in the *Commentary on Ecclesiastes* of Olympiodorus, but that in the *Catena* of Polychronius it is falsly attributed to Didymus.

place the *Metaphrase* in the history of exegesis, either as a kind of "preliminary reading," a "minimal exegesis" of Ecclesiastes,[92] or as an attempt at "transforming this 'rough' Greek document into a 'smooth' Greek work," while at the same time making it more palatable to Christian readers."[93] I believe that it is more appropriate to see it as a kind of *protrepticus*, that is, an appeal to its readers to take up the philosophical life with full seriousness. Origen is said to have written *scholia* on Ecclesiastes,[94] and we have fragmentary *scholia* also from Dionysius of Alexandria, another student of Origen.[95] Given the fact that these are the earliest extant Christian reflections on Ecclesiastes,[96] the common link with Origen seems more than mere coincidence.

(39) Origen speaks in the prologue to his *Commentary on the Song of Songs* of the ways in which the wisdom writings associated with Solomon concern the major themes of philosophy:

Wishing, therefore, to distinguish one from another those three branches of learning, which we called general just now—that is, the moral, the natural, and the inspective, and to differentiate between them, Solomon issued them in three books, arranged in their proper order. First, in Proverbs he taught the moral science, putting rules for

92. This is the final suggestion of Françoise Vinel, "La Metaphrasis in Ecclesiasten de Grégoire le Thaumaturge: entre traduction et interprétation, une explication du texte," *Cahiers de Biblia Patristica* 1 (1987): 213.
93. John Jarick, *Gregory Thaumaturgos' Paraphrase of Ecclesiastes* (Atlanta: Scholars Press, 1990), 311, 315–16.
94. Jerome, Letter 33 to Paula, quoted in Crouzel, *Origen*, 38. Nautin, *Origène*, 374, thinks that Origen commented on the biblical books "par séries homogènes et, à l'intérieur de chaque série [followed] en principe l'ordre de la Bible," with the result that there were only *scholia* on Ecclesiastes for lack of time (*ibid.*, 375), which Nautin dates to about A.D. 247/48 (*ibid.*, 381, 437); there would also, Nautin thinks, have been homilies on Ecclesiastes, though for some reason he supposes a different order of sapiential books in this context (*ibid.*, 403), and the homilies would have been delivered several years before the *scholia* were composed (*ibid.*, 411). Those hypotheses seem to me to lack support.
95. Sandro Leanza, "Pour une réédition des Scolies à l'Ecclésiaste de Denys d'Alexandrie," in ΑΛΕΞΑΝΔΡΙΝΑ: *Mélanges offerts au P. Claude Mondésert* (Paris: Cerf, 1987), 239–46, says that new evidence from the *catenae* shows that Dionysius's commentary covered the entire book of Ecclesiastes, not just the opening chapters as Eusebius and Jerome thought.
96. Hippolytus has been said by Jerome (*de viris inlustribus* 61) to have written on Ecclesiastes, but the work is lost, and even in the fourth century it was hard to get reliable information about Hippolytus and his writings.

living into the form of short and pithy maxims, as was fitting. Secondly, he covered the science known as natural in Ecclesiastes; in this, by discussing at length the things of nature, and by distinguishing the useless and vain from the profitable and essential, he counsels us to forsake vanity and cultivate things useful and upright.[97]

The reader of Gregory's *Metaphrase* will find that he makes no attempt to use Ecclesiastes to teach "physics," even in the form known by the ancients. Gregory's interpretation is closer to the way Origen describes Ecclesiastes a little later in the prologue to the *Commentary on the Song of Songs*:

And so from Proverbs he goes on to Ecclesiastes, who teaches, as we said, that all visible and corporeal things are fleeting and brittle; and surely once the seeker after wisdom has grasped that these things are so, he is bound to spurn and despise them; renouncing the world bag and baggage, if I may put it in that way, he will surely reach out for the things unseen and eternal which, with spiritual meaning verily but under certain secret metaphors of love, are taught in the Song of Songs.[98]

I believe that Origen was presenting Solomon as the complete philosopher, more ancient than the Greeks, and that this included the portrayal of Solomon as a philosopher of nature, based on 1 Kings 4.33: "He spoke of trees, from the cedar that is in Lebanon to the hyssop that grows out of the wall; he spoke also of beasts, and of birds, and of reptiles, and of fish." In Gregory's description of Solomon, Solomon has "wisely penetrated the whole nature of the earth," and understood "the natures of things" (989C, 992A). But in my opinion, probably neither Origen nor Gregory used Ecclesiastes as a basis for presenting the philosophy of nature; rather, they used Solomon's alleged mastery of natural philosophy to add force to his injunction to forsake the world and pursue philosophy.

(40) Of all the recent published discussions of the *Metaphrase*, the most penetrating is that of K. W. Noakes.[99] He points

---

97. Origen, *comm. in Cant.* prologue, 3, in the translation by R. P. Lawson, Origen, *The Song of Songs: Commentary and Homilies* (Westminster: Newman Press, 1957), 41.
98. *Ibid.*, in Lawson, 44.
99. K[enneth] W. Noakes, "The Metaphrase on Ecclesiastes of Gregory Thaumaturgus," in *Studia Patristica*, volume 15.1, ed. Elizabeth A. Livingstone (Leuven: Peeters, 1984), 194–97.

out the extent to which the *Metaphrase* "supplement[s] the account of ascetic theology learned from Origen given in the Panegyric," that is, the *Address of Thanksgiving*.[100] Part of Gregory's technique for accomplishing this transformation of Ecclesiastes is reading the book as punctuated by dialogue: not all of its words represent Solomon's considered views; some passages are what he thought at another time, or even the views of opponents.[101] Origen employs this prosopological exegesis explicitly in his reading of the Song of Songs.[102] I interpret the *Metaphrase* as employing this technique in 993B, 996C-97A, 1009CD-12A, and 1016AB, and enunciating Solomon's response to foolish views in such passages as, "For at that point I thought that all beings earned the same deserts. . . . But now I know that these were fools' opinions, both erroneous and misleading" (1009C). Gregory is deliberately and systematically reading "Ecclesiastes as a prophetic work addressed to the whole Church of God," as Noakes observes.[103] It is in that spirit that I think its contents should be integrated into an overall assessment of Gregory's theology.

Canonical Epistle

(41) The authority of this work was recognized in the second canon of the Council of Trullo in 692.[104] Its abrupt beginning may be due to its having been an encyclical letter.[105] Since this

---

100. *Ibid.*, 195.
101. Noakes (*ibid.*, 194) recognizes this device at work in Gregory's handling of Eccles 11.9 (1016AB). T. A. Perry, *Dialogues with Kohelet* (University Park: Pennsylvania State University Press, 1993), 18-19, postulates a dialogue internal to the text of Ecclesiastes itself, but does not believe that Gregory Thaumaturgus recognized it.
102. For a thorough discussion of this way of reading Scripture, see Marie-Josèphe Rondeau, *Les commentaires patristiques du Psautier (IIIe-Ve siècles)*, Orientalia Christiana Analecta 220.2 (Rome: Institutum Studiorum Orientalium, 1985), 21-89; she discusses Origen's treatment of the Song of Songs on 41 and 44-45. A briefer introduction can be found in Michael Slusser, "The Exegetical Roots of Trinitarian Theology," *Theological Studies* 49 (1988): 463-68.
103. Noakes, 194.
104. Johannes Dräseke, "Der kanonische Brief des Gregorios von Neocäsarea," *Jahrbücher für protestantische Theologie* 7 (1881): 737.
105. Dräseke, "Der kanonische Brief," 728. He derives the idea from Martin J. Routh, *Reliquiae sacrae*, 2nd ed. (Oxford, 1846-48) 2:447.

Canonical Epistle is one of the foundation documents of the canon law of the Eastern Churches, its editing would require a complete critical edition of that legal corpus. Such an edition is at least unlikely; for the time being we must make do with the work of Routh and Dräseke,[106] the collection by J.-B. Pitra,[107] and the ΠΗΔΑΛΙΟΝ.[108] The following translation is based upon a text collated from all the above editions. Like Dräseke, I suspect the division into canons of being a later development, so I have reduced it to paragraph numbers.[109] The eleventh "canon" has a different character from the others, being concerned with definitions rather than situations, and apparently presuming a development of church architecture for which there is little evidence at the time. Many commentators (e.g., Dräseke[110]) think that it is a later explanatory addition, based perhaps on parallel passages from the canonical letters of Basil of Caesarea,[111] and serves as a glossary to Gregory's canons 5, 7, 8, and 9; that interpretation makes sense to me. Other authors treat it as an integral part of the letter.[112]

---

106. Dräseke's edition of the text appears on pp. 730–36 of his article, Dräseke, "Der kanonische Brief." He makes extensive use of the work published by Routh, *Reliquiae sacrae*, 3:251–83.

107. J.-B. Pitra, *Iuris ecclesiastici graecorum historia et monumenta* 1 (Rome, 1864) 562–66.

108. Agapios Hieromonachos and Nikodemos Monachos, ed., ΠΗΔΑΛΙΟΝ (Zakinthus, 1864) ed. S. X. Raphtani (reprint, Athens, 1975), 553–61. An English translation by D. Cummings of the 1908 edition of Agapios and Nikodemos was published as *The Rudder (Pedalion)* (Chicago: Orthodox Christian Educational Society, 1957); the *Canonical Epistle* of Gregory Thaumaturgus comes second in the "Canons of the Holy Fathers," 725–38, but is divided differently from the Migne text, in that the *Pedalion* makes two canons out of the first section.

109. Johannes Dräseke, "Johannes Zonaras' Commentar zum kanonischen Brief des Gregorios von Neocäsarea," *Zeitschrift für wissenschaftliche Theologie* 37 (1894): 249-250; cf. Peter Heather and John Matthews, *The Goths in the Fourth Century* (Liverpool: Liverpool University Press, 1991), 5: "It thus seems not unlikely that Gregory's letter was originally continuous, and that it was broken up into a number of Canons, some with titles, when its authority was recognized."

110. Dräseke, "Zonaras' Commentar," 249–50.

111. Basil of Caesarea, *ep.* 188, canons 4 and 7; *ep.* 199, canons 22 (the second closest parallel), 27, 34, 44; *ep.* 217, canons 56–59, 61, 64, 66, 75 (the closest), 77, 80–83.

112. Fouskas, Γρηγόριος, 169–72, which gives a full account of the scholarly differences. In the end (174), Fouskas gives as his personal view that "canon 11 is genuine at least in substance," though its form may be due to a later writer.

(42) As indicated in the brief life of Gregory presented above, this letter is associated with the incursion of raiders from across the Black Sea into northern Asia Minor in the mid-250's. The sections on property rights predominate, and testify to a strong concern that the rights of each person are the responsibility of all, even in a time of general hardship. This emphasis on property contrasts with the canons of Ancyra and Neocaesarea from soon after the end of the persecution under Diocletian and Galerius, which devote their attention almost entirely to issues of sacrificing and sexual morality.

To Theopompus, on the Impassibility and Passibility of God

(43) This remarkable treatise has featured in a number of modern studies on the philosophical problem of the suffering of God.[113] As Henri Crouzel remarks, the authenticity of this work of Gregory has not been seriously contested. He himself finds in it no trace of events or topics later than the third century, and considers it probable that Gregory Thaumaturgus is not only its author but the central figure in the dialogue itself.[114] Luise Abramowski, in her article mentioned above, agrees with the third-century date of the treatise, but believes that it should be assigned not to Gregory Thaumaturgus but to an otherwise unknown "Gregory the Teacher."[115] Given the frequency with which

---

113. One of the first to devote extended attention to it was J. K. Mozley, *The Impassibility of God: A Survey of Christian Thought* (Cambridge: University Press, 1926), 63–73. Studies since then include Henri Crouzel, "La Passion de l'Impassible: un essai apologétique et polémique du IIIe siècle," in *L'homme devant Dieu: Mélanges offerts au Père Henri de Lubac* (Paris: Aubier, 1963) 1:269–79; Richard Creel, *Divine Impassibility: An Essay in Philosophical Theology* (Cambridge: Cambridge University Press, 1985); Joseph M. Hallman, *The Descent of God: Divine Suffering in History and Theology* (Minneapolis: Fortress Press, 1991), 46–49; Herbert Frohnhofen, ΑΠΑΘΕΙΑ ΤΟΥ ΘΕΟΥ: *Über die Affektlosigkeit Gottes in der griechischen Antike und bei griechisch-sprachigen Kirchenvätern bis zu Gregorios Thaumaturgos* (Frankfurt: Peter Lang, 1987); and Theo Kobusch, "Kann Gott Leiden? Zu den philosophischen Grundlagen der Lehre von der Passibilität Gottes bei Origenes," *Vigiliae Christianae* 46 (1992): 328–33.
114. Crouzel, "La Passion de l'Impassible," 269, 277.
115. Luise Abramowski, "Die Schrift Gregors des Lehrers 'Ad Theopompum' und Philoxenus von Mabbug," *Zeitschrift für Kirchengeschichte* 89 (1978): 273; cf. 277, 280.

Gregory Thaumaturgus appears as "the Teacher" in his *Life* by Gregory of Nyssa,[116] I see no reason why Gregory the Teacher and Gregory Thaumaturgus should not be one and the same.

(44) It survives only in Syriac translation, and was first published by Paul de Lagarde in 1858.[117] In 1880, Victor Ryssel gave the text publicity and made it accessible beyond the world of Syriac scholars by publishing his own German translation of the *To Theopompus* in his monograph on Gregory.[118] Still wider circulation came with the 1883 republication of the Syriac text by Johannes Pitra, with a Latin translation by P. Martin.[119] Both Lagarde and Pitra publish the text as it is contained in the sole surviving manuscript, British Museum Syriac addition 12156.

(45) As to the English translation provided in this volume, I must admit that I am not qualified to produce on my own a translation from the Syriac.[120] The present translation began from both Martin's Latin and Ryssel's German, with assistance from textual comments on the Syriac made by Professor Abramowski of Tübingen.[121] Dr. Sebastian Brock of Oxford University generously took that translation and compared it carefully to the Syriac text, making the corrections which were necessary throughout. Because Dr. Brock's familiarity with early Syriac texts and his expertise in interpreting the specialized terminology found in Christian texts are recognized as unsurpassed in the English-speaking world today, I confidently offer the translation printed here to the English-speaking reader.

116. Seven times: 921A, 925C, 937B, 941D, 949C, 952C, 953A.
117. Paul de Lagarde, *Analecta syriaca* (Leipzig, 1858), 46–64. A new edition of the Syriac is awaited; see Luise Abramowski, "Zur geplanten Ausgabe von Brit. Mus. add. 12156," in *Texte und Textkritik: eine Aufsatzsammlung*, edited by Jürgen Dummer, Texte und Untersuchungen, vol. 133 (Berlin: Akademie-Verlag, 1987), 23–28.
118. Ryssel, *Gregorius Thaumaturgus*, 71–99, with extensive notes in the appendices.
119. Johannes Baptista Pitra, *Analecta sacra spicilegio Solesmensi* (Paris: Ex publico Galliarum typographeo, 1883), 4:103–20, 363–76.
120. I am comforted by the similar admission from Crouzel, "La Passion de l'Impassible," 269, n. 5: "Notre ignorance du syriaque nous oblige d'étudier l'`À Théopompe' à travers la traduction latine de P. Martin: grâce à l'obligeance de Mgr Ducros, vice-recteur de l'Institut Catholique de Toulouse, nous avons pu cependant vérifier sur le syriaque les passages importants."
121. Abramowski, "Die Schrift," 273–90.

To Philagrius, on Consubstantiality

(46) While I believe that this small treatise is the work of Gregory Thaumaturgus, it must be admitted that there are plenty of difficulties involved in its evaluation. These difficulties begin with the title, which here is taken from the Syriac transmission.[122]

(47) "On Consubstantiality" is a phrase which seems more appropriate to a post-Nicene context,[123] and was probably added as an inscription in order to identify the subject matter for later readers. The addressee, "Philagrius," has also been the object of much controversy. Ryssel himself wished to see it as a corruption of the name of the philosopher Porphyry,[124] but this suggestion has attracted no support.[125] This discovery that this treatise was widely known in Greek transmission[126] under the attribution to Gregory Nazianzen (as *ep.* 243) or to Gregory of Nyssa (as *ep.* 26) changed matters, because the Greek title is Πρὸς Εὐάγριον, "To Evagrius." Which name was original could no longer be answered without a consideration of the authorship and the priority of the attributions.

(48) Neither the editor of Gregory of Nyssa's letters[127] nor the modern editors of the works of Gregory Nazianzen[128] think that this work can be by their fourth-century Gregories; Sinko says that it cannot be by Nazianzen because the latter explicitly

---

122. The Syriac text, based on two manuscripts, may be found in Pitra, *Analecta sacra*, 100-103, with a Latin translation by P. Martin on 360-63.
123. Friedrich Baethgen, however, says that prior to the condemnation of Paul of Samosata this terminology would have been perfectly possible; see his review of Ryssel's book in *idem, Göttingsche gelehrte Anzeigen* pt. 44 (1880): 1399.
124. Ryssel, *Gregorius Thaumaturgus*, 110-15.
125. Baethgen (1404-5) and G. Lechler (*Literarisches Centralblatt für Deutschland* 1880, no. 20:643) in their reviews of Ryssel roundly criticized this element of his treatment, and Ryssel partially retracted the suggestion in *idem*, "Zu Gregorius Thaumaturgus," *Jahrbücher für protestantische Theologie* 7 (1881): 571-72.
126. This fact was first published by Johannes Dräseke, "Zu Victor Ryssel's Schrift," *Jahrbücher für protestantische Theologie* 7 (1881): 379-84.
127. Georgius Pasquali, *Gregorii Nysseni epistulae*, Gregorii Nysseni Opera 8.2 (Berlin, 1955), ii.
128. Thaddaeus Sinko, *De traditione orationum Gregorii Nazianzeni*, Meletemata Patristica 2.1 (Cracow: G. Gebethner, 1917), 154-58; Paul Gallay, *Saint Grégoire de Nazianze: Lettres* 1 (Paris: Les Belles Lettres, 1964), xxi, says, "D'ailleurs, la lettre 243 est reconnue universellement comme inauthentique."

rejected both comparisons for the Trinity used in the *To Philagrius*.[129] Nevertheless, François Refoulé would like to assign it to the circle of Gregory of Nyssa, as influenced by Marcellus of Ancyra, sometime prior to 382, and take the addressee as Evagrius Ponticus, the deacon of Gregory Nazianzen who became a monk in the Egyptian desert.[130] Refoulé sets himself in opposition to Manlio Simonetti, who claimed that both the doctrine and the style of argument in *To Philagrius* fitted a third-century pupil of Origen, and matched the sentiment quoted by Basil of Caesarea, *ep.* 210, as coming from an otherwise unattested work of Gregory Thaumaturgus.[131] Simonetti replied, saying that if it was the work of any of the Gregories it must be by Gregory Thaumaturgus, since neither Nazianzen nor Gregory of Nyssa could have proposed such a modalistic and nominalistic notion of the Trinity. If however one were to look for some unknown figure, as Refoulé had done, Simonetti thought it would be someone in the second half of the third century, not a hundred years later.[132] Both Refoulé and Simonetti, however, were strongly affected by the difficulty of squaring the *To Philagrius* with the *Creed* attributed to Gregory Thaumaturgus by Gregory of Nyssa in his *Life*.

(49) Another suggestion as to the work's authorship was made by Reinoldus Weijenborg, who said that it came from the sect of a modalist bishop of Neocaesarea named Atarbius; so far as I know, Weijenborg never wrote the promised study of the text.[133] Henri Crouzel thought that perhaps Weijenborg had

---

129. He is referring to PG 46.1105CDE.

130. François Refoulé, "La date de la lettre à Évagre," *Recherches de science religieuse* 49 (1961): 520–48.

131. Manlio Simonetti, "Gregorio Nazianzeno o Gregorio Taumaturgo?" *Rendiconti, Istituto Lombardo di scienze e lettere, classe di lettere e scienze morali e storiche* 86 (1953): 101–17. The passage from Basil reads as follows in the translation by Deferrari: "They made an attempt too by letter on my friend Anthimus, bishop of Tyana, on the ground that Gregory had said in his exposition of the faith that Father and Son are in thought two, but in hypostasis one. The men who congratulate themselves on the subtility of their intelligence could not perceive that this is said not in reference to dogmatic opinion but in controversy with Aelian" (Basil of Caesarea, *The Letters*, trans. Roy J. Deferrari [Cambridge: Harvard University Press, 1962], 207–9).

132. Manlio Simonetti, "Ancora sulla lettera ad Evagrio," *Rivista di cultura classica e medioevale* 4 (1962): 371–74.

133. Reinoldus Weijenborg, "De authenticitate et sensu quarumdam epistu-

thrown some light on the situation in Neocaesarea in Basil's time, but withheld comment on his suggestion that *To Philagrius* might belong to that context.[134]

(50) Michel van Esbroeck has contended for a similar fourth-century context for the treatise, and grouped it with the text quoted by Basil in *ep.* 210 and two other short *spuria* of Gregory Thaumaturgus.[135] Van Esbroeck promises a fuller publication of the texts in question, one of which (CPG 1787) exists only in Arabic and Ethiopic transmission.[136] For the other text, CPG 1781, besides the hard-to-find article by C. P. Caspari, in which he compares that brief text with one by Gregory of Nyssa "On what it means to be in the image and in the likeness of God," there is now a critical Greek edition of both those texts by Karl-Heinz Uthemann.[137] I do not find the similarities among the texts which van Esbroeck presents to be so striking as to indicate a common provenance. For one thing, *To Philagrius* lacks the explicit "Trinity"-language of CPG 1781 and 1787. I see no reason here to change my earlier view that the *To Philagrius* should be assigned to the third-century Gregory Thaumaturgus.[138]

(51) Two facts about the tradition of the Greek text point, in

---

larum s. Basilio Magno et Apollinario Laodiceno adscriptarum," *Antonianum* 34 (1959): 291, n. 10.

134. Henri Crouzel, "Grégoire le Thaumaturge et le Dialogue avec Elien," *Recherches de science religieuse* 51 (1963): 429–30.

135. Michel van Esbroeck, "Sur quatre traités attribuées à Grégoire, et leur contexte Marcellien (CPG 3222, 1781 et 1787)," in Hubertus Drobner and Christoph Klock, *Studien zu Gregor von Nyssa und der christlichen Spätantike* (Leiden: E. J. Brill, 1990), 3–15.

136. CPG 1787. The entry in the *Clavis Patrum Graecorum* notes "Textus hic ortus uidetur s. v exeunte," which would make it a century later than van Esbroeck's evaluation, "C'est une fois de plus un texte à verser au dossier du IVe siècle..." (van Esbroeck, "Sur quatre traités," 13).

137. C. P. Caspari, "Et Gregorius Thaumaturgus tillagt Fragment med Begyndelsen: 'Af det, der finder Sted hos os, kan man erkjende det, der er over os,'" *Theologisk Tidsskrift for den evangelisk-lutherske Kirche i Norge* 8 (1882): 53–59; Karl-Heinz Uthemann, "'Die Ἄπορα des Gregorius von Nyssa'? Ein Beitrag zur Geistmetaphysik in Byzanz mit einer Edition von CPG 1781," *Byzantion* 63 (1993): 237–27; the text edition is on 311–17.

138. Michael Slusser, "The 'To Philagrius on Consubstantiality' of Gregory Thaumaturgus," in *Studia Patristica* 19, ed. Elizabeth A. Livingstone (Leuven: Peeters, 1989), 230–35. I refer the reader who wishes more detailed discussion to this article.

my opinion, to the greater claims of Gregory Thaumaturgus to its authorship. First, in the manuscript tradition of Gregory Nazianzen, *ep.* 243 (*To Philagrius*) appears in an appendix to his main works, and nearly always in close proximity to the *Metaphrase on Ecclesiastes*, Gregory Thaumaturgus's best-attested work, and the brief *Glossary on Ezekiel* (which I have translated here among the *dubia*).[139] Second, in the six manuscripts of Gregory of Nyssa containing *ep.* 26 (our text) which I have located in catalogs, the oldest has *ep.* 26, lacking its first paragraphs, immediately after the *Life of Gregory Thaumaturgus*;[140] only the latest and most fragmentary of the other five does not also contain the *Life*. These are small pointers, but on this difficult question even slight external attestation is better than none at all.

(52) In view of the incorrectness of the manuscript attributions to Gregory Nazianzen and Gregory of Nyssa, I suspect also the indication in their manuscript tradition of the addressee as "Evagrius": Nazianzen's famous deacon-turned-monk named Evagrius, and the "Evagrius" who sometimes features in the manuscript title of Gregory of Nyssa's oration *On his own ordination*,[141] are more likely to have displaced an original "Philagrius" than the other way around.

(53) The text translated here is that printed by Migne as *ep.* 26 of Gregory of Nyssa (PG 46.1101–7), compared with that printed by the Maurist editors of Gregory Nazianzen.

To Tatian, on the Soul

(54) This little treatise stands in the *Clavis Patrum Graecorum* under the "Spuria" of Gregory Thaumaturgus as CPG 1773, and also under the name of Maximus Confessor at CPG 7717. While

139. Of the 54 Gregory Nazianzen manuscripts which I have located in catalogs, 34 have the three named texts grouped together, 29 of those in the order *ep.* 243, *Glossary*, *Metaphrase*; in two more, *ep.* 243 and the *Metaphrase* are together without the *Glossary*. In several others which lack the *Metaphrase*, *ep.* 243 is at the end of the manuscript.

140. Cod. Milan, Bibl. Ambros. 862 (Martini-Bassi, 960), 11th century. Nearly an entire Migne column of the Greek text is missing.

141. See Ernst Gebhardt, "Titel und Zeit der Rede Gregors von Nyssa 'In suam ordinationem,'" *Hermes* 89 (1961): 503–7.

Dräseke had no difficulty accepting it as a work of Gregory,[142] Jules Lebreton ascribes it to "an unknown author who used the work of Nemesius [of Emesa] on the nature of man and perhaps also a fragment of St. Gregory Thaumaturgus."[143] The parts which Lebreton sees as possibly traceable to Gregory are chapters 5–7; his reasons are the use of arguments from Plato which are not found in Nemesius, the citation of a fragment of chapter 5 by Nicholas of Methone as coming from Gregory, and the comparatively personal style of the section, "the only one where the author puts himself in the picture and seems to be speaking to a definite addressee."[144] More recently, A. Whealey has conjectured that *To Tatian, on the Soul* comes from a circle close to St. Justin Martyr and that the "Tatian" in question was Justin's Syrian student who wrote the *Oratio ad Graecos*.[145] His point that there is no reason to insist that any of the treatise is posterior to Nemesius of Emesa is well taken.[146]

(55) The manuscript tradition is very confused. The work appears in Greek manuscripts attributed to Gregory of Nyssa[147] and Gregory Nazianzen,[148] as well as to Gregory Thaumaturgus and Maximus; the *Clavis Patrum Graecorum* points to Syriac and Arabic transmission under the names of Aristotle and Ibn Sina. Compounding the difficulty of studying the work is the fact that even the Greek manuscripts vary widely in their contents. In this

---

142. Johannes Dräseke, "Zu Gregorios' von Neocäsarea Schrift 'Über die Seele,'" *Zeitschrift für wissenschaftliche Theologie* 44 (1901): 87–100.

143. Jules Lebreton, "Le traité de l'âme de saint Grégoire le Thaumaturge," *Bulletin de littérature ecclésiastique* 8 (1906): 83.

144. Lebreton, "Le traité de l'âme," 81.

145. A. Whealey, "'To Tatian on the Soul': A Treatise from the Circle of Tatian the Syrian and Justin Martyr?" *Recherches de théologie ancienne et médiévale* 63 (1996): 136-45. Whealey's main argument stems from the comparison of the language of our little treatise with that of Justin in his acknowledged works. His parallels are necessarily constricted by the brevity and plain character of *To Tatian on the Soul*, but, even allowing for that, I do not find his parallels strong enough to indicate common authorship.

146. *Ibid.*, 137–38. In addition, it is possible that the perceived similarities stem from the doxographical tradition.

147. Codex London British Museum Old Royal 16.D.I, and Codex Vaticanus Gr. 1907.

148. Codex Gr. Marucellianus A 155; cf. Girolamo Vitelli, *Indice de' Codici Greci Riccardiani, Magliabechiani e Marucelliani* (Firenze-Roma, 1894).

volume, I have settled for translating a text collated from that printed in Migne's *Patrologia* under Gregory Thaumaturgus (PG 10.1137–46) and that printed under Maximus (PG 91.353–62). With the exception of three arguments at the end of chapter 4, the differences are minor.

(56) It is possible that this work has been attributed to Gregory Thaumaturgus in some manuscripts because he wrote it, or at least (as Lebreton suggests) a part of it. If it is by our Gregory, it adds little to our picture of his theology; and if it is not, one wonders why it came to be attributed to him. The most significant point of contact between this and the works whose provenance is less doubtful is the explicit avoidance of scriptural evidence concerning the soul. In that respect, whether genuine or spurious, it corroborates the impression that Gregory's work was believed to be exoteric and directed to an audience either unfamiliar with or uncommitted to the biblical writings.

Glossary on Ezekiel

(57) In many of the chief manuscripts of Gregory Nazianzen there is a brief text of uncertain authorship, the so-called *Significatio in Ezechielem* (CPG 3060). It looks like a glossary, containing some textual observations and keys to allegorical interpretation, but also a few bits of legendary information. The text lacks both a formal beginning and a conclusion, but it does not seem to be a fragment of a larger text, because it deals only with chapter one of Ezekiel and hence cannot have had much before it, and ends with a few general statements which contrast with the style of the earlier glossary. Thaddeus Sinko harshly but defensibly described it as "a farrago of Origenistic scholia,"[149] and therefore it is understandable that neither he nor anyone else has taken a serious interest in determining its authorship more closely.

(58) The external evidence is only of an indirect kind. The *Glossary* is found in a characteristic place in an appendix to the

---

149. Sinko, *De traditione*, 166–67: "Demonstratum est enim, opusculum non esse explicationem Ezechielis I 1 ad artem et ad praecepta revocatam, sed farraginem scholiorum ex Origenis scholiis excerptorum et sine ulla ratione ita iuxta se positorum, ut diversas pericopas diversasque res sine ullo nexu explicent."

manuscripts of Gregory Nazianzen which Sinko classified as "family N."[150] It is nearly always together with two other works which do not belong to Gregory Nazianzen, *To Philagrius on Consubstantiality* and *Metaphrase on Ecclesiastes*.[151] The latter is assigned with great assurance to Gregory Thaumaturgus,[152] and the former, as we have seen, is assigned to Gregory Thaumaturgus in two Syriac manuscripts. Two Armenian manuscripts at Venice contain what appears to be our work, but under the name of John Chrysostom, although the author of the manuscript catalogue corrects (*sic*) that to Gregory of Nyssa.[153] To balance those suggestions of John Chrysostom and Gregory of Nyssa as the author of our text, Bernard de Montfaucon, in his notes to his edition of Origen's *Hexapla*, cites our text as the work of Gregory Thaumaturgus.[154] Although Montfaucon does not give any reasons for this attribution, he was a great expert, and his long-forgotten view may carry some weight.

(59) So can the author of this document be determined, and if it can, is any of the nominees so far suggested a likely candidate for the dubious honor? There are enough points of contact with Origen's work to make it quite likely that the author of the *Glossary* knew at least the Hexapla, if not also Origen's approach

---

150. Sinko, *De traditione*, 151. Justin Mossay refers to this group of MSS as the "recueil de 52." Cf. *idem*, *Grégoire de Nazianze. Discours 1–3*, SC 247 (Paris: Cerf, 1978), 54–55.

151. In an extended search of manuscript catalogues, I have found only two manuscripts in which the *Glossary* is found by itself: cod. Paris. gr. 531 and cod. Paris. suppl. gr. 154, both of the eleventh century. In both cases manuscripts of Gregory Nazianzen are involved, and in cod. Paris. suppl. gr. 154 the *Glossary* is still in an appendix.

152. Most notably on the evidence of Jerome (PL 23.1049B).

153. Muyldermans, "Répertoire," 229. According to Muyldermans, "Miscellanea Armeniaca," *Le Muséon* 47 (1934): 295, Sarghissian comments on the presence of the *Glossary* in another manuscript, "En fait, on ne connaît pas l'auteur de cette 'élucubration.' Pareille prose a eu cependant un succès relatif de la part de plus d'un commentateur arménien des oeuvres d'Evagre. . . . L'auteur du commentaire dont il s'agit içi, demeure également inconnu. D'après une note du catalogue de Venise (2e vol., col. 854), il fait précéder son exégèse sur la vision d'Ezéchiel d'un court aperçu sur la vie et les oeuvres du moine de Scéte."

154. Bernard de Montfaucon, *Hexaplorum Origenis quae supersunt* (Paris, 1713), 2:269, 271 refers to "Gregorio Neocaesariensis in Ezechielem" as one of the sources he uses, and twice cites our text verbatim in his notes to Ezek 1.7 and 1.16. He does not say whether he is working from a manuscript or from a printed book.

to the allegorical interpretation of several scriptural images. There is not enough evidence, in my opinion, to allow us to conclude that the material for this glossary was simply extracted from writings of Origen. A student of Origen's would be a reasonable candidate, but at this point we need to be cautious about assuming the extent to which his students picked up various traits of his theology and scholarship. Wolfgang Bienert has challenged, quite properly in my view, the conventional assumptions about Origen's domination of third-century theology even in Alexandria.[155] Because of the company which the *Glossary* keeps in the manuscript tradition, Gregory Thaumaturgus might be a candidate, but I confess that I have not been able to turn up any parallels in his other works.

(60) Perhaps we should resist the desire to ascribe the *Glossary* to any known author, and postulate a hitherto unknown figure, or one so obscure that only his bare name occurs in the literature. But if the *Glossary* was not thought in antiquity to belong to some well-known and respected author, why did anyone bother to preserve a work of such slight literary or theological interest as this early Christian glossary on Ezekiel?

(61) The translation which I have made for this volume is of the Greek text printed in the Maurist edition of Gregory Nazianzen (Paris, 1778), 1:870–72.

Letter of Origen to Gregory

(62) Many authors[156] take this letter to Gregory, which appears in the *Philocalia*, chapter 13, as having been written by Origen to Gregory Thaumaturgus, but I am skeptical. Although Eric

---

155. The argument is set out at length in his book, Wolfgang A. Bienert, *Dionysius von Alexandrien: Zur Frage des Origenismus im dritten Jahrhundert.* "Patristische Text und Studien, Band 21." (Berlin: Walter de Gruyter, 1978), 1–25, especially in his introduction. His conclusions (222–23) are quite nuanced and note the persistence of Origen's thought in Alexandria despite the reluctance of most of its bishops to endorse it, much less extend it.

156. Crouzel, "Gregor I," 785, and, *idem, Remerciement,* 79–92; see also *idem,* "Faut-il," 300–18; Fouskas, Γρηγόριος, 82–83 (he dates it also, between A.D. 235–37); Johannes Dräseke, "Der Brief des Origenes an Gregorios von Neocäsarea," *Jahrbücher für protestantische Theologie* 7 (1881): 102–26.

Junod himself denies the self-sufficiency of the argument he presents, I find it very persuasive: at only two places in the *Philocalia*, here and in chapter 27, do its compilers, Gregory Nazianzen and Basil of Caesarea, omit a full textual reference to the work which is about to be cited. Junod says, "This silence makes us doubt that the addressee of the letter was the Wonderworker. For if he had been the addressee, how could Gregory and especially Basil not have known? The latter was in contact with the community of Neocaesarea, and he had a special veneration for the memory of its bishop."[157]

(63) This letter is included in an appendix here nonetheless, both because it has so long been associated with the relationship between Origen and Gregory Thaumaturgus and because it throws light on Origen's way with the young men like Gregory Thaumaturgus who came to learn philosophy from him. In many details it corroborates the picture given by the *Address* of what study with Origen was like. Jesus Christ is mentioned in the last paragraph as the source of certain gospel admonitions, and in the context of our knowledge of and participation in God, but in this (admittedly brief) text as in the *Address* the Passion and Resurrection of Jesus are not mentioned.

157. Eric Junod, "Particularités de la Philocalie," in *Origeniana*, ed. Henri Crouzel, Gennaro Lomiento, and Josep Rius-Camps (Bari: Istituto di Letteratura Cristiana Antica, 1975), 186–87. In n. 18, he adds that he shares Pierre Nautin's view that the letter was addressed to a Palestinian studying at Alexandria.

THE LIFE OF GREGORY THE WONDERWORKER

ON THE LIFE AND WONDERS OF OUR FATHER AMONG THE SAINTS, GREGORY THE WONDERWORKER

by Gregory, Bishop of Nyssa

1. Introduction.

THE OBJECT OF MY ADDRESS [893A, H3][1] and of the present assembly are one and the same. For Gregory the Great furnishes you with the occasion for gathering together, and me with that of speaking. As I see it, one and the same power is required both for achieving virtue in deed and for describing what is good worthily in a speech. Consequently the same ally must be called upon for help as the one through whose aid he achieved virtue in his lifetime. This, I am convinced, is the grace of the Holy Spirit, which empowers both for life and for discourse those who with its help endeavor at each of them. So since that brilliant and widely admired life was achieved by the power of the Spirit, we need to pray that the same assistance will come upon this discourse as was present in his life, [893B] in order that the panegyric may not be found unworthy of his accomplishments, but may display [H4] so noble a man to those who are here in his memory just as he was seen on the occasion of his deeds by those who were there at the time.

(2) Now if it were valueless to remember those who were outstanding in virtue, and no incentive toward excellence to those who listen, then likewise it would be superfluous, unprofitable, and no use to anyone for someone to furnish a laudatory discourse, since he would deliver it in vain and fatigue

---

1. The bracketed numbers are keyed to the columns in Migne and the pages of Heil's edition.

the ears to no purpose. But there is such grace attaching to the discourse, if it be done right, that the benefit to the hearers will be much like that which the beacon fire furnishes to those who are steering towards it from the open sea, directing those who are sailing aimlessly on the ocean in the dark. Therefore I think we both need to take equal care in this endeavor, [893C] you in listening and I in speaking. For it is clear that when his life of virtue, like a beacon fire, shines out to our souls through recollection, it becomes a path toward the good both for the one who describes it and for his hearers. We human beings are so constituted that we naturally prize everything praiseworthy and valuable, and desire to possess it.

(3) So that is how lofty the subject of this discussion is. But I am in no danger whatsoever in risking this subject, whether my discourse can rise to heights appropriate to such great deeds [896A] or not; the resulting tribute will be the same to our hero either way. For if the speech captures the marvels, it will completely dazzle your ears with his achievements; if it should fall short, even then the hero's glory would shine forth, for it is the highest tribute to a man to demonstrate that he exceeds our power to praise him adequately.

(4) No one who has been trained in divine wisdom [896B] should seek to praise someone who is spiritually renowned by using the artificial devices of the encomium,[2] in the manner of those outside. For discernment of the good is not based on what we and the others have in common, nor does [H5] one find that those who live according to the world and those who have transcended the world value the same things alike. To the former, what seems great and worthy of attention includes wealth, pedigree, glory, worldly powers, the founding stories of their homelands, and narratives which intelligent people would shun: victories, battlefields, and the horrors of war.

---

2. According to George A. Kennedy, *Greek Rhetoric under Christian Emperors* (Princeton: Princeton University Press, 1983), 63, "an encomium celebrates mortals and is worked out in accordance with art.... Headings are: proemium; *genos*, divided into nation, city, and laws; deeds, divided into those relating to soul, body, and fortune; synkrisis, or favorable comparison with another; epilogue, for example a prayer." The reader will note many of these headings reflected in Gregory of Nyssa's oration.

(5) To our mentality, on the other hand, just one native land deserves honor, paradise, the first home of the human race; just one city, the heavenly one, fashioned of living stones, with God for its creator and builder; just one excellence of lineage, kinship to God [896C]—which no one gets automatically (like a good pedigree in the natural order of things, which often flows even to the wicked through this automatic succession) but which one acquires only by free choice.[3] "For as many as received him," says the voice of God, "to them he gave the power to become children of God."[4] What could be more excellent than such a pedigree? All that the others have for their lineage are myths and fabrications, and deceits of demons mixed up with mythical tales,[5] but our lineage has no need of stories. For whoever looks up to heaven and takes in its beauties and all creation with the eye of the soul, all the wonders it can comprehend of such things, will find there the tales of where we come from; [896D] or rather not of that native land itself but of the colony which we had colonized from the life above before we were given this present world.[6] But if such is the colony, think what the metropolis on which it depends must be, what beauty that has, what its palaces are like, what happiness belongs to those who dwell there. For if created phenomena [H6] are such as to be beyond praise, what must we think of that which is above them, which the eye cannot see nor the ear perceive nor the mind guess at?[7]

(6) The godly rule for encomia uses these traits of spiritual renown to counter the inanities of the world, deeming it shame-

---

3. See Gregory of Nyssa's *Catechetical Oration*, ch. 33 (to which compare Justin, *1 Apol.* 61), and ch. 38–39, for birth by free choice rather than necessity.
4. John 1.12.
5. The notion that demons interpolated misleading material into ancient texts is also suggested by Justin, *1 Apol.* 54–57.
6. Lucas F. Mateo-Seco, "El cristiano ante la vida y ante la morte: Estudio del Panegírico de Gregorio de Nisa sobre Gregorio Taumaturgo," in *The Biographical Works of Gregory of Nyssa*, ed. Andreas Spira (Philadelphia: Philadelphia Patristics Foundation, 1984), 197–219, at 205–6 discusses this passage and proposes that the "colony" is paradise, the "metropolis" heaven. Gregory of Nyssa in the *Dialogue on the Soul and Resurrection* takes a very negative view of any preexistence of souls.
7. Cf. 1 Cor 2.9.

ful that those singled out in the latter are exalted on account of earthly [897A] advantages. So let some worldly man with a view to material happiness try to earn praise from people for reasons such as these: if someone's ancestral land was rich in cattle, if the sea nearby is more than enough for those who exploit it for wealth, if contrasting courses of stones beautify its buildings. But one who looks to the life above, for whom purity of soul is beauty, and freedom from possessions is wealth, and virtue is the ancestral land, and the very palaces of God the city—such a one will turn earthlings' love of honor into a reproach.

(7) Therefore we too, refraining from such considerations, will not begin the praises of the great Gregory with his lineage, nor summon his ancestors to help with the encomia, knowing that no praise is true unless it is proper to those who are being praised. [897B] But we call "proper" that which lasts so long that it cannot be taken away. Therefore prescinding from everything such as wealth, glory, honor, luxury, pleasure, relatives and friends, we remain concerned only with the disposition toward wickedness or virtue: we consider only the virtuous to be blessed.

(8) And let no one think that I have nothing worth saying about this man's native land or forebears, [H7] pretending to overlook these things to conceal some disgrace.[8] For who is there who [897C] does not know the popular designation of the sea, applied by everyone to this nation above all, by which the virtue of those who have always lived here is attested? For alone out of all land and sea this is called the "Friendly Sea,"[9] either because the name conveys to them the high regard foreigners have toward those who dwell there, or because it is the kind of place which blesses ungrudgingly with what they need to live, not only its inhabitants and natives, but also those who resort there from all over the world. Such is the nature of the region, that it produces abundantly everything necessary for life, and does not lack goods from other places, since the sea makes theirs the goods from everywhere. [897D]

(9) The whole nation is such that someone might look at any of its parts by itself and suppose that it excels the others; but

---

8. Of course, it is quite possible that Gregory of Nyssa had little or no information about Gregory on these topics.

9. I.e., ὁ Πόντος Εὔξεινος, the Greek name for the Black Sea.

nonetheless, by the common judgment of the nation, the most outstanding place in their whole region is the city of the great Gregory, which a famous emperor, one of the first of the Romans, Caesar by name, for love and affection for the whole district, permitted to be called after himself.[10] But these things are irrelevant to our purpose if they give the impression that, because of them, that great saint is proved nobler if the countryside sags under the weight of its harvests, if the city is decked with monuments, if it seems that goods from all over are brought abundantly by the nearby sea. [900A]

(10) Neither shall I call to mind in this discourse his ancestors who set the stage for his birth in the order of the flesh, or talk about their wealth, their ambition, their worldly renown. For what would these contribute to the praise—tombs, and monuments, and inscriptions, and dead anecdotes—for one who raised himself above the whole [H8] world, though there is no other way to associate with his renown those whose kinship, on the natural level, this man renounced? For they were led astray in the error of idols, but he, fixing his gaze on the truth, has added himself to the kinship from on high through faith. [900B]

2. *Gregory's youthful dedication to virtue.*

(11) But while we pass over his origins and the city where he first lived, as furnishing us with nothing relevant to our present narrative, we shall however begin our tribute here where he made the beginning of his life of virtue. For when he was bereft of the natural care to his youthful body by his parents' death, at just the time when in most people the mind sins, since it is too young to be experienced in the judgment of the good, he showed from the very first what he would be like at full maturity. And just as the best seedlings, when they rise quickly from first growth to straight young saplings, already give their growers promise of their later beauty, so too he, at an age when for others [900C] the soul is in great danger on account of ignorance, since

---

10. The reader will recognize that Gregory of Nyssa is actually praising his audience in this passage. Formerly known as Sebaste, the capital of Pontus was given the name Neocaesarea in the first century. It is today called Niksar.

youth more often than not slides easily down toward frivolous and stupid things—at that point, by the first choice of his own life, he manifested in his own person that David speaks truly, "The just will flourish like the palm tree." For this tree alone grows up from the earth with its crown full-sized, and as it grows in height receives no increment to its breadth with the passage of time. So he too flourished from his first appearance, emerging perfect and mature immediately in the choice of his life. For, forsaking all that youth goes wild over—riding, hunting to hounds, jewelry, clothes, gambling, [H9] luxurious living—he was from the first complete in the possession of the virtues, consistently choosing what was best for his age. [900D]

(12) The first of the virtues he set out to acquire was wisdom. Teamed up with it by implication was its counterpart, temperance. A strong support to both was self-control, and modesty and freedom from anger were both completed by a disdain for possessions. For vanity and arrogance have no other origin if greed does not bring such passions in its train. [901A] The Logos drove the patriarch Abraham, who was learned in Chaldean philosophy, and understood the harmonious and orderly disposition and movement of the stars,[11] to reckon the possession of knowledge of these things as inferior to the surpassing contemplation of the good. He considered that if what was perceptible to the senses is so great, what must those things which are above sense be? Thus, he drove him to acquire what he sought by advancing via worldly[12] wisdom and becoming more lofty through that, so as somehow thereby to approach what is imperceptible. In just the same way[13] also this Great One,[14] when he had assiduously acquainted himself with the worldly philosophy, through the things by which Hellenism convinces most people, by these same things he was led to the understanding of Christianity, and forsaking the mistaken religious observance of his ancestors he began to seek the truth about reality, [901B] since he had

11. Josephus, *Antiquities* 1.8.2.
12. Literally "the outside" wisdom or philosophy, as often in Christian literature; cf. 1 Cor 5.12.
13. I.e., like Abraham.
14. ὁ μέγας, as Gregory of Nyssa frequently terms the Wonderworker.

learned, from the very things at which those outside labor, the incoherence of Greek doctrines.

(13) For after he saw Greek and barbarian philosophy alike divided into different conceptions in their opinions of the divine, and the leading exponents of the positions not converging toward one another but competing to consolidate each position separately by subtlety of speech, he left them to refute each other as if in a civil war. He for his part embraced the solid doctrine of faith, which has its foundation in no fancy logical footwork or artificial reasonings but rather was announced in simplicity of expression with equal respect for all, [H10] and which manifests its trustworthiness precisely by being above knowledge. For if what was said were such that it could be comprehended by the power [901C] of human thoughts, it would in no way differ from Greek wisdom. For they are of the opinion that what they are able to comprehend is the same as what is. But since comprehension of the transcendent nature is inaccessible to human reasonings, on this account faith replaces thoughts, extending itself to those things which are above reason and comprehension.

(14) For these reasons, just as Scripture says about Moses, "He was schooled in all the wisdom of the Egyptians,"[15] so also the Great One, coming through all the schooling of the Greeks and knowing by experience the weakness and incoherence of their doctrines, came to be a disciple of the gospel, and even before being initiated through the mystical and incorporeal birth, he so perfected his life that he brought no stain of sin to the baptismal cleansing. [901D]

(15) During his stay in Egypt in the city of Alexander, to which young people who cared for philosophy and medicine stream from all corners of the world, his peers found the sight of a young man endowed with discretion beyond his years hard to bear. For the approbation given to one who is pure was a rebuke to the defiled. Since the intemperate might have some defense if they seemed not to be alone in their attitude, they conceived the idea of a plot to cast some blame upon the life of the Great One,

---

15. Acts 7.22.

and they put forward for his discrediting a woman prostitute who had been [904A] thrown out of a brothel in disgrace. While he, as was his custom, was engaged in examining in a dignified way, together with the leading men, on some subject in philosophy, the woman approached coyly and coquettishly, and giving the impression that she was very well known to him by everything she said and did.[16] Then she said [H11] she had been cheated of her wages, adding also with effrontery the occasions for which she accused him of deprivation of her pay.

(16) But while they who knew his life well were vexed and stirred with anger against the woman, he was not agitated along with those who were provoked to anger on his behalf, nor did he revile her as someone who was very upset might reasonably do. He did not summon character witnesses nor reject the accusation with an oath, nor denounce the wickedness of those who had contrived these attacks against him; [904B] but turning to one of his comrades he said in a quiet and controlled voice, "You, give her the money, so she may not long continue to disturb our present pursuit of reason by importuning us."

(17) When the one so directed learned from the prostitute how much money she was asking from him, he readily counted it all out, and the plot of the licentious against the wise one came to an end, and the slut's reward was already in her hands. At that moment there came from God a testimony to the young man's discretion, and the refutation of the false charge made by his peers. For as she received the money in her hands she was racked by a demonic spirit, wailed in a loud, inhuman, animal cry and fell face down [904C] in the midst of the gathering; an awful and fearful sight to those present, her hair wildly disheveled and torn out by her own hands, her eyes rolled back into her head, and her mouth dribbling foam. And the demon which was choking her did not cease till that Great One had called upon God and interceded for her. [904D]

(18) Such are the stories they tell of the Great One's youth, preliminaries worthy of the events of his later life. In fact, the wonder is so great that even if there were nothing further to add,

---

16. This last six-word phrase is set apart by Heil as a probable later addition.

from this alone he would have grounds second to none for praises among those who have been outstanding in virtue: rich, young, wandering far abroad, sojourning in a populous city, in which, on account of the way young men pass their life in enjoying as much pleasure as possible, [H12] purity was a rebuke to those who lack discretion. He did not have a mother [905A] taking care of all the practicalities of life, nor a father disciplining his daily conduct; yet he raised himself up through freedom from passion so far towards virtue that the Ruler of the Universe became a witness to his actions by refuting the woman's false accusation with a painful blow.

(19) And what better theme could one come up with for an encomium? How could one wonder at this man as he deserves? Did he not dominate his nature by reason, and harness youth to thought like some domesticated animal, and become superior to all the natural passions which are awakened, and arouse against himself the envy which naturally besets all good people? Did he not then rise above this, too, not standing up to defend himself against the plot of his companions, even doing a kindness to the one who was helping them [905B] attack his reputation, by prayer delivering her from the demonic passion?

(20) From history we know Joseph to have been the same sort of person: he was offered a golden opportunity to do wrong with the wife of his master, when she became infatuated with the young man's beauty, and no man would have been a witness of his recklessness. But he too, conscious of the divine eye, preferred to seem to be wicked than become so, and to submit to what evildoers did rather than become an evildoer.[17] But perhaps he even had more to boast of than that story, for as regards turning away from defilement there is a difference between the abomination of adultery and appearing blameworthy in a lesser offense. Now since he judged that, even when there was no danger from the laws, the very pleasure from sin by itself was more to be feared [905C H13] than punishment, he either outdid Joseph in the nobility of the marvel or at least will not be judged second-rate by comparison.

17. Gen 39.6–23.

(21) But that is the kind of preface his life had. What was the life itself like?

(22) After he had passed through the whole education of worldly wisdom, he met a certain Firmilian, from a prominent Cappadocian family, a man of similar moral principles, as he showed by his subsequent life, since he became an ornament of the church of Caesarea, and he manifested to his friend what he wanted to do with his life: to focus on God. When he learned that his friend was preoccupied with the same strong desire, he forsook all concern with worldly philosophy and went with him to the one who at that time was giving instruction in the philosophy of the [905D] Christians (this was Origen, often mentioned in books). Thereby he showed not only his love of learning and hard work but also his serenity and moderation of character, for though he was full of so much wisdom he did not disdain to use another teacher for studies in divine things.

3. *Gregory's return home and ordination.*

(23) And when he had spent with the teacher a period of time appropriate to the studies, although many tried to detain him abroad and they all asked him to stay with them, he, putting his country first, went back up again to his homeland, bringing with him the manifold wealth of wisdom and knowledge, which he imported like a [908A] merchant in worldly affairs who has done business with all the best people. For that matter, to one who judges matters aright, it will not seem entirely insignificant for his reputation that he took no notice of a public appeal from so great a city,[18] and did not give in to the effort made by all its brightest men to get this man to stay, and their local rulers' eagerness for that same purpose. All shared the goal that that Great One should stay with them to instill virtue and teach the laws of life.

(24) But fleeing the occasions [908B] for vanity which came from every side, since he recognized that the passion of arro-

---

18. It is impossible to know what city Gregory of Nyssa has in mind here. Origen was teaching in Caesarea, but there is no hint in the *Address of Thanksgiving* that any attempt was made to keep Gregory Thaumaturgus from returning to his homeland.

gance [H14] usually leads on to a life of wickedness, he sought the quiet life in his native land as a kind of haven. The whole people looked to the man, and everyone was expecting him to teach his learning to the public in their common assemblies, where he might acquire a good repute among them as a sort of fruit of his great labors. But that Great One, knowing whence it was fitting for the true philosophy to be made public by those who seek to understand it accurately, so as never to be consumed in soul by some ambition (for the praise of hearers is devastating, sapping the healthy tension of the soul with a certain arrogance and vainglory), for this reason made silence his example, displaying the treasure which lay within not by words but by deed. Separating himself [908C] from the commotions of the marketplace and from town life altogether, he lived in a remote place alone with himself, and through himself with God. He made little account of the whole world and those in it—not busy running kingdoms, not looking for posts of leadership, not listening to anyone tell how some public matter was being managed.

(25) But since he had set his mind on how the soul might be perfected by virtue, he devoted his entire life to this with zeal, and allowing himself to say good-bye to life's affairs he became in our parts another Moses, rivalling him outright in his wondrous deeds. Both left this agitated and beset life, Moses and Gregory each in his own time going off by himself,[19] until to each the reward of the pure life was [908D] manifested by a theophany. But it is said that Moses had a wife along with philosophy, while Gregory made virtue his only consort. So although they both had the same aim, for each of them departed from the crowd with the purpose of penetrating the divine mysteries [H15] with the pure eye of the soul, someone who knows how to size up virtue is entitled to judge which of them was marked more by the passionless[20] life: the one who stooped to the legitimate and permissible participation in pleasures, or the one who transcended even that and gave no opening into his life to material attachment.

(26) Phaidimos, who at that time presided over the church of

---

19. Moses fled to the land of Midian in Exod 2.15, and married Jethro's daughter Zipporah. See Gregory of Nyssa, *Life of Moses* 19–20.
20. That is, the life free of irrational and alienating emotions.

Amaseia [909A] and enjoyed a God-given power of foreknowledge from the Holy Spirit, tried as hard as he could to get hold of the great Gregory and make him a leader of the church, so that he might not lead such a good life inactive and without benefit. But the latter, sensing what the priest was about, managed to hide by shifting from one retreat to another. After having tried everything, the great Phaidimos, although he used every stratagem and idea, was unable to recruit the man to the priesthood, since he had been protected by many visions from being caught by the hand of the priest. Both of them were equally persistent in their efforts, the one eager to capture, the other to evade his pursuer. For the former saw a holy offering to bring to God, while the other feared lest [909B] the introduction into his life of the thought of the priesthood might be a burden impeding his way to philosophy.

(27) For this reason Phaidimos, overcome by some divine impulse concerning the task he was facing, disregarding the intervening distance by which he was separated from Gregory (he was three days' journey away), but looking to God and saying that both of them at that moment were equally present to the sight of God, laid on Gregory his word in place of his hand, consecrating to God one who was not present bodily, and allotting to him that city which up to that time happened to be so strongly gripped by the deception of idols that, [H16] although the number of those who dwelt in the city and its environs was beyond counting, not more than seventeen could be found who had received the doctrine of faith.[21] [909C]

4. *Gregory's initiation through a heavenly vision.*

(28) So when he had thus willy-nilly come under the yoke, and later all the proper ceremonies had been carried out on him, and having requested a little time from the one who had

---

21. On this strange ordination, see the analysis by K. N. Papadopoulos, "Λειτουργικὰ σημειώματα," *Kleronomia* 12 (1980), 5–6, who proposes that Phaidimos designated Gregory a presbyter without ordaining him, on the grounds that confessors did not need ordination to the presbyterate. Later Gregory would have been ordained bishop. I doubt if Gregory of Nyssa was so concerned to save canonical precision.

summoned him to the priesthood to come to an understanding of the exact purport of the mystery, he no longer, as the Apostle says, thought it right to pay heed "to flesh and blood,"[22] but asked that he be given by God a manifestation of what is hidden. And he did not feel confident in preaching the word until the truth had been revealed to him in some visible way. [909D]

(29) For while he was concentrating during the night on the doctrine of faith, and turning over all sorts of thoughts in his mind (for even then there were those who were falsifying the true doctrine, and through the plausibility of their proposals often making the truth unclear even to experts)—to him, then, as he was lying awake and pondering, someone appeared in a vision, in human shape, elderly looking, very dignified in garb, displaying every virtue in [912A] the grace of his countenance and the calmness of his appearance. Astonished at the sight, he got up from his bed to learn who this might be and why he had come. When the latter calmed his distress of mind with a quiet voice and said that he had appeared to him by divine command on account of the matters about which he was uncertain, so that the truth of the orthodox[23] faith might be disclosed, he took heart at the word and looked to him with joy and amazement.

(30) Then as the figure suddenly extended his hand and by the line of his [H17] fingers indicated to him what appeared at his side, he turned his eyes to where the hand was pointing and saw, across from the one he had seen, another [912B] vision, in female form, larger than human size. Astonished once again, he lowered his eyes to himself and was at a loss at the sight, not able to bear to look at the manifestation. For the paradox of the vision lay precisely in this, that although the night was far advanced, light illumined the appearances for him, like something bright lighting a lamp. Therefore since he was not able with his eyes to bear the vision, he heard through a kind of word those who had appeared to him discussing with each other the doctrine about which he was pondering, so that he not only was instructed as to the true knowledge of the faith but also recognized the

---

22. Gal 1.16.
23. τῆς εὐσεβοῦς πίστεως.

ones who had appeared by their names, since each of them addressed the other by their proper name.

(31) For he is said to have heard [912C] from the one who appeared in female form as she urged the evangelist John to show the young man the mystery of the truth; and that the latter said that he was ready to indulge the mother of the Lord also in this, since it pleased her. And when he had thus uttered the doctrine, balanced and clearly defined, they again vanished from view. And he is said to have written down that divine initiation[24] as soon as possible, and afterwards to have used it as the basis for his preaching in the church and to have left that God-given teaching to his successors as a kind of inheritance, by which the people there are initiated to this day, thus remaining unaffected by every heretical wickedness.

(32) Now the words of the initiation are these [912D]:

One God: Father of the living Word, subsistent wisdom and power and eternal impress;[25] perfect begetter of perfect; Father of only-begotten Son. [H18]

One Lord: only from only; God from God; impress and image of the Godhead; effective Word; wisdom embracing the structure of the universe, and power which makes the entire creation; true Son of true Father; invisible of invisible, and incorruptible of incorruptible, and immortal of immortal, and eternal of eternal.

One Holy Spirit: holding existence from God, and manifested through the Son (namely to human beings); perfect image of the perfect Son; life [913A] the cause of living things;[26] holiness who makes sanctification possible; by whom is manifested God the Father, who is over all and in all, and God the Son, who is through all.

Perfect Trinity: in glory and eternity and sovereignty neither divided nor estranged. [H19]

(Therefore there is nothing created or subservient in the Trinity, nor anything introduced which did not exist before but came later. Therefore neither did the Son fall short of the Father, nor the Spirit of the Son; but the same Trinity remains always undisturbed and unaltered.)[27]

---

24. Here, and in the passage which follows, the term μυσταγωγία, "mystagogy," and its cognate verb are used, with a view to the baptismal faith transmitted to neophytes.

25. Heb 1.3.

26. Many sources have next "holy fountain," but Heil does not consider that to belong to Gregory of Nyssa's original text.

27. Even those who do not accept L. Abramowski's argument that this initia-

Whoever would like to be convinced of this should listen to the church, in which he proclaimed the doctrine, where the very inscriptions of that blessed hand are preserved to this very day.[28] Do these not rival [913B] in the marvelous nature of their grace those divinely fashioned tablets of stone? I refer to those tablets on which the legislation of the divine will was engraved. For just as the word says that Moses, having left the world of appearances and calmed his soul within the invisible shrines (for this is what "the darkness" stands for),[29] learned the divine mysteries, and in person instructed the whole people in the knowledge of God, the same dispensation is to be seen in the case of this Great One. He had not some visible mountain of earth but the pinnacle of ardent desire for the true teachings; for darkness, the vision which others could not comprehend; for writing-tablet, the soul; for the letters graven on the stone tablets, the voice of the one he saw; through all of which both he and those initiated by him enjoyed a manifestation of the mysteries. [913C]

(33) He was filled with a certain boldness and confidence through that vision, like an athlete who, since he has enough experience from competition [H20] and strength from training, strips confidently for the race and prepares for combat against his competitors; now he likewise, suitably anointed in soul by his care for himself[30] and by the assistance of the favor which was revealed to him, thus undertook his struggles—for his whole life in

---

tion was fabricated by Gregory of Nyssa (see her article, "Das Bekenntnis des Gregor Thaumaturgus bei Gregor von Nyssa und das Problem seiner Echtheit," *Zeitschrift für Kirchengeschichte* 87 [1976]: 145–66) must recognize that this section, placed in parentheses by Heil in his critical edition, matches passages from Ps.-Basil, *Eun.* 5 (PG 29.753B) and Gregory Nazianzen's *Oration* 40.42 (PG 36.420A), which are cited by Heil in his apparatus.

28. While this is sometimes proposed as conclusive evidence that Gregory of Nyssa did not fabricate the language of this "mystagogy," I find it unlikely on practical grounds at least: an inscription of more than one hundred words (even if one omits the apparent parenthetical sections) would be both unusual and hard to read in a third-century provincial church building, and it is hard to picture Gregory of Nyssa going over and transcribing it. A more likely scenario, in my opinion, is that there was an inscription which read ΕΙΣ ΘΕΟΣ, ΕΙΣ ΚΥΡΙΟΣ, ΕΝ ΠΝΕΥΜΑ ΑΓΙΟΝ, ΤΡΙΑΣ ΤΕΛΕΙΑ—the words before the colons in my translation. Gregory of Nyssa could well have seized upon this as the basis for an authoritative, orthodox interpretation.

29. Exod 24.12–15. See Gregory of Nyssa, *Life of Moses* 46.
30. I.e., by his spiritual discipline.

the priesthood deserves to be called nothing less than struggles or contests in which through faith he combatted every power of the Adversary.

5. *Gregory's first conquest: a temple and its custodian.*

(34) Immediately after he arose from his remote retreat, he felt an inner impulse toward the city in which he would have to organize the church for God. [913D] He knew that the whole region was held fast by the deception of demons, and that a temple of the true God had never been built, but that the whole city and its environs were filled with altars, temples, and images, since the whole nation shared the same eagerness to beautify the sacred precincts of idols and the holy places and perpetuate idol-mania among men with the help of processions, sacred rites, and abominations performed on the altars. Like a noble soldier through whom the momentum is changed when he joins the battle-line, thus also this Great One begins his achievement of mastery with the demons themselves. How?

(35) On his way to the city from his place of retreat, as night was falling and a fairly heavy rain made him stop, [916A] he entered some temple with his followers. That temple was a notable one, where the temple custodians were visibly possessed by the attending demons while a kind of divination and oracle was being produced by them. Entering the temple with his companions, he immediately brought terror on the demons by the invocation of the name of Christ, and when with the sign of the cross he had purified the air which was filthy with the stench of sacrifices, he passed [916B H21] the whole night according to his custom, keeping vigil in prayers and hymnody, so that a house made abominable by the blood on its altars and its images was transformed into a house of prayer.

(36) When he had passed the night in this fashion, at dawn he was set to continue further on the journey. But when the temple custodian at dawn presented the customary service to the demons, he said that the demons appeared to him and said the temple was barred to them because of the one who was resting in it. He, using various exorcisms and sacrifices, tried by these

means to get the demons to move back into the temple. But when, despite everything he tried, the effort was ineffective, since the demons no longer responded to his invocation as they used to, the temple custodian, aroused with anger [916C] and rage, seized that Great One, threatening every kind of terrible thing: to haul him off to the authorities, to use force against him, to denounce his effrontery to the emperor, that, although he was obviously a Christian and an enemy of the gods, he dared to be in temples, and that his entrance had turned away the power at work in the sacred precincts and the mantic operation of the demons no longer visited the sites as usual.

(37) But in a high-minded fashion he shook off the rash and ignorant rage of the temple custodian, and counting on the assistance of the true God against all the threats, he said that he was so much convinced of the power of the One fighting on his behalf that he could drive them away from wherever he wished and make them settle [916D] in whatever places he might will, and promised to furnish immediate demonstrations of what he had said. [H22] The temple custodian, marveling and very dismayed at the magnitude of his power, summoned him to show his power by these things and to make the demons enter the temple again.

(38) When the Great One heard this, he tore off a little piece of paper[31] and gave it to the temple custodian, inscribing a word of command to the demons. Now the letters in this phrase read thus: "Gregory to Satan: Enter!" The temple custodian, taking the petition, placed it on the altar, then presenting the [917A] sacrifices and pollutions which are their custom he saw again what he had seen before the demons were evicted from the sanctuary.

(39) When these things happened he began to grasp the fact that Gregory possessed a divine power, by which he appeared to have overwhelming superiority over the demons. Eagerly catching him again before he got to the city, he demanded to learn from him the mystery, and who that God is who has a nature to

---

31. Naturally not paper in the modern sense, since it was not yet known in the West; but "writing material" would not be idiomatic English.

which demons are subject. When the Great One told him briefly the mystery of true religion, the temple custodian was affected in a way normal for one uninitiated in things divine, and he supposed that it was far beneath our idea concerning God to believe that the Divine had appeared to human beings in the flesh.[32] But when [Gregory] said that this faith was not confirmed by arguments, but commanded assent by the wonders that [917B] had happened, the temple custodian sought to see a further marvel from him, so as to be convinced of the faith through an event. Then it is said that the Great One did the most unbelievable wonder of all.

(40) For when the temple custodian asked that one of the great huge rocks they could [H23] see, impossible for human strength to move, should be transported to another place solely through the power of faith at Gregory's command, it is said that that Great One, nothing daunted, immediately ordered the rock as if it were a living thing to be translated to the place which the temple custodian had indicated. But when this had happened, the man straightaway believed in the word and left everything: people, home, wife, children, friends, priesthood, [917C] shrine, possessions; instead of all that had belonged to him, he claimed for himself the association with the Great One and a share in his labors and that divine philosophy and instruction.

(41) Faced with this, let every artificial conceit of the wordsmiths be silent which would by eloquence exalt the impressiveness of wonders to the skies. For the wonder in what has been recounted is not of such a kind that the narrator's power can make it lesser or greater than it is. For what could one say to add to the wonder, beyond what has already been said? How might one diminish for the hearers their astonishment at the event? A stone causes people who served stones to forsake stones. A stone becomes a preacher of the divine faith and a guide to salvation for unbelievers, not announcing [917D] the divine power by some sound or word, but proving the God proclaimed by Gregory to his creatures. All creation we believe is in equal measure subject to him, not just such as is endowed with sensation, spirit, and

---

32. Note that "the mystery of true religion" here includes the Incarnation, a point unmentioned in the "mystagogy" described earlier.

soul, but even if there is anything beyond these, it accepts the order of the servant just as if it were not lacking in sensation. What kind of hearing [H24] does a stone have? What sense does it have of the authority of the one commanding it? What locomotory power is in it? With what members and joints is it equipped? But the power of the one commanding serves all these kinds of functions for the stone, and when that temple custodian saw it, all of a sudden he understood and began to loathe the deceit of the demons which has ensued upon the error of the human race, and he was converted to the true God, inferring from what his servant [920A] had done how inexpressible is the power of the Lord. For if the servant had such power as by a word to move the immovable, and by a command to prevail against things without sensation, and to give effective orders to things without souls, how great an effective scope of power should we understand the ruler of all to have, whose will became the stuff and structure and power of the world and everything in it, and of those things which are above it?

6. *Gregory enters Neocaesarea and builds a church.*

(42) So then that Great One, beginning with the victory against the demons and bringing with him the temple custodian as a sort of trophy against the defeated, astonishing people in advance by his reputation, thus entered the city with confidence and boldness, not boasting in chariots and horses and mules and the crowd of his [920B] followers but guarded on all sides with virtues. The inhabitants of the town poured out en masse as to some account of a new marvel, and all were eager to see who that Gregory is who, though a human being, has power like an emperor over those whom they deemed gods, apparently able to order the demons to and fro [H25] like slaves wherever he might will, and leads their priest, as if he had bound him under some power, to look down on the honor he previously enjoyed and exchange all of his possessions for his companionship. [920C]

(43) While all received him in this frame of mind outside the town, when he got to the people he passed them by as if they were inanimate matter, though all were looking intently at him; by turning to none of those who met him and going straight into

the city, he induced much greater astonishment in them, appearing to the viewers to exceed his reputation. For his way of entering a large city for the first time was unprecedented, since he was not astounded at such a great crowd gathered on his account but proceeded as he would through a desert, looking only to himself and to the road, turning to none of those crowded around him—this seemed to the people greater than the feat involving the stone. For this reason, though as was said earlier, [920D] before his arrival there were few who had embraced the faith, he entered surrounded on all sides by an escort as if the whole city honored his priesthood.

(44) But since he had freed himself at one stroke of everything, as if it had been a kind of burden, when he took up philosophy, and he no longer had any of those things which are necessary for life, neither field, nor building site, nor house, but was himself all he had—or rather virtue and faith were heritage and home and wealth to him—so therefore he was in the city but had no dwelling [921A] anywhere, either belonging to the church or of his own. While the people around him were in consternation [H26] and at a loss as to how he might find someone to give him shelter, the Teacher[33] said to them:

Why are you at a loss as to where we should rest our bodies, as if you were outside the shelter of God? Does God seem too small a house for you, if it is "in him that we live and move and have our being"?[34] Or are you cramped by the vault of heaven and seek another lodging than this? Let each one of you strive to have one house of your own, one built by the virtues and reaching to the heights. Grieve only at this, that such a dwelling not be ready for you. For the confines of earthly walls bring no profit to such as live in virtue; [921B] let the quest for walls be more fittingly undertaken by those defiled in wickedness, since the house is often a concealment for the shame of secret deeds. But for those whose life has been set right through virtue, walls have nothing around which to throw a veil.

---

33. Gregory of Nyssa calls the Wonderworker either "the Great (One)" or "the Teacher." This helps to explain the puzzle noted by Luise Abramowski in her article, "Die Schrift Gregor des Lehrers 'Ad Theopompum' und Philoxenus von Mabbug," *Zeitschrift für Kirchengeschichte* 89 (1978): 273–90, that both that text itself and Philoxenus referred to Gregory as "the Teacher."

34. Acts 17.28.

(45) When he had said these things to his companions, there stood up one of the most prominent men, reckoned among the leaders in family, wealth, and other advantages; the man's name was Musonius. As he knew that many were bent on the same effort, that they might welcome the man into their homes, he anticipated the others and preempted the favor for himself, urging the Great One to accept his hospitality and honor his house by entering it, so that he might be more noble and renowned in the life beyond this one, since time would pass on even to his descendants the memory of such an honor. [921C] But when many others gathered and besought him on similar matters, judging that it was just to give the favor to the one who asked first, he went to stay with him, after placating the others through kind words and reciprocating their compliments.

(46) If our telling of the stories about him is narrative and rather plain, since our discourse deliberately omits the embellishments [H27] which some subtlety of thought might discover in the events, that very fact may itself be, to those who judge matters rightly, no small [921D] evidence of the fact that the wonders done by the one being commemorated have in no way been embellished by invention, but that the remembrance of the facts in his regard suffices for the most perfect eulogy, like natural facial beauty unadorned by any cunning of cosmetic art.

(47) Although there were very few who had previously been catechized in the doctrine, before the day was over and the sun had set enough were added by the first encounter so that the crowd of those who had come to believe was sufficient to constitute a congregation. In the morning the common people were again at the doors, the same people plus women and children and those old in years and some of those whose body was plagued by demons or some other affliction; and he was in their midst, [924A] sharing by the power of the Spirit in accord with the need of each in the crowd: proclaiming, discerning, directing, teaching, healing. For most of all he won the multitude over by proclamation, because vision coincided with hearing and the tokens of divine power illumined it through both. For his word amazed the hearing as his mighty deeds with the sick amazed the eyes. The mourner was comforted, the young person brought to

wisdom, the elderly comforted by fitting words. He taught servants to be dutiful to their masters; people with power, to care benevolently for their subjects; the poor person, that the sole wealth was virtue, which everyone could possess according to his ability; the one proud of his wealth was in turn admonished to be steward, not lord, of his possessions.

(48) By distributing to women what was beneficial, to children [924B] what was appropriate, to fathers what was properly dignified, and by being all things to all,[35] [H28] by the collaboration of the Spirit he at once constituted for himself so great a people that they wanted to build a temple, everyone assisting to this goal with their goods and their bodies. This is the temple which is pointed out to this day, which that Great One, halting as soon as he arrived, laid as a kind of foundation and groundwork for his priesthood, completing the work by some sort of divine impulse and higher aid as is evidenced at a later time. For when there was a very severe earthquake in the city in our own times, and almost everything was completely destroyed, all public and private [924C] buildings ruined, that temple alone remained unshattered and unshaken, so that through even this it is manifest with what sort of power that Great One undertook his affairs.

7. *Gregory settles a feud between two brothers over a lake.*

(49) Now these were appointed by divine power as a testimony for later ages to the Great One's faith. But even back then, since everyone in the city and its environs was astonished by the apostolic marvels [924D] and believed that everything he said and did he accomplished and said by divine power, they did not suppose that when the disputes of daily life arose they had any more exalted court of appeal, but every judgment and every complicated entanglement was solved by his counsels. Whence by his grace there was good order and peace for the community and for each and every one, and great increase of good things both private and public, since no wickedness destroyed their mutual understanding. But it would not be inopportune to recall

---

35. Cf. 1 Cor 9.22.

one of his judgments so that, as the proverb says, the whole woven garment might be manifested to us by the fringe.[36]

(50) The divine Scripture also, though Solomon issued many judgments to his subjects, [925A] yet managed to portray the man's whole insight through one of them.[37] For when judging between the two mothers, [H29] since the wrong was unprovable, each of them in identical fashion disowning the dead child but clinging to the living one, he knew how to trace the hidden truth in a roundabout way. Since there was no witness to the wrong and both women were equally suspect of lying or telling the truth, he summoned Nature[38] as his witness of the truth, uncovering the mind's purpose through his wisely conceived threat. By pretending to order that, when the living and the dead alike had been cut in half by a sword, half the children should be allotted to each mother, he handed over to Nature the judgment of the truth. [925B] For when one gladly welcomed the edict and urged the executions on, while the other, deeply moved in her maternal emotions, agreed to yield, asking that the child be spared (for she would take it as a blessing if the little one could somehow be saved), the king took this as the criterion of truth and granted the winning verdict to the one who willingly gave way, reasoning that the one who did not care about the killing of the infant was proved by Nature not to be the mother of the one whose death she advocated. Now what judgment of the great Gregory shall we in turn narrate?

(51) Two brothers, young in age, who were in the process of dividing their inheritance between them, laid claim to a marshy lake, each competing to have the whole thing and neither ready to admit the other [925C] to possession in common. So the Teacher became the master of the legal proceeding, and on the actual spot he applied his own rules, promoting reconciliation through arbitration, [H30] urging the young men to come to agreement through affection and to prefer the reward of peace to gains in income. For he said, "The former lasts forever for

---

36. This is not a scriptural proverb.
37. Cf. 1 Kings 3.16–28.
38. This view of "nature" as something which can be trusted to manifest the truth is also reflected in the *Metaphrase on Ecclesiastes* 1 (989C–92A).

both the living and the dead, but the enjoyment of the latter is temporary, and the condemnation for wickedness is eternal," and probably many similar things to check the undiscipline of youth. [925D]

(52) When the exhortation proved ineffective and youth was inflamed and flared up into greater anger, swollen by hope of gain, on each side an army was formed from among their servants, and murderous mobs commanded by anger and youth, and the time of engagement was set, with the battle to be joined from both sides on the following day. The man of God, remaining on the banks of the marshy lake and spending the whole night in vigil, worked a kind of marvel worthy of Moses over the water, not dividing the depths in two parts by a blow of his staff, but drying up the whole thing [928A] altogether. At dawn he showed the marshy lake as solid ground, dry and without moisture, as if it had in its bosom not even a speck of water, although before the prayer it was flooded. And when he had settled these things by divine power he again withdrew by himself, but the sentence of his deeds dissolved the rivalry for the young men. Since that over which they were preparing to fight each other no longer existed, peace replaced anger and once again Nature showed itself in the brothers.

(53) Even now the visible signs of that divine decision are to be seen. For at the water line of the old marshy lake some traces of the overflowing water are still preserved to this day. But what then was so far submerged beneath the water has all been transformed into groves and habitation and meadows and plowed lands.[39]

(54) I think that the renowned Solomon himself [928B H31] would not dispute as to first prizes against this judgment. For which does more for virtue: to save the infant suckling from two maternal breasts, though its well-being would have been entirely equal whether its nourishment had been sought from the one who bore him or from the other? Or to produce a saving solution for two young hotheads, who were just arriving at the affairs of life in the prime of youth, when in that same bloom of life

---

39. Robin Lane Fox, *Pagans and Christians* (San Francisco: Harper and Row, 1988), 531–32, describes what may be the geographical occasion for this miracle-story.

anger was provoking them to murderous thoughts against each other? They were just about to show their contemporaries a painful spectacle by engaging in battle against each other, at which there was reason to believe, either that they would both be destroyed by each other, or that one of them would be plunged into the horror [928C] of fratricide—not to mention those who would have been fighting on either side with the same rage, whose assault on each other would be limited only by the death of their antagonists. So he who by prayer dissolved the sentence of death determined against them by evil's high command, and changed their nature back to itself, and transformed their eagerness to kill into positive peaceful sentiments—how much more fitting to marvel at his judgment than at him who unmasked the prostitute's wicked deed?

(55) In the case of the miracle of the water, how water enough to float a boat was transformed all at once into dry land, the marshy lake becoming a plain, and how what was the local sea now returns to the production of crops, I think it would be better to keep silent on this than to tell it without being [928D] able to do justice to the marvel. For of the wonders we have learned about in Scripture, which is so remarkable as to be able to enter into comparison with this one on equal terms? Joshua son of Nun made the Jordan River stop, but only as long [H32] as the Ark was in the water. As soon as the people had crossed to the other side and the Ark had come through he gave the river back its usual flow again.[40] The bottom of the deep in the Red Sea was denuded of water when the sea was driven back to either side by the Spirit, but the duration of the marvel was the passage of the army through the deep on the [929A] dry strip. But after that the surface of the sea became one again, and the temporary gap was flooded over.[41] So this remains a unique event which occurred in such a way that the marvel did not lose credibility because of the passage of time, since it continues to be testified to by visible traces. That is the way the affair of the marshy lake is both described and shown.

40. Josh 3.14–4.18.
41. Exod 14.21–29.

8. Gregory sets a limit to the river floods.

(56) But another, later such marvel is pointed to and recalled as his. A certain river flowed through their region whose very name indicated the wildness and savagery of the stream. The locals called it "The Wolf"[42] because it did so much damage. It is large even as it flows down from its sources in Armenia, on account of the mountain heights which furnish it with an abundant flow, and a deep curve which undermines the bases [929B] of the cliffs is made much more savage by the torrents of winter as it gathers to itself all the runoff from the mountains. On the upper plain of the region it traverses, often confined by banks to either side, it overflows its banks in places on either side, flooding with its stream all the adjacent ground, so that it is a continual source of unexpected dangers to the inhabitants of the place, when the river overflows into the fields in the dead of night [H33] or even in broad daylight. As a result, not only trees and sown crops and cattle would be destroyed by the rush of the waters, but the danger used to touch the inhabitants themselves, shipwrecked in their own houses without warning in the overflow of the water.

(57) Now when the marvels already accomplished by the Great One [929C] had become known to the whole nation, those who lived along that part of the river rose up and they all in a body, including women and children, became the Great One's suppliants, begging to be provided with some deliverance from the desperate evils, on the ground that God was able to accomplish in him all those things which human ingenuity cannot manage. For it was their custom to omit none of those things which belong to human counsel and power, and to plan with rocks and earthen dikes and anything else against such evils, but even after they had done everything they were unable to withstand the onslaught of the evil. And so that he should be as strongly impelled to mercy as they could make him, they asked him to come see the misfortune in person and learn how it was not possible to move their settlement, [929D] and that their death was always waiting in the force of the water.

---

42. I.e., the Lycus.

(58) So he came to the spot—for no fear could impede his zeal for good—having requested neither a wagon nor horses nor anything else which could transport him; but with the help of an ordinary staff he walked the whole way, philosophizing all the while with his traveling companions concerning the highest hope, for always in his discussion with them, as we noted, he made other things subordinate to the most important concern. Anyway, as the flooding stream was shown him by his guides and the sight itself made the problem obvious (for the place had been dug out into a deep gully by the onslaught of the waters), he said the following to his companions [932A H34]:

It does not belong to men, brothers, to mark off the movement of the water with limits. Such a work belongs only to divine power, to enclose within limits the rush of the waters. For thus the prophet says regarding God, "He placed a boundary which it might not transgress."[43] Only to the Lord of creation is the nature of the elements submissive, staying continuously in whatever places it has been ordained. So since it is God who legislates the limits for the waters, only he by his own power may also constrain the disorder of this river. [932B]

He spoke, and having become as if filled by a very divine inspiration, and with a loud voice entreating Christ to come to his assistance for the task before him, he firmly planted his staff which he carried in his hand at the point where the bank was breached.

(59) The ground there, which was very moist and spongy, gave way at once to the weight of the staff and the hand of the one planting it, so that it sank easily all the way down. Then having entreated God that this should become a kind of bar and hindrance to the disorderliness of the river, he returned again, having shown by deed that all that he did was accomplished by divine power. For immediately, not after a long time, the staff took root in the bank and became a tree; this tree furnished a boundary to the stream and even today the tree is a visible sign [932C] and reminder to those who live nearby. Whenever heavy rains and winter storms make that Lycus rise as usual and begin to rage, frothing passionately in its flow, then, when around the trunk of the tree it attains its highest point of flood, it again piles

---

43. Ps 104.9; cf. Gen 1.9.

higher in the middle and reduces its flow, and as if fearing to approach the tree it passes the area by with arched crest.

(60) Such was the power of the great Gregory, or rather of the God who works the marvels in him. Like something tame, [H35] the nature of the elements was shown as apparently altered by his commands, so that a marshy lake was transformed into cropland and the torrents were domesticated as the staff assured safety for the residents. Right up to the present [932D] the tree is called "the Staff," a memorial of Gregory's grace and power preserved for the local people for all time.

(61) Which of the marvels of the prophets would wish to be put up against these for comparison? The dividing of the Jordan, for instance, which Elijah accomplished by a blow of his cloak before his ascension, and after him Elisha, who inherited both his cloak and his spirit?[44] On these occasions, the stream having been divided only for the prophets in time of need, [933A] the Jordan became fordable, the flow dividing itself enough to provide the prophets' feet space to pass through on the dry bottom, though for a later time and the rest of people it was just as before. But the river Lycus, driven once and for all from its disorderly course, makes Gregory's wondrous deed permanent by remaining for all subsequent time as the Great One's faith had made it at the moment of the miracle, and what the occurrences accomplished was not the astonishment of the onlookers but the salvation of those who lived near the river. So while the marvel is the same—for to the prophets and to the imitator of the prophets the nature of the water was equally subject—if one may speak boldly, what the latter did wins in philanthropy, [933B] by which the safety of the neighbors was [H36] assured, since the stream was restrained once and for all and remains stable afterwards.

9. *Gregory gives Comana a bishop, Alexander.*

(62) When throughout the region such great wonders had been reported and were believed to have been worked through the power of faith in Christ, everybody was longing to share the

---

44. 2 Kings 2.6, 14.

faith corroborated by such deeds. The proclamation was advancing strongly and the mystery was at work and the pursuit of the good was intensifying, since the priesthood was being established everywhere, so that everywhere the faith might abound and increase. An embassy came to him from a certain neighboring city asking him to visit them and to organize a church among them through the priesthood.[45] The name of the town was Comana,[46] [933C] to which the people unanimously asked the Great One to come.

(63) He came and stayed among them a few days, and by his actions and words to them kindled further their hunger regarding the mystery. When it was time for their embassy to reach its goal and for someone to be designated high priest of their church, then the recommendations of all those in office were concentrated on those who seemed to stand out in eloquence and family and other superficialities. For they supposed, since those things also were qualities of the Great Gregory, they should also not be lacking to the one who entered upon this office.[47] [933D] But when they had been divided several times in their votes, everyone preferring someone different, the Great One was waiting to receive some guidance from God on the matter in hand.

(64) And as Samuel is reminded not to be dazzled by physical beauty and height [H37] in the choice of the one who was to rule[48] but to seek out a royal soul, even if it should happen to be in an ugly body, so he likewise, seeing beyond what the people voting liked regarding each candidate, looked to one thing only: if someone even before the proclamation,[49] by concern for his life and for virtue, conducted himself as a priest in his manner.[50]

---

45. Here priesthood is portrayed as a requisite for the constitution of a church, as earlier we saw the necessity of a congregation of the people: see above, p. 61.
46. This Comana Pontica lay near the present town of Tokat.
47. Literally, τὴν χάριν ταύτην, "this grace."
48. See 1 Sam 16.7.
49. Lampe's *Patristic Greek Lexicon*, s.v. ἀνακήρυξις, takes this as his "proclamation as bishop"; in other words, ordination should not be the start of his conversion; but in the present context it could refer to the proclamation of the gospel in Comana.
50. For an extended exposition of Gregory of Nyssa's views on the qualifications to be sought in a bishop, see his *ep.* 13, to the church at Nicomedia.

So they brought forward their candidates with encomia, promoting each his own, while he kept ordering them to look also to those who were most perfected in their way of life (for it is possible even among such [936A] people to find someone famous in life who is most exalted in the wealth of the soul). One of those who was in charge of the voting deemed this decision of the Great One to be an outrage and a mockery if, when none of those rated superior to the others on the basis of eloquence and honor and the outward evidence of their life had been admitted to the priesthood, some of the laborers might be thought more worthy of such an office.[51] He came to him and said, full of sarcasm, "If you order these things—that such people as these should be overlooked, though they were picked from the whole city, but that from the rabble someone should be advanced to the eminence of the priesthood—you might as well call the charcoal-burner Alexander to the priesthood, and if it seems right we could, by switching to him, all agree [936B] with each other in our votes, the whole city."

(65) He said this, therefore, dissembling his own view with his sarcastic intervention, while finding fault with the failure of earlier speakers to produce a decision. But his words gave the Great One an idea, that it was not without God's help that Alexander came to the mind of those deliberating. "And who is [H38] this Alexander," he said, "whom you have called to mind?" Then when one of those sharing in the laughter brought into their midst the aforementioned man, clad in dirty rags, and not fully at that, displaying at once the trade he was in, and covered with soot on his hands and face and the rest of his body from the charcoal, the others were expecting a hearty laugh when this Alexander stood up in their midst. But to that penetrating [936C] eye the sight furnished great astonishment: a man in extreme poverty and unkempt body, who respected himself and was comfortable with this appearance, which was most ridiculous to uneducated eyes. For that is the way he presented himself.[52]

51. I.e., "grace," as in note above.
52. There are many textual problems, including apparent scribal glosses, in the next half-page. The reader who is curious about them should study the apparatus to Heil's edition.

(66) Not by necessity of poverty had he come to such a life, but rather he was a kind of philosopher, as his later life revealed. But he pursued anonymity, being superior to the general eagerness for success, and counting his physical life as nothing since he had a strong desire for the higher and truer life.[53] And so as to accomplish [936D] to the highest degree his goal of virtue, he contrived to be unnoticed by being such as to hide himself in the lowliest of occupations as if it were some ugly mask.

(67) (In another version, though he was outstanding in his youth, he thought that it was dangerous to his goal of moderation to display the beauty of his body like someone flaunting his natural endowment, for he knew that such was for many the start of grievous [937A H39] falls. Therefore, so as he might neither suffer anything he did not will nor make himself an occasion of passion for others' eyes, for this reason he gladly donned charcoal-burning as a kind of ugly mask, and through it he trained his body for virtue by hard work, and concealed his beauty with coal dust and at the same time employed the earnings from his labors in keeping the commandments.)

(68) Having sent him out of the meeting, after he learned all the facts about him with exactitude, he first gave him to his companions, ordering them what they should do, while he himself, addressing the meeting again on those things under consideration, instructed the assembled people, setting before them the doctrines concerning the priesthood and thereby sketching out the life according to virtue. And he expanded on these words, [937B] keeping the gathering occupied until his servants, their job completed, arrived bringing with them Alexander, cleansed from the grimy soot by a bath and clothed in the Great One's garments (for this is what they had been ordered to do).

(69) But when they all turned toward Alexander and were amazingly affected toward what they saw, the Teacher said to them:

You have suffered nothing new, misled by your eyes and entrusting the judgment of the beautiful to sense alone. For sense is a risky criterion of the truth of real things, since it itself blocks the way into the depth of understanding. And this was pleasing to the demon who is the enemy of

---

53. The contrast here is between βίος and ζωή.

the true religion, [937C] for the 'chosen instrument'[54] to lie entirely idle, concealed by ignorance, [H40] and for there not to arrive in your midst a man who would be the overthrow of his dominion.

Having said this he advanced the man to God through the priesthood, having perfected him by grace according to the statutory form.[55]

(70) But while everyone was looking toward the new priest, encouraging him to make some discourse to the church, Alexander immediately showed in the first moments of his rule that Gregory's judgment of him was unerring. He gave a speech full of penetrating insight, but less ornamented with flowery language. Whereupon some insolent youth visiting them from Attica ridiculed the ugliness of his diction, that it was not ornamented with Attic refinement; he was chastened, they say, [937D] by a very divine vision in which he saw a flock of doves shining with some extraordinary beauty and heard someone saying that these were Alexander's doves which he had held up to ridicule.

(71) What in these events is more amazing than the other? The fact that the man[56] was not abashed by the opinion of the worthies and not swept along with the testimonies of leadership? Or the wealth concealed in the coals, to which there followed the testimony of the right judgment straight from God through the rhetor's vision? For to me each of these in itself seems to be fit to contend with the other, but there is hardly any need to rank all the events we recall in terms of marvelousness. For to oppose the impulse of the leadership was [940A] a most manifest indication of his unshakable high-mindedness; to him all worldly appearances were looked down on equally, and whether toward the greater and more illustrious or toward the humble and unrecognized he behaved appropriately. Since he accorded special esteem to virtue alone and judged only the life of wickedness to be worthy of rejection, he saw as of no value all those things which

---

54. See Acts 9.15.
55. This should probably not be taken as evidence for a settled ordination ritual in mid-third century Pontus; more likely it reflects late fourth-century concerns.
56. I.e., Gregory.

in terms [H41] of this life are judged worthy of pursuit or of contempt. What he did at that time proves it.

(72) As he sought to find the one most pleasing to God, he did not suppose that wealth and prestige should be relied on for testimony, nor the distinctions of this world, none of which the divine word enumerates in its lists of goods. Not only is it worthy of praise and marvel that he disregarded [940B] what the powerful sought, but he also outdid himself in what followed. If he had only dismissed the unworthy vote without furnishing the rest of what they needed, he would have impeded an evil but he would not have accomplished the good. But he, since he discovered the good in addition to not agreeing to the worse, perfected the good through both, by not letting evil through and by bringing the good to effective existence. So the good work of the Great One for that city was of both kinds, as he prevented the error they were committing out of ignorance and revealed through himself the good which had been hidden from them. [940C]

10. Gregory not deceived by a sham "dead" man.

(73) Although everything went well for the Great One according to his purpose with the assistance of the Spirit, it might not be inopportune also to narrate a minor incident about the road, as the grace which accompanied the man is manifested by everything. Since it was very clear to everyone that more than anything else the man was concerned to see to all that could comfort the needy, two Jews,[57] either looking for profit or even plotting some reproach against the man as an easy prey to deception, [H42] stood watch beside his road home. One of these, appearing to have died, stretched out on his back on the shoulder alongside the public road. The other, bitterly bewailing the one lying there, feigned the cries of mourners and called upon the Great One as he passed by, saying that [940D] this poor man who had suddenly been overtaken by death was lying naked and unprepared for burial. He asked the Great One not to overlook

---

57. The identification of the two as Jews probably reflects an opposition to Judaism shared by Gregory of Nyssa and his hearers.

the duty of piety in his regard, but to take some pity on his need and provide from his means that the final dignity be given to the body. He begged in these and similar terms, and [Gregory] without hesitation threw the double cloak[58] which he was wearing onto the one lying there, and continued on his way.

(74) After he had passed by, when those who played the trick on him were by themselves, the confidence man exchanged his feigned grief for laughter and told the one on the ground to get up, cackling with pleasure at the gain they had acquired by the deception. [941A] The other remained still, hearing nothing of what was said. When the first gave a loud shout and kicked him with his foot, the one on the ground still neither heard the sound nor felt the blow, but remained stretched out as before. For he was dead from the moment the garment landed on him, being truly in that death which he had pretended so as to deceive the Great One. So the man of God was *not* mistaken, but the garment was useful to the one who took it for the very purpose for which it was donated by him.

(75) But if such a work of the Great One's faith and power seems to be quite repulsive, let no one be alienated once he looks at the great Peter. He too displayed the power which was in him not only through the good works he performed, as when he showed the people the one who was lame from birth running and leaping,[59] [941B H43] or cured by his own body's shadow the ills of the sick on whom the sun cast it along the road, by striking the apostle's body at an angle;[60] but he also condemned to death Ananias, who behaved scornfully towards the apostle's indwelling power.[61] I imagine this was so that, by the fear it caused, all insolence in the people might be chastened at the terrible example and instructed so that it might not happen to them too.

---

58. This διπλόη was doubled fabric; it could be made in children's sizes (see 1 Sam 2.19). One author has seen in the present passage an ancestor of the story of Martin of Tours, who cut his military cloak in half to clothe a beggar: Paul Devos, "Le manteau partagé. Un thème hagiographique en trois de ses variantes," *Analecta Bollandiana* 93 (1975): 157–63.
59. Acts 3.8.
60. Acts 5.15.
61. Acts 5.1–11.

(76) Suitably, therefore, the imitator of Peter, who had shown the greatness of his power through many beneficent marvels, made the one who tried to use deception against the Spirit tell the truth against himself. In my opinion it was necessary that the [941C] overthrower of falsehood transform even the falsehood in the deceiver into truth, so that it might thereby be manifest to all, both that everything said by the Great One was true and that whatever he took to be true was not false. Thus the Jews, by mocking the Great One's power in the manner just described, became a lesson for others not to venture deception, since God is the accuser of their reckless deeds.

11. *Gregory heals a possessed boy.*

(77) Later, once when there was an open-air gathering in a country spot nearby and everyone was feeling astonished at his teachings, some lad cried out to those standing there [941D] that the Teacher was not saying these things of himself but another standing next to him was delivering the words. When the child was brought forward after the gathering had broken up, it is said that the Great One said to those present that the lad was not clean from a demon, and suddenly taking off the linen cloth [H44] that was on his shoulders and endowing it with the breath of his own mouth thus he threw it over the lad. When this happened the boy shook and cried out and fell down and was thrown about and suffered all the passions which come from demons. Then when the saint placed his hand on him and calmed the shaking, his demon flew away, and when he was normal again, he no longer said that he saw a second speaker by the saint. [944A] Now this too is one of his great marvels, that he accomplished the healing types of miracles without any special fuss; but for the deliverance from demons and the cure of bodily ills the breath from his mouth was sufficient, brought to the sufferer in a linen cloth.

(78) To go through in order all the marvels worked by him would require a long book and a discourse exceeding the time we have now, but since I have been reminded of one or two more things told about him I shall close the discourse with these.

12. *Gregory cannot be found by the persecutors.*

(79) The time came when the divine proclamation had circulated everywhere and all in the city and its environs had been converted to the true faith in the doctrine; when the altars and the temples and the idols in them had been overturned, [944B] and human life had been cleansed from the defilements associated with idols, and the disgusting burning of sacrifices had been extinguished, and the gore on the altars and the defilements from live sacrifices had been washed away; and when everyone in every place was zealously erecting handsome temples in the name of Christ. Anger and envy entered the man in charge of the Roman Empire at that time because the ancestral cults of error were falling into neglect,[62] [H45] while the mystery of the Christians was growing and the church was swelling to a multitude everywhere in the civilized world, increasing to great size through those constantly devoted to the word. Thinking his own bitterness strong enough to withstand the divine power and to check the preaching of the mystery [944C] while destroying the congregations of the churches, and then to bring those who had progressed in the Word back to idols again, he sent the governors of the provinces an edict decreeing a fearful threat of punishment against them if they would not mutilate with manifold tortures those who worship the name of Christ, and lead them by fear and the coercion of tortures back to their ancestral worship of demons.[63]

(80) When this fearsome and godless proclamation had been promulgated to all the governors, what had been ordered to this end by the tyrant's cruelty permeated throughout the realm. Someone was governing the people in that place who was such that no power of enforcement was lacking for the evil onslaught,

---

62. This may seem exaggerated; but even what seem like small changes in religious practice could have significant effects, as can be seen by Pliny's letter to Trajan (*ep.* 10.96).

63. The decree in question is described in general enough terms to apply either to that of Decius (250) or that of Valerian (257). W. H. C. Frend, *The Rise of Christianity* (Philadelphia: Fortress Press, 1984), 319, assigns it to the persecution of Decius. There is no evidence that in either persecution local governors were threatened with punishment if they failed to persecute the Christians.

[944D] since he personally felt bitterness and hostility toward those who believed in the Word. There issued from him a monstrosity among public ordinances, that they would either have to renounce the faith or be punished with punishments of every kind, including death. The keepers of the common good at that time had no other public and private duty and mission except harassing and punishing those who held the faith.

(81) The terrors lay not only in the threats that were uttered, but in addition the cunning preparation of the instruments of torture brought consternation and [945A] filled people with fear even before they had experienced them. They thought of swords and fire and beasts and pits and limb-twisting racks, and iron chairs on the fire, and wooden stakes [H46] on which the stretched-out bodies of the victims were torn in shreds with the applications of fearful claws, and lots of other inventions for torturing bodies many ways. All of those laying hold of these forces had a single aim—not to be outdone by each other in excess of ferocity. And some were making accusations, others identifications; and some were searching for those in hiding, while others went after those in flight. But many, eyeing the possessions of the faithful, under the guise of religious piety drove out [945B] the adherents of the faith, with a view to getting hold of their businesses.

(82) There was total confusion among the people and much helplessness, as they all looked on each other with suspicion, since the loyalty of children to their parents did not endure in the terrors, nor did Nature guarantee to children the faithfulness of parental care. Families split over religion were divided against each other, and a child with Greek ideas became the betrayer of his believing parents, and the father still in unbelief turned accuser against his believing child, and a brother, for the same cause, would war against Nature, judging it holy that his own kinsman should be punished if he clung to the true religion.

(83) Whence the desert places became full of those who were driven out,[64] while the houses were empty of inhabitants. Many of the public buildings were turned over to their needs, for

64. This exodus into an unsettled region during persecution may have contributed to the rise of monasticism, though other causes are generally given more prominence.

[945C] the prisons were inadequate to house the crowd of those who were being punished for the faith. All the marketplaces and meeting places, public and private, instead of their customary joyousness, shared in such sorry sights of those who were dragged in and those who were being killed, as some were laughing at what was happening, others were weeping. There was no pity for children nor respect for grey hairs, nor reverence for virtue, but, as in slavery, every age was delivered to the enemies of the faith. Nor did the natural weakness of their kind grant to women to remain outside such struggles, but there existed one law of [H47] cruelty against everyone, condemning whoever was hostile to idols to the same degree of consequences, without regard for nature.[65]

(84) Then [945D] that Great One, seeing the weakness of human nature, how most people were unable to fight to the death for true religion, advised the church to pull back a little from the fearful attack, thinking it better that they should save their lives by flight than that, by standing in the battle line of the contest, they should become deserters from the faith. And so that people might be as strongly persuaded as possible that it was not dangerous to their soul to save their faith through flight, by his own example he embodied the advice to go away, since he himself withdrew from the approach of danger before the others.[66] The especial goal of the rulers was this, that by capturing him like a general they might shatter the whole battle line of the faith, and for [948A] this reason his enemies were trying very hard to take him into custody.

(85) He had gone to a certain uninhabited hilltop, taking along the former temple guardian who had in the beginning been drawn to the faith and now served the office of deacon.[67] When their pursuers in great numbers were hard on their heels, since someone had let them know the place in which he was

---

65. It is unclear whether the differential in nature between men and women is meant here, or Gregory of Nyssa's usual concern with the natural obligations which bind people together.

66. Dionysius of Alexandria (Eusebius, *h.e.* 7.40) and Cyprian of Carthage (*ep.* 20.1) reacted to the persecution of Decius as Gregory did, by taking evasive action, but were criticized for doing so.

67. ἤδη τῇ χάριτι τῆς διακονίας ὑπηρετούμενον; cf. notes 47 and 51 above.

concealed, some, by encircling the foot of the hill, guarded lest he have any escape if he took that course; the others, going up on the mountain and searching every inch, were already in view of the Great One and headed straight for him. But he, [948B H48] having ordered his companion to stand with firm and unwavering confidence towards God and to believe in salvation, holding up his hands in prayer like him, and not to let his faith be driven away by fear even if the pursuers got very close, made himself an example of that command for his deacon, looking to heaven with steadfast gaze and hands stretched straight upward. And that is the way they stood.

(86) When the others had run up to them, looking all over the place and searching every stand of bushes and every pile of rocks and every bend of the stream with all diligence, they went back again to the bottom of the hill, assuming that their quarry, frightened into flight, [948C] was in the hands of those posted down below. As he was not found with this group and he was not with the others either, the spy kept indicating the location of the Great One's refuge by signs, while the searchers maintained firmly that they had seen nothing except two trees standing a short distance apart. When the searchers had left, the informant, left behind, and grasping that the Great One and his companion were in prayer, and recognizing the divine protection by which they were taken to be trees by their pursuers, fell down before him and believed the word; and the one who a short time before had been a pursuer became one of the fugitives.

(87) They stayed in the wilderness a long time, for the war against the [948D] faith was prevailing, since the governor was raging viciously against those dedicated to the doctrine of the true religion, and everyone had taken to flight, since after what happened with the Great One the persecutors themselves were losing hope that he would ever be captured. At that point, turning their raging bitterness against those who stayed behind, they searched through the entire people for all, men and [H49] women and children alike, to whom the name of Christ was holy. They dragged them to the city, and filled the prisons, accusing them of true religion rather than any other wickedness, so that the courts were no longer engaged in any of the common affairs.

This alone was the rulers' concern: to bring all outrages and every kind of torture they could think of against the adherents of the faith. [949A]

13. *Gregory's clairvoyance about the persecution is demonstrated.*

(88) Then it became even clearer to everyone that the Great One planned nothing without divine assistance. For as he guarded himself for the people through flight, all those who were struggling for the faith had a common ally. Just as we hear regarding Moses that, though he stood far from the Amalekites' battle line, by prayer he endowed his people with power against their adversaries,[68] in the same way he too, surveying what was happening with the eye of his soul, called on divine assistance for those struggling in the confession of the faith.

(89) Once when he was praying to God with his companions according to his custom, and was suddenly stricken with amazement at the struggle and the tumult, it was quite clear to those present how abstracted he was and involved in the vision and straining to listen [949B] as if some sound were coming to him. When a considerable interval had elapsed as he remained the whole time in the midst without bending or moving, then, as if the vision before him had come out well, he again returned to normal and gave praise to God in a ringing voice, uttering the triumphant and grateful hymn which we often hear the psalmody of David saying: "Blessed be God, who has not given us [H50] as prey to their teeth."[69]

(90) When those around him were wondrously affected and asked to learn what vision had presented itself to his eyes, it is said that he told them he had seen a great collapse at that hour, when the devil had been bested by some young man in the contests for the true religion. Since they still did not understand what he said, [949C] he explained to them more exactly that by a great assistance at that hour a certain noble youth had been

---

68. Exod 17.8–13.
69. Ps 124.6.

contending in the struggles for the faith, having been brought to the governor by the police. He even added his name, calling him Troadios, and that after many tortures which he had endured nobly he had put on the crown of his testimony.[70]

(91) The deacon was flabbergasted at what he heard and did not dare to disbelieve any of what had been said, yet still thought that it exceeded human nature, since he was so far from the city and no one had come down to announce what had happened to him, to speak to his companions concerning what had happened there like one who had been present at the events; he begged the Teacher to permit him [949D] to see the events for himself and not to be hindered by him from visiting the place where the wonder occurred. But when [Gregory] said that it was frightening to be among murderers and to experience repugnant things, often from the Adversary's abuse, the deacon said that he would put his trust in the assistance of his prayers, uttering to him this appeal: "You commend me to your God, and no fear of enemies will lay hold of me." When [Gregory] through prayer had sent God's help along with him as a companion, he confidently set out on the road, paying no attention to anyone he met.

(92) Having arrived in the city by evening and being dirty from [952A H51] his journey, he thought it was necessary to wash off the dirt by a bath. That place was in the control of a certain homicidal demon who habitually visited the bath, whose destructive power was effective against those who came after dark, and for this reason after sunset that bath was unused. When he got there he asked the person on duty to open the door and let him enter, and not to begrudge him the comfort of the bath. He testified that none of those who had ventured at that hour had returned from the water on his own two feet, but that the demon had overpowered them all after nightfall, and that many had already out of ignorance suffered fatal injuries; weeping and graves and lamentations had received them, rather than the refreshment they expected. Though he explained these things [952B] and more, that man felt no less desire but insisted, coercing him in every way to let him inside. Then, using a subterfuge so as not

---

70. I.e., martyrdom.

also to be endangered by the stranger's ignorance, he handed him the key and distanced himself from the bath.

(93) When he was inside and stripped, various kinds of fear and the germs of panic were contrived by the demon: various apparitions made of mingled fire and smoke showed themselves in the shape of men and beasts, flashing upon the eyes, sounding in the ears, crowding his breath, and engulfing his body. Making the Sign upon himself and calling on the name of Christ, he [952C] traversed the first chamber unscathed. When he entered the inner one he encountered terrible sights, since the demon had been transformed into the most fearful apparition, and at the same time he thought the room was being shaken by an earthquake and the pavement beneath torn asunder to reveal the naked flame below, and that flaming sparks were flying up [H52] from the waters, and again the Sign and the name of Christ were an adequate armor for him, and the aid furnished through the Teacher's prayers dispersed the terrors of the sights and happenings. When he had left the water and was headed for the exit he was again hindered, since the demon was holding the doors shut. Once again even this impediment was undone of its own accord through the same power, as the door opened to the Sign. But since he thought that [952D] everything had yielded to himself, it is said that the demon cried out to him with a human voice not to think that it was his own power through which he had escaped destruction; for the voice of the one who had commended him to his protector had given him his impassibility.

(94) After he had been preserved in the above fashion, he was a source of astonishment to the people who ran the place, since none of those who had risked the water at that hour had ever reappeared among the living. When he had told them his story and learned that the brave deeds of the martyrs in the city had happened just as the Great One out in the wilderness had said earlier, after adding to the marvels told about him [953A] through the things he had seen and heard and learned by personal experience regarding the power of the Great One's faith, to which the demon had testified, he ran back to the Teacher, having left to his own and to those to come later a common protection, namely, that each should commend himself to God through

the priests. Even now throughout the church, but especially among them, the same formula is a memorial of the aid which helped that man then.[71]

14. How Gregory honored the martyrs' memory.

(95) When that tyranny had been broken by God's help and peace again made room for the human life in which it was easy for all to devote themselves to the divine in freedom, and when he had descended again to the city and visited the whole countryside round about, he gave [953B H53] to peoples everywhere an increase of devotion toward the divine by decreeing festivals in honor of those who had borne up bravely for the faith. Taking up the bodies of the martyrs here and there, gathering together on the anniversary by the yearly cycle, they rejoiced as they kept festival in honor of the martyrs.

(96) And this too was a proof of his great wisdom, that in re-educating his whole generation to a new life at one time, while taking charge of nature like a sort of charioteer and harnessing them safely by the reins of the knowledge of God, he allowed his subjects to cavort a little in the yoke of faith through merriment. Since he understood that in bodily rejoicing the immaturity and lack of discipline of the multitude remained stuck in the error of idolatry, [953C] in order that first of all the main thing might then be achieved in them, namely, to look to God instead of to vain religious practices, he let them rejoice at the memories of the holy martyrs, and experience good emotions, and exult, so that when with the passage of time their life had been naturally transformed to what is more noble more and more strict, their faith would be directed to that end. This is already achieved, even in the multitude, as all feelings of gladness have been transferred from the pleasures of the body to the spiritual form of rejoicing.[72]

---

71. Gregory of Nyssa may not have been too early to reflect the widespread practice of using Gregory the Wonderworker's reputation in the preparation of spells and amulets; see the section on *Gebetsliteratur* by Heinzgerd Brakmann in the article, Henri Crouzel, "Gregor I (Gregor der Wundertäter)," *Reallexikon für Antike und Christentum* 12 (1983): 791–93.

72. This may describe a desirable state of affairs rather than an actual one. For a sense of what the martyrs' feasts were like in Gregory of Nyssa's time, see As-

15. Gregory's departure from this life.

(97) Building the church community in this fashion, [953D] and concerned to see everyone transferred from idols to the saving faith before his departure from this life, since he foreknew his own departure he zealously searched throughout the whole city and the area round about, wishing to learn if any still remained outside the faith. Therefore since he knew that those who were faithful to the ancient error were not more [H54] than seventeen in number, he looked up to God and said, "This is very sad, that there should be something lacking to the full number of the saved." But it is worthy of great thanksgiving, that he leaves as many idolaters to the one who would take over the church after him as he himself had found Christians.

(98) After praying for growth to perfection for those who already believed, and for the conversion of unbelievers, he thus [956A] left this human life for God, having charged his closest associates not to use the place reserved to him for burial. For if when he was alive the Lord did not have any place to lie down, but spent his life sojourning with others, neither would he be at all ashamed at his sojourn after his death. "But let it be said of my life in times to come," he said, "that Gregory was not named for someplace while he lived, and after death rested in strangers' graves, keeping himself from every earthly possession to the point of not even receiving burial in his own place. For his only possession would be that honor which does not bear within it any trace of selfishness."[73]

16. Another story from early in Gregory's career.

(99) Let each of those who happen on the discourse wonder at the sudden transformation of the whole people from Greek

---

terius of Amaseia, *Homilies I–XIV*, edited by C. Datema (Leiden: E. J. Brill, 1970), homilies 9–12.

73. Paul Koetschau, "Zur Lebensgeschichte Gregors des Wunderthäters," *Zeitschrift für wissenschaftliche Theologie* 41 (1898): 241, proposes that Gregory of Nyssa's sermon ended here, followed only by the brief doxology which furnishes the last sentence of the text printed in Migne. The intervening material would have been added later.

vanity to the acknowledgment of [956B] the truth, and let no one fail to believe who has regard for the dispensation by which such a transformation of views from falsehood to truth took place. For now, as I resume, I will narrate what happened in the early days of his priesthood, which the discourse has passed by in its hurry to reach the rest of the marvels.

(100) There was a popular feast in the city, held according to ancestral custom for some demon [H55] of the local inhabitants. Almost all the people flocked to it, the whole region making festival with the city. The theater was filled with those assembled, and the crowd of those who had streamed to it overflowed the seats on all sides, and while everyone was craning to look down in front[74] for the sights and sounds, the stage was full of [956C] commotion, and the jugglers were unable to give their performance, since the hubbub among the packed audience not only curtailed the enjoyment of the music but also gave the jugglers no chance to put on their acts. Then a common cry broke out from the whole people, calling on the demon to whom the feast was dedicated and asking him to find more room for them. When they all shouted together the cry rose on high, and the words seemed to come from the whole city as from a single voice, offering this prayer to the demon—the prayer ran word for word, "Zeus, give us space!"—that Great One, when he heard the sound of them calling on the demon by name, from whom they asked that free space [956D] should be given to the city, sent word to them by one of the bystanders that even more free space than they were praying for would be given them.

(101) When this pronouncement from him had been delivered like a heavy sentence, a pestilence followed that popular festival, and suddenly wailing was mingled in with the dancing, so that the celebrations were changed into sorrows and misfortunes for them as, instead of flutes and clapping, continuous lamentation took over the city. The affliction fell abruptly upon the people, penetrating faster than they expected, feeding on their houses like fire, so that [957A] the temples were filled with

---

74. In Greek: to the ὀρχήστρα.

those laid low by the disease who had fled there in the hope of a cure, and the springs and streams and cisterns were full of those [H56] burning with thirst because of the weakness brought on by the disease. But the water was too weak to quench the flame from deep within, leaving those once afflicted with the disease feeling just the same after the water as before. Many went off to the tombs on their own, since the survivors were no longer as numerous as those in their graves.

(102) People were not without warning of the onslaught of the disease; but when a certain portent reached the house about to be stricken, then death ensued. When therefore the cause of the disease became apparent to all, namely, that the demon which they had invoked was fulfilling in an evil way the prayer of the foolish, [957B] effecting this terrible urban clearance by means of the disease, then they came as suppliants to the Great One, begging that the onslaught of the evil might stop through the God whom he knew and preached, whom they confessed was the only true God and had power over everything. For when that portent of the ruin to come appeared at a house and made them despair of life on the spot, there was one way for those in danger to be saved: that the great Gregory enter that house and by prayer drive out the disease which was invading the house. Since the report spread swiftly to all through those who first encountered this salvation, they abandoned all the things they had previously pursued out of thoughtlessness—oracles [957C] and expiatory sacrifices and wasting time with idols—for all were looking to the great priest and each was drawn for his own sake to the salvation of the whole people. His reward from those who were saved was the salvation of their souls.

(103) When the true religion of the priest was manifest in such an experience, there was no more delay in assenting to the mystery for those who through deeds had been taught the power of the faith. Thus for those people sickness proved stronger than health. While they were healthy they were too weak in their thoughts for acceptance of the mystery, but by bodily illness they were made [H57] healthy enough for faith. When the error of idols was thus refuted, all were converted to the name of [958D] Christ, some led by the hand to the truth through the disease

that came upon them, still others by putting up faith in Christ as a bulwark against the plague.

(104) There are other marvels of the great Gregory preserved in memory to this time which we have not set down in writing out of consideration for unbelieving ears, lest people be harmed because they think the truth in the extraordinariness of the accounts to be a lie.[75]

---

75. There follow in various manuscripts a number of different doxologies. A reader who is interested in them should consult the apparatus to Heil's edition.

THE GENUINE WORKS OF ST. GREGORY THAUMATURGUS

ADDRESS OF THANKSGIVING TO ORIGEN

An address of St. Gregory the Wonderworker to Origen, which he spoke in Caesarea in Palestine, after studying with him for many years, and just before he departed for his own country.[1]

IT IS GOOD TO KEEP SILENT; most people usually wish others would, and I would be happiest now if I were gagged and forced to be silent willy-nilly. (2) For I am out of practice, and I lack experience of these beautiful and gracious speeches, spoken, or rather composed, from carefully chosen, elegant nouns and verbs one after another in an unbroken stream. I may even lack the natural ability to elaborate this elegant and truly Hellenic work. (3) Be that as it may, it must be eight years now since I myself spoke or wrote an oration, large or small, or heard someone else give one of his own composition either in writing or orally, or even present panegyrics or argumentative speeches in public, except these wonderful men who have embraced the good philosophy. (4) They themselves care less for eloquence and finding just the right words; relegating words to second place, they wish to investigate the facts themselves as they really are and to expound them accurately. (5) Not, I think, that they are unwilling—they are eager—to fashion fair and precise thoughts in fair and graceful language. But perhaps they cannot easily combine in one and the same soul, so puny and human, the sacred and godlike power of thought with eloquence in the spoken word, accomplishments for two men, each a specialist, since they are contrary to each other. (6) For silence is the friend and partner to thinking and discovery, but someone who seeks to speak well and confidently will not find that skill except in words and in their constant employ.

---

1. Although this treatise has been known also as "The Panegyric to Origen" (Migne, Quasten, Fouskas), the modern preference is for "Address of Thanksgiving" (Koetschau, Altaner, Crouzel, Marotta), a title based on 3.31 and 4.40.

(7) In addition, another branch of study weighs heavy on my mind, and makes me tongue-tied whenever I wish to say even something brief in the accent of the Greeks: our wonderful laws, by which now the affairs of everyone in the Roman Empire are regulated, and which are neither compared[2] nor learned by heart without exhausting effort. While they are wise and precise and far-ranging and remarkable and, in a word, very Hellenic, still they have been expressed and transmitted in Latin, which is powerful and magniloquent and quite in conformity with the imperial power, but nonetheless difficult for me. (8) I do not suppose it is either possible or desirable to have it any other way. But since our words are nothing other than images of what is going on in our souls, we ought to acknowledge that the case is the same for those who are capable speakers as for good painters who are outstandingly skillful in their art, and are also rich in their palette of colors; they can produce not only copies but also designs which are different and gorgeous in their varied pigments, without any limitations.

2. We,[3] on the other hand, are like the poor; we do not have these varied preparations, and either never had them or perhaps lost them as, restricted to charcoal and potsherds, the common everyday nouns and verbs, we copy out faithfully, as best we can, the originals of what is going on in our souls, indicating them in the words we have at hand, trying to show the outlines of the soul's impressions, even if they are not clear or fully worked out, as is the case with charcoal drawings;[4] but if something which

---

2. Crouzel has "concilier," Marotta "armonizzare." The Greek word συγκείμενοι can mean either of those, or compare, or compose. We know little of what went on in Roman legal education at the time. According to Joseph Modrzejewski, "Grégoire le Thaumaturge et le droit romain. À propos d'une édition récente," *Revue historique de droit français et étranger* 49 (1971): 321–22, on the one hand, Gregory's testimony shows how important Roman law had become since the edict of Caracalla in 212, but it also reflects the persistence of local laws in the provinces, under the protection of Roman authority.

3. I shall try to reproduce in the translation Gregory's shifts between first person singular and plural, despite the fact that it is sometimes jarring in English, because passages in the plural are sometimes taken as inclusive of Athenodorus his brother; see the introduction, pp. 17–19.

4. Eugenio Marotta, "I neologismi nell'orazione ad Origene di Gregorio il Taumaturgo," *Vetera Christianorum* 8 (1971): 241–42, says that this metaphor indicates the opacity of a mediocre oration by comparison with that of a true orator.

looks good and sounds fine appears from somewhere, we greet it with pleasure, since we were not expecting it. (9) There is in the third place, however, something else which hinders and dissuades and more than all the rest restrains me, and simply orders me to keep quiet: the topic itself, for whose sake I was eager to speak, but now I delay and vacillate. (10) For I am proposing to speak about a man who looks and seems like a human being but, to those in a position to observe the finest flower of his disposition, has already completed most of the preparation for the reascent to the divine world. (11) I am not coming to praise his family origin or his bodily development, and then delaying and putting it off out of excessive caution, nor his strength and good looks; such things form the praises for young men, which demand less careful consideration of whether or not what is said is worthy. (12) For to make a speech full of pretention and solemnity, with misgivings lest it be too restrained or too effusive, for deeds which are not lasting and permanent but quickly change and pass away, would not interest me even if I were invited to speak, since these are profitless and vain things, and of such I would not willingly set out to speak. On the other hand, if that were requested, the discourse would not require any special precaution or reflection lest I appear to say something inadequate. (13) But now I call to mind his most godlike feature, where his inner being connaturally touches God (since although for the moment it is enclosed in what is visible and mortal, yet it is struggling with the greatest industry to become like God), and I also plan to touch on some wider matters and on the gratitude which I have to God for the fact that I chanced to meet up with such a man (beyond all human expectation, either that of others or even my own, since I neither intended nor even hoped for it). As I prepare to treat of such great things, small and completely simple as I am, do I not have good reason to step back, hesitate, and voluntarily keep silence?

(14) And in fact keeping quiet seems to me clearly the safest thing, lest under the pretext of thanksgiving but perhaps out of rashness I might, by speaking about august and holy things in irreverent, cheap cliches, not merely fall short of the truth; I might even be responsible for defrauding those who believe that things are the way the speech, weak as it is, would describe them,

a caricature rather than like the realities in its power. (15) Still, O dear chief, everything about you would be undiminished and unimpeached, and especially the divine aspects, remaining as they are, unshaken, not in the least harmed by our small, unworthy words. (16) But I do not know how we will avoid appearing bold and rash as we foolishly tackle, with little intelligence and preparation, matters which are great and perhaps over our heads. (17) And perhaps if elsewhere and in other company we had been ready to blurt these things out, we would have been just as bold and daring, but our rashness would not be due to insolence, since we would not be flaunting these things in your presence. (18) But now we shall fill up the measure of folly, or rather we already filled it up when we dared to enter with unwashed feet (as the saying goes)[5] into ears which the divine word itself does not visit shod in the stout leather of riddling and obscure phrases, as in the ears of most men, but entering barefoot (as it were), clear and manifest, it settles there. But we, bringing our human words like dirt or mud, have dared to dump them on ears which have been trained to listen to divine and pure sounds. (19) So is it enough to have sinned this far, and should we now control ourselves and go no farther with this address, but desist from it? Would that it were so. (20) Nevertheless, may it just once be permitted to my boldness first to express the cause which stimulated me to begin this struggle, the only possible excuse for this rashness of mine.

3. (21) Ingratitude is clearly despicable, in my view—the most despicable thing of all. (22) For someone who has experienced something good not to try to return the favor, even if he can manage no more than verbal thanks, he must plainly be obtuse and insensitive to his benefits, or thoughtless. (23) But whoever once becomes sensitive and aware of the good things he has experienced, if the memory is not also recorded for later times, if he should not also present some thanks to the author of the benefits, such a one is lazy, ungrateful and impious, sinning in a fashion for which neither great nor small may be excused: (24) if

---

5. The second-century writer Lucian of Samosata cites this phrase as proverbial in *Demonax* 4 (Loeb Classical Library, 1.144), *Rhetorum praeceptor* 14 (4.152), and *Pseudologista* 4 (5.378).

someone is great and accomplished, because he does not raise his voice with all thanks and honor for his great blessings; if he is humble and insignificant, because he does not praise and honor with all his might the one who blesses not only the great but the humble. (25) It is incumbent on those who are superior and advanced in power of soul, as it is on those with huge resources and great wealth, to return the largest and most lavish honors they can to their benefactors. (26) But the humble and those in straitened circumstances may not be neglectful or remiss, or hang back as if they could bring nothing worthy or correct; (27) like poor but honest folk, they should bring honors out of the capacity they have, in proportion to their own ability, not to that of the one they honor. These honors will be just as acceptable and pleasing to the one honored, and he will not deem them secondrate compared to the big and numerous ones, if they are offered with great enthusiasm and complete sincerity. (28) Thus it says in the holy Bible[6] that a certain humble, poor woman arrived with the rich and the powerful, who from their riches gave big expensive gifts, while she alone contributed a small, even tiny amount, but still everything she had. She earned recognition for the largest gift.[7] For I do not think the holy Word[8] weighed the munificence and worthiness by the quantity of wealth given, which is external, but rather by the intentions and goodwill behind it. (29) So we should not give way at all to fear lest our thanksgiving be unequal to the benefit, but on the contrary boldly attempt to offer in return tributes which, even if they are not adequate, are what we can manage. If our discourse falls short of perfection, yet it may be partially successful because it puts an end to the appearance of outright ingratitude. (30) For to keep complete silence under the plausible pretext of being unable to say anything worthwhile would be really odious; the attempt to repay is always praiseworthy, even if the one who offers thanks cannot manage what is worthy. So even if I am incapable

---

6. Greek, ἐν ἱεραῖς βίβλοις.
7. Mark 12.41–44.
8. Greek, ὁ ἱερὸς λόγος. Here it is hard to know whether Gregory means Scripture, the divine Logos, Jesus Christ as portrayed in the gospel passage, or some combination of those.

of speaking worthily I shall not keep silent, but be content if I fulfil everything of which I am capable.

(31) Now here is my discourse of thanksgiving. I would not wish to speak it to the God of the universe, even though thence we have all the sources of good things, and thence also we should begin our thanks or our hymns and praises. (32) But not even if I offer myself in my entirety, not such as I am now, profane and unclean, commingled and blended with accursed and unclean wickedness, but stripped as clean, as bright, and as pure as possible and unmixed with anything bad—not even, I say, if I were offering myself whole and bare, as if offering a newborn, could I by myself offer any gift worthy of the honor and recompense due to the Director and Cause[9] of all things. (33) Neither any individual nor everyone together can praise him fittingly, even if all became clean at one and the same time, rising above themselves, or rather returning to him all together in one spirit and one harmonious impulse. (34) For a person might be able to understand one of his works most excellently and perfectly, and if he was capable, speak about it worthily; but as regards that very ability with which he is endowed, since he got it from none other than God, there is no other higher source whence he could obtain the means to offer thanksgiving.

4. (35) But the praises and hymns to the universal king and guardian, the continual fountain of all good things, we shall transfer to one who even in this respect heals our weakness and who alone is able to make up our shortcomings, our souls' champion and Savior, his first-begotten Word, the Demiurge and Pilot[10] of all things. (36) He alone can send up continuous and

---

9. Marotta has "Signore e Creatore" (Lord and Maker), which is fair, but Gregory's actual words (ἡγεμόνι καὶ αἰτίῳ) have a less directly biblical ring to them.

10. There are precedents for this Platonic terminology in Christian theology; cf. Athenagoras, *Legatio* 22.12, ed. William R. Schoedel (Oxford: Clarendon Press, 1972), 52–53: "It is as if a man were to regard the very ship in which he sailed as performing the work of the pilot. Without a pilot it is nothing more than a ship even though it has been equipped with everything; just so, neither are the elements of any use, no matter how beautifully ordered, without the Providence of God. For the ship will not sail of itself, and the elements will not move without the Artificer [demiurge]"; and Theophilus of Antioch, *Ad Autolycum* 1.5. Christ is designated as "pilot" in a slightly different sense in *Martyrdom of Polycarp* 19.2.

unfailing thanksgivings to the Father for himself and for the universe, each individually and all together. He is the truth, and both the wisdom and the power of the Father of the universe[11] himself, and is also with and in him and united to him completely; so there is no way that, either through lack of attention or wisdom, or some weakness, like someone estranged from himself, he might either lack the power to praise, or have it but deliberately (which is blasphemous to say) allow the Father to go unpraised. (37) He alone is able to fulfill most perfectly the full worth of the praises he deserves. The Father of the universe, who made him one with himself, and by means of him all but[12] self-describes himself, would both honor and be honored, in a way, with a power entirely equal to his own; this[13] it fell to his only-begotten to possess, first and only out of all that exists, the God-Word who is in him. (38) All other things are able to give thanks and true worship only if, when we make our offering for all the good things the Father has given us, we attribute the power of worthy thanksgiving to him[14] alone, confessing that the only way of true piety is to remember the cause of all things entirely through him. (39) Therefore, since the boundless providence over all, which protects us in great things and small, has also brought us to this point, let him, the enduring Word, be confessed worthy of thanks and hymnody, since he is most perfect and living, and the animate Word of the first Mind itself.

(40) But of all the human race, let this our thanks be directed particularly to this holy man[15] here. Should I wish to extend my hymn further, it would go to him who, out of all the unseen, godlike ones who watch over human beings, was appointed by some great decree to govern and nurture me and be my guardian from

---

11. This expression, which ought not to be confused with the "intratrinitarian" Father, is very frequent in earlier writers. One of the most instructive parallels is Justin *1 Apol.* 63.11–15.

12. Crouzel and Marotta both translate μονονουχί as if it meant "so to speak" (see H. Crouzel, *Remerciement à Origène, suivi de la Lettre d'Origène à Grégoire.* SC, vol. 148 (Paris: Cerf, 1969), 50, for an explanation).

13. I.e., honor, or the unique position described in the previous clause as a whole.

14. Here and in the rest of this paragraph "he" and "him" refer to the Word.

15. I.e., Origen.

childhood, (41) the holy angel of God "who feeds me from my youth," as that man[16] beloved of God says, clearly referring to his own.[17] (42) But he, being great, appropriately had one of the greatest: either some unnamed one, or perhaps even the angel of the great council[18] himself, the common Savior of all, was himself assigned by reason of his perfection to be his only guardian; I am not sure of this, but he both knows and praises his own great one, whoever it might be. (43) Next to the Pilot whom all have in common, however, we also praise this one[19] who since our childhood has been our personal pedagogue. (44) Besides being good in all respects whatever, he was my tutor and protector. What was worthwhile was not apparent to me or my closest friends, for we were blind and saw nothing of the future, so as to be able to judge what was needed, but it was clear to him, who foresaw everything that would be good for our souls. Back then and still today he raises and trains and leads me by the hand, (45) and in addition to everything else he arranged (the most important thing of all) to introduce me to this man, who was not close to me by family or any human blood relationship, nor a neighbor or a resident of a nearby region, not even from the same nationality—factors which often give people an occasion to get to know each other and become friends. (46) In short, although we were unknown to each other, unrelated, foreigners, and separated by a great distance, however many nations, mountains, and rivers lay between us, with truly divine and wise foresight he contrived this meeting as my salvation by leading us to the same spot. I guess he foresaw this earlier, from my first birth and nurturing. (47) How that happened would take long to recount, and not only if I spoke exactly and tried to omit nothing; but even if I skip most of it I would like to recall briefly a few of the highlights.

16. I.e., Jacob.
17. In Gen 48.15, Jacob calls on "the God (LXX θεός) before whom my fathers Abraham and Isaac walked, the God (LXX κύριος) who has led me all my life long to this day, the angel who has redeemed me from all evil."
18. τὸν τῆς μεγάλης βουλῆς ἄγγελον; cf. Isa 9.6 LXX = Isa 9.5, and also Jer 39.19 LXX = Jer 32.19, Κύριος μεγάλης βουλῆς. Justin applies this phrase in the same way (*Dialogue* 76.3, 126.1).
19. The "pilot" is the Logos (see above, 4.35, and footnote), and "this one" is Gregory's own appointed angel.

5. (48) From birth our parents gave us our first upbringing, including the misguided customs of my native land. That we were about to be freed of them I don't think anyone anticipated, nor was it my hope, since I was a little child not yet able to reason, under a superstitious father. (49) Then came loss of my father and orphanhood, which may even itself have been what started me on the road to knowing the truth. (50) For at that point for the first time I was turned over to the saving and true Word;[20] I forget how, more under compulsion than of my own accord. For what power of judgment did I have, when I was fourteen? But from that point on this holy Word immediately began to dwell with me; at the very point when the reason common to all comes to maturity, then first did it come to dwell with me.[21] (51) As I reckon it now, even though I did not do so then, I consider it no small sign of the holy and wonderful providence in my regard that this encounter was thus proportioned to my years, (52) so that everything that preceded that age, all the works of error, had been transmitted to childishness and ignorance. That way, the holy Word was not transmitted in vain to a soul not yet reasonable, (53) but to one which had become reasonable already. Even if it did not yet belong to the divine and pure Word, yet it would not be devoid of the awe which that Word imparts. So both the human and the divine reason began in me at the same time, the latter coming to my aid by that power which I cannot describe but which is proper to it, the former receiving its aid.[22] (54) The thought of it fills me at once with both happiness and fear, heartened by how I was led but afraid lest, even after having been favored in these ways, I might fail at the end all the same.

20. This passage could refer either to the attainment of full use of reason, or to some connection with Christianity. Marotta, "I neologismi," 59, n. 32, thinks it was an interior conversion.
21. Stoics are reputed to have advocated the notion that rationality properly speaking begins at fourteen, by the accumulation of sensations and mental images; see Iamblichus, *de anima* (from Stobaeus, ed. Wachsmuth 1.317), and Tertullian, *de anima* 38.1 (ed. Waszink, 54).
22. This role of the Logos in giving aid to the Christian is a fairly common theme in early Christian writing; for examples, see Justin, *2 Apol.* 4(5).1 and *Dialogue with Trypho* 30.3.

(55) But I do not know how my discourse got stuck at this point, since I wish to narrate methodically the remarkable dispensation[23] by which I came to this man. So if at first I summarize as I hurry on to what followed, I do not pretend to give the one who so arranged matters the praise he deserves, or thanksgiving and true worship, lest we be thought vulgar for calling it that while saying nothing worthy; I am simply stating the case and making formal acknowledgment, or something in a more appropriate category.

(56) It seemed good to my mother, the only one of my parents left to care for us, that, when we had been educated in the other subjects, like children who were not ignobly born and nurtured, we should also study with a rhetor, since we were to be rhetors. And in fact we did study with one, and would have become rhetors ourselves before long, said the experts at the time; I myself cannot say if this is correct, nor would I wish to. (57) But there was no talk of these things,[24] nor any inkling yet of the causes which would bring us here. But although those closest to me had no idea and I myself had no such ambition, the divine pedagogue and true guardian, ever alert, (58) came and gave one of my teachers an idea (incidentally he was the one entrusted with teaching me the Latin language, not to the level of fluency, but so as not to be completely unacquainted with this language, and he happened not to be unacquainted with law). (59) Putting this idea into his head, he[25] encouraged me through him to study Roman law. And that man did so with eloquence, and I was persuaded, more to gratify the man than because I wanted to learn the profession. (60) Taking me on as a student he began to teach enthusiastically, but in passing he said what turned out to be the truest thing of all: that the study of law would give me the best "passport"[26] (this was the very word he

---

23. *Oikonomia*, the dispensation of providence, in this case a particular providence.
24. I.e., of Origen and his circle. Marotta and W. Metcalfe, *Gregory Thaumaturgus. Address to Origen*, take this passage in much the same way, but Crouzel applies it to the previous remark about Gregory's prowess at rhetoric: "On n'avait aucune raison de parler ainsi..."
25. I.e., Gregory's heavenly pedagogue.
26. Greek, ἐφόδιον. Metcalfe, *Address to Origen*, uses "passport" and the Greek

used), whether I wanted to be a rhetor who contended in the law courts, or some other kind. (61) That is what he said, speaking with human factors in mind, but he seems to me to have spoken inadvertently under a more divine inspiration than he realized. (62) For when with mixed feelings I became a student of these very laws, the links had already been forged: the city of Berytus was both the motive and the first stop on the way here, the most Roman city not too far away from where I was, and well-regarded as a center for learning these laws.[27] (63) Other matters transferred this holy man from the city of Alexandria in Egypt, where he had his former home, and moved him to this region, too, as if to meet us. I do not know how to explain these things either, and gladly refrain from trying.[28] (64) But so far there was nothing about our legal studies which made my coming here and my becoming involved with this man inevitable, as one could also go off to the city of the Romans. (65) So how was this too arranged? The governor of Palestine at the time[29] suddenly summoned my brother-in-law, my sister's husband, alone—to his dismay, since it separated him from his wife—and took him away to be his assistant and share in the labors of ruling the people, for he was a legal expert, and still is for that matter. (66) When he got there, he did not wait long before sending for his wife, since he had been separated from her painfully and unwillingly, and he brought us along with her. (67) So when we were thinking of moving I don't know where, but of moving somewhere other than this, suddenly there came a soldier with orders to escort and give our sister safe passage to join her husband, and also to bring us along with her as traveling companions. (68) We would give joy both to our brother-in-law and especially

---

term as well; other modern translators prefer to translate it with the Latin word *viaticum.*

27. Berytus is the modern Beirut. The implications of this passage for the state of Roman law in the third century are clarified by Modrzejewski, "Grégoire le Thaumaturge," 313-24.

28. Origen was forced to leave Alexandria by Bishop Demetrius, his old patron; see the attempts at reconstruction of the events by Henri Crouzel, *Origen: The Life and Thought of the First Great Theologian* (San Francisco: Harper and Row, 1989), 17-24, and Pierre Nautin, *Origène: Sa vie et son œuvre* (Paris: Beauchesne, 1977), 69-70, 427-31. The date was about 231-33.

29. This official, ὁ τότε ἄρχων τῶν Παλαιστίνων, has not yet been identified.

our sister, that she should not make the journey without dignity or with excessive worry, as well as to our friends and relatives who congratulated us and pointed out the not inconsiderable bonus that we might come to Berytus, there to set about the study of law. (69) Clearly everything was moving us: doing right by our sister, our own studies, and even the soldier (since we mustn't forget him) who carried the authorization for several to use the public conveyances,[30] and tickets for a greater number of us than just my sister alone. (70) These were obvious, but the truest benefits remained concealed: our fellowship with this man; the true things[31] we could learn through him about what belongs to reason; our own souls' advantage for salvation that led us here, blind and ignorant, but so fortunately for us. (71) Clearly it was not the soldier but some divine traveling companion, a good guide and protector, the one who gives us safe passage our whole life like a long journey, who set aside the other considerations (including Berytus, on account of which we fancied we wanted to travel) and stopped when he had brought us here. He was the effective agent in everything until by every means he would unite us with this man who has done us so much good. (72) And when he had come through so much and handed over the dispensation[32] to this man, the divine messenger perhaps rested here as well, not from weariness or fatigue, for the race of the divine servants is tireless, but because he had handed over to a person who would fulfill all possible providence and guardianship.

6. (73) He took us in hand from the first day, the first real day for me, the most precious of all days if I may say so, when first the true sun began to rise on me. At first, when like wild animals or fish or some kind of birds caught in a trap or a net we tried to extricate ourselves and slip away, wanting to leave him for Berytus or for home, (74) he contrived by every stratagem to bind us close; he employed every kind of argument, attached every line

30. Gregory is referring to the imperial post, the *cursus publicus*, which was used exclusively for official communication.
31. This is a difficult text to construe without emendation. For balance with the other members of the series of phrases, I would prefer to emend τὴν to τὰ and take ἀληθῆ as neuter plural, modifying μαθήματα.
32. See above, 5.55, note 23.

(as the saying goes), and exercised all his powers. (75) He lauded philosophy and those who love philosophy with lengthy praises and many other appropriate things, saying that the only ones truly to live the life which befits rational beings are those who strive to live uprightly, who know themselves first for who they are, and next what the genuine goods are which a person ought to pursue, and the truly bad things one must avoid. (76) He castigated ignorance and all the ignorant; most people, the eyes of their mind squeezed shut like baby animals, have no knowledge of what they are and wander like brute beasts without any idea of what good and evil are or any desire to find out. With great excitement they vie for possessions, fame and popular acclaim, and physical attractiveness (77) (as if these were a good, reckoning them to be worth a great deal, and even everything) and all the skills which can procure these things for them, and such careers as provide them, including military and judicial experience and legal expertise. As he made these last points, which really shook us, with full force and very artfully, he added, "... while they pay no attention to our most important feature: reason." (78) I cannot recount here how many such words he uttered in favor of the life of philosophy, not just one day but most of those first days when we went to hear him. We were pierced as by a dart by his discourse even from the first, for he combined a kind of winsome grace with persuasiveness and compelling force. But we still vacillated and pondered: on the one hand we resisted taking up the life of philosophy, still not entirely convinced, and on the other hand for some unknown reason we were unable to depart, but were constantly drawn toward him by his words as if under some greater constraints. (79) For he said that no true piety toward the Ruler of the universe—which humanity alone of all animals on earth was honored and deemed worthy to be able to have, as probably everyone, wise or ignorant, grasps if he has not completely lost his wits to some brain injury—no true piety at all, properly speaking, was possible to anyone who did not lead a philosophic life. (80) As he poured out more arguments like these one after another, and by his arts brought us in the end to a complete standstill like men under a spell, he was supported in his words, I know not how, by some divine power.

(81) And indeed he sank into us the spur of friendship (not easily resisted but sharp and most effective) and of courtesy and good disposition; his kind attitude toward us showed in his very tones as he addressed us and conversed with us. He was not trying to bewilder us with words anyway; his purpose was honest and benevolent and helpful, to save us and make us participants in the good things of the philosophic life, (82) and even more in those with which God has endowed him more than most, or perhaps even anyone in our time: namely, the saving Word, the Teacher of true piety. Although he visits many, and conquers all that he encounters (for nothing can withstand him, since he is and will always be the king of all), yet he is hidden, and not easily (or even with difficulty) known to the multitude, so that if asked about him they could say anything clear.

(83) Like a spark landed in the middle of our soul, the love for the most attractive Word of all, holy and most desirable in its ineffable beauty, and for this man who is his friend and confidant, was kindled and fanned into flame.[33] (84) Gravely wounded by it, I was persuaded to neglect all the affairs or studies for which we seemed destined, including even my precious law, and my native land and friends, those back home and those we were to visit. Just one thing seemed dear and beloved to me, the life of philosophy and this divine human being, its chief exponent. (85) "And the soul of Jonathan was knit to that of David."[34] I read this only later in the sacred Scriptures, but at the time I felt it no less exactly than it was stated, as it was prophesied in most exact terms. (86) For Jonathan was not knit to David as a whole, but his "soul," the higher parts, which are not cut off when the apparent and visible elements have been cut off from a person, and which will not be coerced by any means, for they never

---

33. Richard Valantasis, *Spiritual Guides of the Third Century* (Minneapolis: Fortress Press, 1991), 27–28, sees this passage as an explicit reference to a sexual relationship between Origen and Gregory. His argument is not altogether convincing, and it is also difficult to be sure what behaviors and what metaphors for relationship would at that time have characterized a friendship which was sexual as distinct from one which was not.

34. 1 Sam 18.1. This verse is not in the standard Greek MSS of the LXX, but is found in the recensions of Origen and Lucian along with the rest of 1 Sam 17.55–18.6.

move involuntarily. (87) For the soul is free and not imprisoned in any way, even if "you keep yourself shut up in your room."[35] For in its primary sense, it is its nature to be wherever the mind is, and if it seems to you to be in a room, you are imagining it there in some secondary sense. So it is never prevented from being in whatever place it wishes to be; but rather, in actual fact, it can only be, and reasonably be thought to be, where the works proper to itself alone are found, and relative to that. (88) So has not "the soul of Jonathan was knit to that of David" perfectly articulated in a very few words what I experienced? Those things which, as I said, will never be forced apart involuntarily will not easily be parted even voluntarily by an act of will. (89) For I surmise that the power to break these sacred and loving bonds belongs not to the inferior party, who is fickle and easily misled and could not do the binding by itself in the first place, but to the superior one,[36] who is stable and not easily shaken, and is more capable of fashioning these bonds and this sacred knot. So likewise it was not the soul of David which "was knit" by the divine word to the soul of Jonathan, (90) but just the opposite: the soul of the inferior is described in the passive as being knit to the soul of David. The greater, since it is self-sufficient, would not choose to be knit to its inferior, but the inferior, in need of assistance from its better, ought to be attached to the superior as one "knit." That way the latter, remaining independent, takes no harm from its association with its inferior,[37] while the other, undisciplined in itself, when it is linked and conformed to the greater is held under the sway of the greater without being injured in the least by the constraints of its bonds. (91) So also it was the role of the one who excelled, and not of the lesser, to forge the bonds; it is proper to the inferior to be knit and to be as it were powerless to

---

35. Koetschau refers the reader to Demosthenes, περὶ τοῦ στεφανοῦ (*De corona*) 97, translated in the Loeb Classical Library edition by C. A. and J. H. Vince (Cambridge: Harvard University Press, 1971), 81: "For every man's death is the goal of life, though he keep himself cloistered in his chamber." Crouzel (*Remerciement*, 130, n. 5) notes another allusion to this text of Demosthenes in the letter of Pope Cornelius to Fabius of Antioch quoted by Eusebius, *h. e.* 6.43.16

36. Greek, τῷ κρείττονι; Gregory often uses this word for God as well, and that implication may not be far from his mind here.

37. Compare *To Theopompus* 6.7.

escape from the bonds. (92) By such constraints *this* David, having bound us, holds us now as ever since that time, nor even if we wished could we be freed from his bonds. Not even if we should move away will he let go our souls, since he holds them thus "knit," to use the terms of holy Scripture.

7. (93) Anyway, having thus caught us from the start and completely encompassed us, when he had accomplished the main thing and it seemed that we would stay, from that point on he behaved like a good farmer who has ground that is untilled or had never been good soil, but salty and parched, rocky and sandy— or maybe not entirely barren and unproductive but even quite fertile, though unwatered and uncultivated, overgrown with thorns and scrub and hard to till.[38] (94) Alternatively, he did as a gardener does with a plant—a wild one which does not bear cultivated fruit but which is not entirely valueless if someone versed in horticulture brings a cultivated shoot and grafts it in, making a cut and then binding them together until they are both nourished as one as they grow further together (take a crossbred tree: it is a combination, but it bears fruit from what is barren, fruits of the good olive on wild roots).[39] Either way, a wild one is hardly valueless to a really skilled gardener, and even a cultivated one which is fruitful otherwise than it should be, or again through lack of cultivation is unpruned, unwatered and dried out, choked by putting out far too many random shoots, and correspondingly prevented from blossoming and bearing fruit. (95) These are the kind of people he takes, and surveying them thoroughly with his farming skill, he understands not only what is visible to all and out in the open to see, but also digs down and tests their innermost parts, questioning and probing and listening to the answers. After he had begun to think that there was something in us which was not useless, unprofitable, and hopeless, (96) he hoed, dug, watered, did everything he could, ap-

---

38. The resemblance to the first two types of ground in the gospel parable of the sower (cf. Mark 4.3–8) may not be coincidental. But as A. Knauber, "Das Anliegen der Schule des Origenes zu Cäsarea," *Münchener theologische Zeitschrift* 19 (1968): 193, points out, the teacher as farmer was also a favorite *topos* of popular philosophy, especially in Stoic circles.

39. Crouzel and Marotta both suggest there may be a reminiscence of Rom. 11.17ff. here.

plied every skill and solicitude he had, and succeeded in domesticating us. When our unruly soul kept sending up and yielding "thorns and thistles"[40] and every kind of wild weeds and plants, as overgrown as it was disorderly and reckless, he cut everything off and got rid of it by proofs and by confrontation. (97) On occasion he would trip us up in speech, challenging us in thoroughly Socratic fashion, every time he saw us fighting the reins like unbroken horses, veering off the road and running aimlessly every which way, until by persuasion and coercion, as by the bit which was the word from our own mouth, he made us stand quietly before him.[41] (98) At first it was hard for us and not without grief, as he was introducing us novices, who had never practiced following an argument, to his own reasoning, and purifying us at the same time.

When he had brought us to a proper frame of mind and prepared us well to accept the words of truth, (99) only then, as into soft, well-tilled soil, ready to push forth what would come from the seeds, he began to plant lavishly. He did the sowing of the seeds at the right time, and all the rest of the cultivation at its right time, appropriately accomplishing each task and with reason's own means. (100) Everything obtuse or duplicitous about the soul, whether it was born that way or had coarsened through overindulgence of the body, he lanced and reduced by the refined arguments and rhetorical devices used for ailments of the mind. (101) These [arguments], starting from the simplest beginnings, twined around each other and turned in all directions, developing into a vast and inescapable web. They woke us up as if from sleep, and taught us the lesson always to pay attention to the questions at hand, never being misled either by amplitude or by subtlety. (102) As for our lack of judgment and impetuosity—we would agree to anything at all, even if it happened to be false, and often contradict what was said even if it was true—out of this too he educated us, with the aforesaid arguments and a variety of

---

40. Koetschau sees here an allusion to Gen 3.18.
41. Gregory seems here to be describing, and with unusual vividness, the impact of dialectic as wielded by a master. The shift of imagery from horticulture to training horses may be a deliberate reminiscence of Plato's *Phaedrus*, with its famous image of the soul as two horses and a charioteer.

others. For this part of philosophy is of general application, accustoming us not to tear testimonies to shreds and reject them out of hand, whether carelessly or by accident, but to examine them with precision, [and] not only those things that are plain to all. (103) For many things which were attractive and impressive at first sight and entered our ears as true under the guise of elegant words, but which are rotten and deceptive no matter how they captivated and passed for truth with us, were soon detected to be unsound and unworthy of credence, poor counterfeits of the truth. And he showed us how ridiculously easily we were misled and rashly appealed to illegitimate arguments. (104) Conversely, other sound and trustworthy things, since they are not couched in plausible language, seemed against reason and most unbelievable; at first sight they were rejected as false and ridiculed undeservedly, but later, to those who worked them out and understood exactly what they meant, what previously had been deemed worthless and disreputable were understood to be the truest things of all and simply irresistible.[42] (105) That is why he taught us to investigate not just the externals which strike one immediately, which are sometimes deceptive and dishonest, but also the inner realities, and to sound each thing lest it ring false; and when we learned to trust ourselves on those things, then to deal with the externals and reach an opinion on each. (106) Thus the part of our soul which judges concerning words and arguments was trained in reasonable fashion, (107) not according to the judgments of elegant rhetors as to whether something is Greek or barbaric in its expression, for that is an insignificant and unnecessary thing to learn. (108) This, however, is most important for all, "both Greeks and barbarians, the learned and the simple,"[43] and (to keep my speech short by not naming all the crafts and occupations one by one) for absolutely every human being who selects any mode of life whatever. Yes, it

---

42. Here Gregory may be describing Origen's efforts to show that the "barbarian" sacred texts of Scripture, properly interpreted, contained more profound wisdom than many accepted Greek philosophical works. See Origen's *Contra Celsum* praef. 5; 1.10–11, 18, etc.; *De principiis* 4.1.7; and Henri Crouzel, *Origène et la philosophie* (Paris: Aubier, 1962), 103–37.

43. Rom. 1.14.

ADDRESS OF THANKSGIVING 109

is a concern for all who would deliberate on any matter whatsoever and seek to avoid being misled.

8. (109) And not [only] this form [was trained],[44] which dialectic by itself might manage to put right, but also the humbler aspect of our soul,[45] as we were amazed by the immensity, wonder, and intricate, all-wise fabrication of the world, and dumbfounded and laid low by astonishment, no longer knowing what to think, like dumb animals. (110) Then he raised us up and put us straight with other lessons, those in physics, explaining each existing thing, and analyzing them with great wisdom down to their most basic elements, and then weaving them together by reason and going over the nature of the entire universe and each of its parts, and the endless alteration and transformation of the things in the world. (111) In the end he brought us, by his clear teaching and the arguments which he had either learned or discovered about the sacred arrangement of the universe and the unsullied nature,[46] to the point where a rational wonder replaced the irrational one in our souls.[47] (112) It is this most lofty and inspired learning which the universally coveted knowledge of nature instills. (113) What need to mention the things which belong to sacred studies: geometry, so dear and unambiguous to all, and astronomy, which cruises the air? Each of these he impressed upon our souls by teaching, or recalling it to our memory,[48] or I do not know how best to express it. (114) As an unshakable base for everything else whatever, he laid down geometry as a kind of sure foundation; then he drew us up to the heights through astronomy, as if, by a kind of sky-high ladder of the two sciences, he were making heaven accessible for us.[49]

44. Gregory is continuing the explanation from 7.106 above. For εἶδος as a constituent of the soul, see Plato, *Republic* 435c.
45. Crouzel describes this lower part of the soul as the principle of the imagination and the passions, comprising both the irascible and concupiscible appetites (*Remerciement*, 141, n. 7).
46. The meaning of this last is unclear: "Nature"? Or even God?
47. Crouzel, following Brinkmann, notes echoes of Plato in this section and the following.
48. Plato, in the *Meno*, *Phaedo*, and elsewhere, taught that learning is a process of remembering what the soul already knew.
49. It is worth comparing the preceding passage to one from the second-century writer Alcinous, *Didaskalikos* 28.4: "The introductory ceremonies, so to

9. (115) Not to mention the topmost matters of all, on whose account the whole race of philosophers labors most, as if expecting to reap from the varied orchard of all the other branches of learning the great, good fruits of philosophy, the divine virtues concerning how to act, which bring the soul's impulses to a calm and steady condition. (116) This, by freeing us from grief and disturbance by any evil, would make us disciplined and tranquil and godlike and truly happy. (117) These things too he labored to instill with his own soothing and wise words, which were nonetheless most compelling, concerning our actions and our ways. (118) And not by words alone but by deeds as well he found a way to bring our impulses under control, by the very process of beholding and coming to understand the soul's impulses and disorders.[50] This knowledge more than anything enabled our soul to be restored from its discord, and to move from confusion to what is settled and disciplined. (119) By seeing itself as in a mirror,[51] it beholds the very origins and roots of evil, its whole unreasonable side, from which unnatural disorders arise in us; and also its best part, the rational, under whose control it remains self-determined, free from harm and disorder. (120) Then, having come to an exact understanding of these things which are in it—all that springs from our inferior part, flooding us with licentiousness or squeezing and choking us with pettiness, such things as pleasures and passionate desires or

---

speak, and preliminary purifications of our innate spirit, if one is to be initiated into the greater sciences, will be constituted by music, arithmetic, astronomy, and geometry, while at the same time we must care for our body by means of gymnastics, which will prepare the body properly for the demands of both war and peace." Alcinous, *The Handbook of Platonism*, trans. John Dillon (Oxford: Clarendon Press, 1993), 38.

50. πάθη, which are passions in the sense of disordered impulses in the person. The correlative term, ἀπάθεια, means freedom from disordered emotions. The rational ordering of impulses or ὁρμαί is basic to Stoic ethics. See the chapter on human action and emotion in John Rist, *Stoic Philosophy* (Cambridge: University Press, 1969), 22–36.

51. On this theme, often found in early Christian spiritual theology, see Athanasius of Alexandria, *Contra gentes* 8, 34; it can also be recognized in Theophilus of Antioch, *Ad Autolycum* 1.2, translated by Robert M. Grant (Oxford: Clarendon Press, 1970), 5: "Just as a man must keep a mirror polished, so he must keep his soul pure. When there is rust on a mirror, a man's face cannot be seen in it; so also when there is sin in a man, such a man cannot see God."

griefs and fears,[52] and every subdivision of evil which comes under these headings—it would cast these things out and remove them from its path. At their start, and at the moment they spring up, it would get the better of them and not let them grow even a little, but destroy them and wipe them out. (121) But since the things which arise from our higher part are genuinely good, these it would nourish and preserve, fostering them from the first and protecting them carefully till they reach perfection. (122) For that is how the divine virtues may come to be in the soul: prudence, able to judge first the very movements of the soul, and from those we get an understanding, in things external to us, of whether they belong to goods or evils;[53] and temperance, the power of choosing these things rightly from the beginning; and justice, which renders to each his due; and the guarantee of all these things, fortitude.[54]

(123) He did not teach us how to act by standard definitions such as "prudence is knowledge about good and evil or about what to do and what not to do";[55] indeed, [he taught us] that this kind of learning is vain and unprofitable, if the word be unsupported by works, and if prudence does not do what is to be done and avoid what is not to be done, but simply provides its possessors with knowledge of these things, like many people we see. (124) Likewise with temperance, that it indeed is an understanding of what to choose and what not to choose, but not at all as the other philosophers teach it, especially the most recent ones. They are forceful and vigorous in argument (I have often been amazed to see them prove that virtue is identical for God and human beings, and that on earth the wise human being is

52. These are the four main Stoic categories of passion or internal disorder, the first two involving excessive dilation of the personality, the latter excessive constriction.

53. Gregory seems to note as the task of prudence both the moral assessment of proposed actions outside ourselves (cf. Galen, *De placitis Hippocratis et Platonis* 7.2) and also making the initial judgment regarding the impulses themselves, which is the key to Stoic ethics (Rist, *Stoic Philosophy*, 27–36, has an illuminating discussion of the role of these judgments).

54. This is a classic enumeration and description of the cardinal virtues.

55. This is close to the definition offered by Chrysippus, as reported by Stobaeus; see H. F. Arnim, ed., *Stoicorum veterum fragmenta* (Leipzig: B. G. Teubner, 1924), 3:262.

equal to the highest God),[56] yet they are unable to transmit either prudence, in such a way that someone might do the works of prudence, or temperance, so that someone might actually choose what he has learned to choose. (125) The same holds for justice, and even for fortitude. (126) This man did not explain to us about virtues in that fashion, in words, but rather exhorted us to deeds, and he exhorted us even more by deeds than by what he said.

10. (127) I plead with the contemporary philosophers, those I know and those about whom I have heard from others, and with other people, not to hold blameworthy what we now say. Let no one believe that I speak out of friendship for this man or still less from animosity toward the rest of philosophers. (128) As much as anyone, I myself wish to be their admirer on account of their words, and it is my own desire to sing their praises and to hear others saying nice things about them. But some things are such that they bring the very name of philosophy into utter contempt with nearly everyone, and I would almost prefer to be completely uneducated than to learn any of these people's teachings, whom I would not deem worth consulting on account of the rest of their life—though perhaps I am wrong to think this.[57] (129) In any case, let no one suppose that I say these things to curry favor, to inflate the praises directed toward this man, or to curry favor another way by speaking against the worldly philosophers. Rather let him be persuaded that, lest we seem to be flatterers, we understate his deeds, (130) and refrain from outfitting[58] ourselves with the verbs and nouns and devices conventional to encomia.

Even when I was a boy learning public speaking from a rhetor, I was unwilling to tolerate eulogizing and delivering an encomium about anyone which was not true. (131) Since even now I do not propose to eulogize, I simply do not think I should exalt

56. Opponents of the Stoics taxed them with holding this latter view: see Plutarch, *de stoicorum repugnantiis* 13, and *de communibus notitiis* 33, in Plutarch, *Moralia* 6.2, ed. M. Pohlenz, 2nd ed. (Leipzig: B. G. Teubner, 1959), 14, 100. But Middle Platonists like Apuleius, *de Platone* 2.23 could speak in a similar way.

57. The expression is ambiguous, but as 10.134 indicates, Gregory thinks, on balance, that even education from bad teachers is better than none at all.

58. Like Crouzel, reading ἐκποριζομένους instead of ἐκποριζομένοις, following the suggestion by Brinkmann.

this man by denouncing others; actually, I would be disparaging him, if I contrasted his blessed life with the failings of others, so as to have something finer to say about him. We are not so foolish as that. (132) Instead, I shall describe in full what I experienced, without any invidious comparisons or overblown language.

11. (133) This man by himself was the first who persuaded me to pursue the philosophy of the Greeks too, convincing me by his own moral behavior to listen to and assimilate moral doctrine, (134) though I would not have been convinced had it been up to the other philosophers, wrongly (I again admit),[59] but very nearly to our misfortune. At first I did not encounter very many of them, just a few vaunted as teachers, but all of them in their philosophizing stopped at words. (135) This man too at first used words to exhort me to philosophize, while preceding the verbal exhortation with his deeds. He did not just recite memorized formulas; on the contrary, he did not even think it worthwhile to speak if he could not do so with a pure intention and striving to put his words into action. He tried to offer himself as an example of the person trying to live a good life whom he described in words, and presented a paradigm, I would like to say, of the sage. (136) But since from the start our discourse promised truth, not pretension, I do not yet call him a paradigm of the sage; even though I would like to say that this is true, I let it pass for now. So he was not an exact paradigm, but he very much wished to become like one, striving with all zeal and enthusiasm, even, if one may say so, with superhuman power.

(137) He wanted to turn us into the kind of people who are masters of the impulses themselves, not just masters of doctrines and well-informed about our impulses. He pushed even the doctrines in the direction of deeds, and placed before us not just a small portion of each virtue but its entirety, if we could but understand, right before our eyes. (138) He even, if one may use the word, *forced* us to act uprightly by our soul's authentic action,[60] to which he persuaded us to assent. He induced us to put

59. See above, 9.128.
60. Greek, ἰδιοπραγίαν, which can mean taking care of one's own business. It is used by Origen in the *Contra Celsum* 5.47, where he refers to "the opinion of the Platonists who hold that justice is an individual act of the parts of the soul"

aside career anxiety and the hurly-burly of public life, inciting us to look carefully at ourselves and to do what was really our responsibility.[61] (139) That this is what "acting uprightly"[62] means and that it is the true virtue of justice is what some of the ancient philosophers expressed when they say that this authentic action is also most effective in procuring happiness for ourselves and those closest to us, if indeed this virtue[63] is about rendering to each according to his deserts, and what belongs to him. (140) For what else would be proper to the soul, what so worthwhile, if not to take care of its own self, not looking to what is outside nor meddling in others' business nor, in short, doing itself the worst injustice, but turning inward to itself, giving itself its due and acting uprightly? Thus he taught us by force, if one may put it that way, to do what is just.[64] (141) In addition [he taught us] that to be prudent is no less a matter of being present to oneself and wishing and trying to know ourselves. This is the noblest achievement of philosophy, which is even attributed to the most inspired of demons as an injunction comprising all wisdom: "Know thyself!"[65] (142) But that it is truly the work of prudence, and this is divine prudence, is well said by the ancients: it really is the same virtue whether it belongs to God or to human beings,[66] since the very soul which practices to see itself as in a mirror,

---

(Origen, *Contra Celsum*, trans. Henry Chadwick, [Cambridge: University Press, 1965], 301). A closer parallel to Gregory's usage in this passage can be found in Clement of Alexandria, *Stromata* 6.125.6: τῷ τελείῳ ... ἐξ ἰδιοπραγίας καὶ τῆς πρὸς θεὸν ἀγάπης ἡ δικαιοσύνη.

61. For a brief, clear elucidation of the Stoic concept of personal freedom and responsibility, see A. A. Long, "Freedom and Determinism in the Stoic Theory of Human Action," in *Problems in Stoicism*, ed. A. A. Long (London: Athlone Press, 1971), especially 189–92.

62. The term is from Aristotle's *Nicomachean Ethics* 1135a16, and was widely employed by later philosophers.

63. I.e., justice—what follows is the standard definition.

64. What concerns Gregory here (and above, section 138) is the fact that one cannot force someone to act in complete freedom.

65. Not demons in the sense of evil spirits, but in the classical Greek sense of powerful spiritual forces; in this case, the source of the inscription at Delphi as reported by many ancient writers, for example, Plutarch, *Letter to Apollonius* 26 (116CD), translated by Frank Cole Babbitt, *Plutarch's Moralia* 2 (Cambridge: Harvard University Press, 1956), 183.

66. This statement does not easily square with what Gregory says above in section 124.

when it also glimpses the divine mind in itself, if it should be worthy of such fellowship, sets out on an indescribable path to this deification. (143) He taught temperance and courage in the same fashion: those are temperate who maintain the prudence of a soul which knows itself, whatever befalls it, for this after all is temperance, a kind of prudence kept intact. (144) Those who are courageous remain true to the aforesaid pursuits in all circumstances, and do not give up either voluntarily or under some coercion, but preserve and hold fast to their words. And that is what this virtue is,[67] the preserver and guardian of principles.[68]

12. (145) And still, despite his wholehearted efforts, he has yet to raise us from our slowness and sluggishness and make us just and prudent and temperate or courageous, since we lack so much, who neither possess nor come anywhere near to any virtue, human or divine. (146) For they are great and lofty, and none can be obtained by anyone unless God breathes in the power. We were not born in such a fortunate condition, nor, we confess, are we yet worthy to reach them, since by reason of indifference and weakness we neglect to do all those things which those must do who aim at the best and court perfection. (147) Therefore we are still on the way to being just or temperate, or to possessing any of the other virtues. But this wonderful man, friend and guide to the virtues, first made us lovers, because we were fiercely in love with love, perhaps the only way he could. (148) By his own virtue he instilled a passionate love for the attractiveness of justice, whose golden countenance[69] he truly displayed to us, for prudence to which all have recourse, for the true and most desirable wisdom, for godlike temperance, which is the soul's good health and peace for all who possess it, for his most amazing courage, (149) his patience with us,[70] and true

67. As John Dillon, *Middle Platonism* (London: Duckworth, 1977), 76, points out, "The Stoics held that one could not possess one virtue without possessing them all."
68. δόγματα: therefore "principles" in the sense of the basic tenets of philosophy.
69. Crouzel, *Remerciement*, 156, n. 1, traces the expression to fragment 490 of Euripides' *Melanippe Sapiens*.
70. Greek, ὑπομονῆς ἡμῶν. Other translators render ἡμῶν as a subjective genitive, which created speculation about a special kind of Christian patience; see Crouzel, *Remerciement*, 156–57, n. 2.

piety in every circumstance, which people are right to call "the mother of virtues." For this is the beginning and the consummation of all the virtues,[71] for from it the rest of the virtues may also most readily be added to us if we want. If we desire and work to acquire for ourselves what everyone must have who is neither godless nor infatuated with pleasure, namely, to be God's friend[72] and supporter, we would also occupy ourselves with the other virtues. Then, not unworthy and filthy but with every virtue and wisdom, we might draw near to God escorted as if by a good guide and very wise priest. I think that everything has no other goal than to come to God, having been conformed to him in purity of mind, and to remain in him.

13. (150) In addition to all his other zeal and hard work, how I would like to extend my discourse on his teaching concerning theology and his reverence, entering into the man's very disposition! With what intelligence and preparation he desired us to learn by heart all the doctrines about the divine, careful lest we be in danger concerning the most important thing of all: knowledge of the cause of all things. (151) He deemed those worthy to philosophize who with every energy had read all the writings of the ancient philosophers and singers,[73] neither excluding nor disdaining any of them (since not yet able to discriminate) (152) except those which belong to the atheists, who, since they have abandoned common human beliefs,[74] say that there is no God or providence. The latter are not worth reading, lest our

---

71. I do not know the origin of the words in quotation marks, but Prov. 1.7 LXX puts εὐσέβεια in parallel with φόβος θεοῦ as the source of wisdom and moral instruction. As Ryssel, Koetschau, Crouzel and Marotta point out, the passage from "true piety" to this note is quoted by Antonius "The Bee" Melissa, in his commonplace book (PG 136.772B).

72. Cf. *Enchiridion Sexti* 86b, τέλος εὐσεβείας φιλία πρὸς θεόν, Henry Chadwick, ed., *The Sentences of Sextus* (Cambridge: University Press, 1959), 22.

73. The Greek ὑμνῳδός is an uncommon term for poets. From what follows, I think that it implies that Origen's curriculum included the Psalms and other biblical writings alongside (or maybe even before) the Greek philosophers, Homer, and Hesiod, despite the entry in Lampe's *Patristic Greek Lexicon*, s.v., which alleges that Gregory is speaking about writers of non-Christian hymns, though Origen uses the same word for the Psalmist. In my opinion, there is no basis for attributing to Gregory a usage so much at odds with Origen's. Cf. section 195 below.

74. Greek, ἐννοιῶν.

soul be defiled in the encounter by hearing doctrines opposed to the service of God before it has attained piety; for even those who approach the temples of what they think to be genuine religion refrain from touching anything unholy.[75] So he did not even consider their writings worth enumerating among men who professed to be religious. (153) But [he did think it worthwhile] to take up and become conversant with all the rest, neither biased in favor of one nation or philosophic doctrine, nor yet prejudiced against it, whether Hellenic or barbarian, but listening to all.[76] (154) This was a wise and very sound method, lest one isolated doctrine from one group or another be the only one heard and promoted: if it should happen not to be true, by entering our soul as "the sole truth" it might mislead us, and by forming us in isolation it might make us its own,[77] no longer able to cast it off or to wash it out, as if we were woolens dyed with some intense dye. (155) For human argument is an awesome tool and very flexible, manifold in its artifices and sharp; it penetrates the hearing to make an impression on the mind and set it and, when it has persuaded those forever captivated that it should be loved as true, remain within it, false and deceptive though it be, like a dominating sorcerer whose own dupe himself comes to his defense. (156) The human soul in turn is easily led astray by argument and quite eager to assent. Even before it exercises judgment and examines something on all sides it is ready, either from its own dullness and weakness or because its reasoning power is inadequate to the tiring precision demanded by serious investigation, to hand itself over without a care to arguments and teachings which are often false and which, being themselves erroneous, mislead those who hold them. (157) Not only that, but even if another argument should wish to put it straight, it is no longer accessible or open to persuasion, but clings to what it has, as if some relentless tyrant held it fast.

75. This would certainly apply to Jewish Temple etiquette, as Gregory may have learned it from biblical writings.
76. The point may be that anyone who is prejudiced against any "barbarian" philosophy will never look at Jewish and Christian revelation. See Justin, *1 Apol.* 46,3 for an early example of Christian reference to biblical figures as barbarians, from the Greco-Roman point of view. Cf. 7.104 and note 43 above.
77. ἰδίους, meaning here something like "closed-minded."

14. (158) Was it not these mutual conflicts and oppositions in doctrines among philosophers that led to the quarrels where they opposed each others' teachings, some prevailing over others and others yielding to yet others? (159) And do not all wish and claim to do philosophy, from the moment they were first won over,[78] and assert that their desire was not less after they had become versed in arguments than when they began? Indeed, that they have an even greater love for philosophy now, when so to say they have begun to "taste" it and to be thoroughly familiar with the arguments, than when as beginners they were first excited by the impulse to philosophize? Yet even though they say these things, do they not still refuse to pay attention to any of the arguments of those who think differently? (160) None of the "old school" thinkers convinced any of the moderns or the Aristotelians to return to him and philosophize according to his philosophy—nor vice versa; no one wins anyone over. (161) For one would not easily be persuaded to agree to other ideas in place of one's own, even though, had he been persuaded to come to the same views as these before he became a philosopher, he perhaps would have loved them first. He would be so in love with such views as no longer even to listen to arguments with an unprejudiced soul, being just as opposed on their account to the very ideas he holds now.

(162) Our noble and most erudite and most discriminating Greeks pursued wisdom along the lines which each, borne by some impulse, encountered from the start, saying that these alone are true and all the rest from other philosophers are deception and nonsense. Each upholds his own, with no more argument than that everyone prefers their own ideas to those of others, there being no need to change and revise one's views as a result of demonstration or persuasion. (163) Truth to tell, each has nothing other than the irrational impulse toward philosophy to support these very teachings, and no other criterion of what he supposes to be true than (paradoxical as it is to say so) uncritical

---

78. The "protreptikos" to which reference is made here was a recognized genre of philosophical address, a sort of combination of prospectus and sales speech to attract students.

accident: each likes the opinions he first encountered, and since he is, as it were, fettered by them, he can no longer accept others.[79] (164) Even if he be able to speak of his own ideas of the universe with valid proof, and of how those of his opponents are false, and even though he be supported by reason, precisely then he is without support, since he gives himself over to the arguments which prejudice him, apparently considering that as an advantage. (165) But these thinkers take chances in other areas, and especially regarding the greatest and most necessary matter of all, the knowledge of God and true piety. (166) And still they stay somehow fettered in the same ideas, and no longer could anyone rescue them easily: it is like a bog on a very broad and treacherous plain, which does not permit those who have once stepped in it to reach safety any longer, either by returning or by getting to the far side; they are stuck in it until the end. (167) Alternatively, it is like a deep, dense, tall thicket into which some wayfarer has strayed: he probably really wants to get himself back to cleared land, but because of the distance and the denseness he is unable to, turning every which way in it and finding various connected paths within, he sets out on several of them, hoping to succeed by one of them right away; but they only lead farther in, never out, since they are just paths around this one thicket. Finally the wayfarer, exhausted and ready to give up, as if the universe were the thicket and no human habitation was left on earth, decides to stay there and set up housekeeping, and make such a clearing for himself as he can in the thicket. (168) Another example would be a labyrinth: there appears to be only one way in, so someone enters through the only door they see, thinking that there cannot be anything complicated about the way out. He proceeds into the very middle, and discovers a marvelous spectacle and a most ingenious contrivance full of paths and fitted out with interconnecting entrances and exits; when he wishes to leave he is no longer able to, but is trapped inside by the contrivance which seemed to him so clever. (169) There is nothing—no labyrinth so involved and complicated, nor thicket so dense and tangled, nor marsh or bog so perilous—that holds

---

79. Origen, in *Contra Celsum* 1.10, makes this point in very similar fashion.

those who enter it so fast as a doctrine, if it be one held by philosophers like these in their isolation.[80]

(170) So lest we go through the same unhappy experience as most do, he did not introduce us to one particular doctrine of the philosophers, nor allowed us to wander on our own, but he introduced us to all in his desire that there be no Greek doctrine with which we would be unacquainted. (171) And he himself went in with us, going ahead and leading us by the hand as if on a hike, in case we met something crooked and deceptive and misleading. He was like an expert who, since from long involvement in arguments he is neither unfamiliar with nor unskilled in any of them, may himself stay safely on high ground, and by extending a hand to others might save them by pulling them out if they are in over their heads.[81] (172) He gathered and presented to us everything which was useful and true from each of the philosophers, (173) but excluded what was false, and for the rest especially people's outlandish views on piety.

15. To such he advised us to pay no attention,[82] even if someone be hailed by everyone as a genius, but to pay heed to God alone and to his prophets. (174) He himself expounded and clarified the dark and enigmatic places, of which there are many in the sacred words. Whether God liked to address human beings this way so that the divine word might not come bare and unclothed into an unworthy soul[83] (such as most are), or whether, although every divine saying is by nature perfectly clear and simple, it seems vague and dark to us who have forsaken God and forgotten how to listen with so much passage of time, I cannot say.[84] Anyway, he clarified and brought it into the light, whether

---

80. Editors have suggested various emendations to the text here, and it may be impossible to construe without some change; my translation presumes κατ' αὐτούς (as in the next sentence) for the MS κατ' αὐτῶν.

81. This last phrase renders βαπτιζομένους, and has to be considered when one wonders whether Gregory was baptized during (or even before) his time with Origen. Crouzel, *Remerciement*, 167, n. 5, sees here an allusion to Plato, *Euthydemus* 277D.

82. Or, if μηδέν were emended to μηδενί, "to pin our faith to no man" (Metcalfe, *Address to Origen*, 81; see Crouzel, *Remerciement*, 168, n. 3).

83. See above, 2.18.

84. These two explanations are classic; the first resembles the justification for parables in Mark 4.11–12 or Paul's explanation in 1 Cor 3.2 of why he had used

ADDRESS OF THANKSGIVING   121

he encountered real enigmas, since he is a formidable and most penetrating student of God, (175) or whether there was nothing intrinsically obscure or unintelligible to him. He is the only living person whom I have either met myself or heard others tell about who could do this, who had trained himself to receive the purity and brightness of the sayings into his own soul, and to teach others, (176) because the Leader[85] of them all, who speaks within God's friends the prophets, and prompts every prophecy and mystical, divine discourse, so honored him as a friend as to establish him as his spokesman. (177) Through this man he brought about instruction in those matters at which he had only hinted through others,[86] and he granted to this man to investigate and uncover the principles of everything that the One most worthy of our trust had royally decreed or declared. (178) Thus whether one be hard and distrustful of soul, or eager to learn, he might, by learning from this man both to understand and to believe, be, as it were, compelled[87] to assent and to follow God. (179) I think that he says these things only by fellowship with the divine Spirit, for it takes the same power to listen to prophets as it does to prophesy, and no one hears a prophet except the one to whom the prophetic Spirit has granted insight into its own words. (180) There is a saying like that right in holy Scripture, saying that only the one who shuts may open, but no one else.[88] But the divine Word opens what has been closed when it clarifies the enigmas. (181) He has received this greatest gift from God and heaven's noblest destiny, to be the interpreter of God's words to human beings, to have insight into the things of God as if God were speaking, and to explain them to human beings

---

language which was easier to digest than straight spiritual doctrine would have been, while the second could refer either to the Fall in Genesis 3 or to Plato's notion of how souls came to the material world, or both.

85. In the New Testament, ἀρχηγός always refers to Jesus; here the divine Word also seems to be meant, though one might have expected a reference to the Holy Spirit.

86. Perhaps Justin's references to Plato and Daniel (*Dialogue with Trypho* 5.4 and 76.1) are examples of what Gregory means here.

87. Here, as above in sections 138 and 140, Gregory finds it necessary to qualify the verb ἀναγκάζειν when it is a case of acts which must be free; he carefully avoids portraying Origen as someone who reduces his students' moral freedom.

88. Koetschau suggests Isa 22.22, Job 12.14, and Rev 3.7 as possible parallels.

as human beings hear. (182) So to us nothing was beyond words,[89] nor was anything hidden and inaccessible. We were permitted to learn every doctrine, both barbarian and Greek, both the most mystical and the most pragmatic,[90] both divine and human; we pursued the ins and outs of all these more than sufficiently[91] and examined them closely, taking our fill of everything and enjoying the good things of the soul. Whatever one might bring up, be it an old axiom of truth or anything else of that sort, in him we possessed the most amazing resource and power, full of the most beautiful insights. (183) In short, he was truly a paradise for us, a copy of the great paradise of God, in which there was no need for them to till the ground underfoot[92] nor to fatten on bodily food, but only, planting themselves or implanted in ourselves[93] by the Cause of all things, to grow in the soul's adornments like beautiful trees, rejoicing and taking our fill.[94]

16. (184) This is truly a paradise of contentment, this is itself true joy and repletion, in which we have been luxuriating during this period which has come to a close. It was not brief in fact but yet it was all too brief, if it will stop at this point, for those who now take their leave and depart from here. (185) For I depart not knowing what is wrong or what sin I have committed, I am banished. I do not know what I ought to say; but I have even begun to babble that I am a second Adam cast out of paradise! How delightful it was to live, listening to the teacher speak as I kept silent! How profitable it would be to live in quietness by

---

89. Greek, ἄρρητον.

90. Greek, πολιτικώτερον, indicating the doctrines about how to regulate social relations.

91. Unfortunately it is impossible to reproduce in translation Gregory's play on words: σὺν πάσῃ περιουσίᾳ ἐκπεριϊοῦσι.

92. Despite Adam's task of tending the garden (Gen. 2.15), he apparently had no need to work the soil (as inferred from Gen. 3.23). Gregory employs this as a typological description of studying with Origen.

93. See Plato, Timaeus, 41E–42A, for the soul sown or engrafted into the body.

94. This passage may reflect one from Origen, in *Selecta in Genesin* in Origen, *Opera omnia*, ed. H. E. Lommatzsch (Berlin: Haude et Spener, 1831–46), 8:57, where 2.15 is paraphrased, "that is, to work in the church the truly interior spiritual works," but the tradition is as old as Philo, *De plantatione* 9.36–39 in Philo, *Philonis Alexandrini Opera quae supersunt*, ed. Leopold Cohn and Paul Wendland (Berlin: Georg Reimer, 1896–1930), 1:335.

ADDRESS OF THANKSGIVING   123

keeping silent even now, rather than—as in the present untoward scene—turning my teacher into a listener. (186) For why did I need these words? Why put all these things into a speech, when it would be better not to go but to stay on? But these faults seem to be part of the ancient deception,⁹⁵ and the sentences on our first ancestors still lie in wait for me. (187) Or again I see myself as disobeying, by daring to contravene the words of God when I ought to stay in the same place with the same people. But I am leaving, fleeing from this blessed life as much as did that man of old from the face of God, as he turned back to the earth from which he was taken. (188) So shall I eat dirt all the days of my life there,⁹⁶ and work the soil, though it bear me thorns and thistles⁹⁷ in the form of the griefs and cares⁹⁸ of which I am ashamed, since I abandon the concerns which are beautiful and good. (189) And back I go again to what I had left behind: the land I came from, my earthly relatives, and my father's house,⁹⁹ while I leave the good land, where I obtained the good homeland I never knew of before, and relatives, whom once I had them I later began to know as soul mates, and the house which truly is our father's, where the father stays and is nobly honored and celebrated by his true sons who wish to remain there.¹⁰⁰ I, on the other hand, neither noble nor worthy, leave all those things as I "turn back"¹⁰¹ and retrace my steps.

(190) A certain son is said to have moved away from his father to a distant land, after receiving from his father the inheritance which would fall to him along with his other brother, because that was what he wanted. By living extravagantly, he dissipated his family wealth and used it all up. Finally in straits he went to work as a swineherd, and when his hunger made him wish he

---

95. Cf. Gen 3.13.
96. By conflating Gen 3.14's curse of the serpent with 3.17's sentence against Adam, Gregory manages to portray his departure in the most treasonous terms.
97. Cf. Gen 3.18.
98. "Griefs and cares" is a common phrase; see Liddell and Scott's Lexicon, s.v. φρόντις.
99. This may suggest that Gregory had resources of property of which Gregory of Nyssa in his sermon knew nothing.
100. Here Gregory begins to allude to the parable of the Prodigal Son (Luke 15.11–32), an allusion which extends through section 191.
101. Cf. John 6.66, not to mention Lot's wife in Gen 19.26.

could share the pigs' feed he did not even get that. So he paid the full penalty for his stupidity in exchanging his father's truly royal table for what he had not imagined, pigs' slops and a life of servitude. (191) We seem likely to incur something like this as we depart without even our entire legitimate inheritance. For while we do not take what we need, we go away nonetheless, leaving behind what we admire and love with you[102] and around you, and receiving worse in exchange. (192) For all the dismal things will await us, tumult and agitation in place of peace, and in place of a quiet and well-ordered life a chaotic one, and in place of this freedom a harsh bondage to marketplaces, tribunals, crowds, and pretentiousness. (193) No longer shall we have any time to devote to divine things,[103] nor shall we tell the words of God; we shall "recite the deeds of human beings" (which a prophetic man deemed simple affliction)[104] and in our case even those of wicked human beings. (194) Truly night in place of day, darkness rather than brilliant light, and mourning rather than celebration will await us; and in place of a homeland the enemies' country where I may no longer sing a sacred song[105] (for how could I, in a land foreign to my soul, where an inhabitant may not draw near to God?), but only wail and groan as I remember all that is here, if even this is allowed to me.

(195) "Enemies" refers to those who entered the great and holy city where the Divine is worshipped, to drag the inhabitants and singers and theologians away captive to their own country, namely, Babylon. But these, when they were brought there, did not want to praise the Divine in song though their captors wanted them to, nor would they sing psalms in an unclean[106] land; instead, hanging up their musical instruments on the willows, they wept by the rivers of Babylon. (196) I see myself as one of them, driven from this holy city which is my homeland, where day and night the holy laws are recited, and hymns and songs and

---

102. In the singular, referring to Origen.
103. Greek, τὰ κρείττω, which in Gregory often refers specifically to the divine realm.
104. Cf. Ps 17.4, but in the LXX version: "so that my mouth will not recite the deeds of human beings."
105. The reference here and in the development which follows is to Ps 137.
106. βεβήλῳ: a pun on Babylon.

mystical doctrines, and the light of the sun is continual,[107] shining on us in daytime as we discuss the divine mysteries and at night when we are inspired by the visions of what the soul saw and did in the daytime; to sum it all up: where the divine inspiration is pervasive. (197) This is what I am driven from, carried captive to a foreign land where it shall not be right for me to play, having hung my own instrument, like theirs, from the willows. I shall be by the rivers, but I shall be digging in the muck and will not want to repeat hymns when I remember them; perhaps I shall even forget, my memories despoiled by the other drudgery. (198) But if it is not only unwillingly that I depart, like a captive, but also voluntarily, since no enemy was involved apart from myself, since I could have stayed, (199) perhaps as I leave here I shall not travel without peril, since I am departing from a city which is safe and peaceful. Probably even as I travel I shall encounter thieves and be captured, and having been stripped naked be wounded with many blows, and lie somewhere half-dead.[108]

17. (200) But why am I grieving this way? There is the Word, the Savior of all, who protects and heals all those half-dead and robbed, the unsleeping[109] guardian of all human beings. (201) And we have seeds,[110] those which you showed us that we already had, and those we received from you, the good thoughts.[111] With these we depart, weeping as we go, but still carrying these seeds with us. So perhaps the guardian who attends us[112] will preserve us; (202) perhaps we shall return to you again, bearing the fruits and the sheaves produced by the seeds[113]—not perfect (how

107. As in the heavenly Jerusalem; cf. Rev 22.5.
108. The reference is to the parable in Luke 10.30–37.
109. As Crouzel, *Remerciement*, 180, n. 3, notes Koetschau suggested this might be a reference to Ps 120(121).4 where "Israel's guardian will neither slumber nor sleep." In the New Testament, this wakefulness is a characteristic of pastoral care (2 Cor 6.5, 11.27; Eph 6.18; Heb 13.17), a notion easily applied to Christ.
110. The proximity of these seeds to mention of the Word (Logos) is not likely to be accidental. The λόγοι σπερματικοί were postulated in Stoicism as generative principles. Christian writers such as Athenagoras (*Legatio* 6.4) and Justin (2 *Apol.* 7(8).3 and 13.3) had already used this notion in the second century.
111. τὰς καλὰς ὑποθήκας, which combines the notion of suggestion from within and a pledge entrusted to someone. There may also be an allusion to 2 Tim 1.14.
112. See 5.71 above.
113. See Ps 126.6.

could they be?), but such as we can produce from the affairs of city life, weakened by some sterile or malevolent force, but not entirely without value for us, if God approves.

18. (203) So let my discourse come to an end here. It is full of boldness where it has least right to be, yet also I think gives thanks reasonably well, given our ability. Although we have said nothing worthy, at least we have not been completely silent, and yet I have done it with tears, in the fashion customary when people take leave of their friends. It is a bit stilted, but contains nothing in the way of flattery, nor perhaps too old-fashioned or elaborate. Of this I am certain, that there is nothing fabricated about it, but it is entirely true, sound in intention and pure and sincere in character.

19. (204) But you, our beloved head, arise and send us off now with prayer. As you saved us by your holy instructions during our stay, save us also by your prayers as we depart. (205) So hand us over and commend us; most of all hand us over to the God who led us to you. Give thanks for the things that have happened for our benefit, and ask him also to lead us by the hand in what is to come, always standing by us, reminding us of his commandments, filling us with holy fear of him, becoming the best of pedagogues. For when we have gone and are no longer in the freedom we had with you, we shall obey him. (206) Ask him also to give us some consolation for losing you, to send an angelic companion to be a good escort. (207) And ask this also, that he turn us around and bring us to you again; this alone will reassure us more than anything else.

METAPHRASE ON THE ECCLESIASTES OF SOLOMON

HESE ARE THE WORDS of Solomon, [988B Eccles 1] the son of David the king and prophet, a king honored beyond all others and a most wise prophet, to the entire Church of God. [989A]

(2) How empty and foolish are the affairs and projects of human beings, as far as they are merely human. For one cannot say that any advantage attaches to these things which human beings strive with body and soul to accomplish as they move about the earth, enslaved to transitory things, never wanting to look beyond the stars with the noble gaze of the soul. And the life people lead is worn down day by day, with the passing seasons and years, and the regular transits of the sun, as they come and go. Reality seems like the passing of the torrents which discharge themselves into the measureless depths of the sea with a great roar.

(3) And the things which were produced by God on our account remain the same, [989B] such as our origin from the earth and return to the earth, the earth's very existence, the sun orbiting around it all and returning again to the same place, and likewise the winds.[1] And though so many rivers empty themselves into the sea and winds blow upon it, they do not force the sea to overstep its bounds, nor do they infringe on it.[2]

(4) And this is how the things which set the boundaries to our life are organized, but the words and deeds which human beings come up with have no measure. There is lots of talk, but no benefit from the pointless babbling, yet the human race

---

1. In PL 10.989B, note 88 on this phrase discusses whether it might be an interpolation, on the basis of the mention of winds later in the sentence. A glance at Eccles 1.6b shows that such suspicion is unwarranted.

2. Here the winds are an intrusion into the LXX text, but for wind as God's way of controlling water, cf. Gen 8.1 and Exod 14.21.

never gets its fill of speaking and listening to others speak, while with their wandering eyes they try to take in every chance occurrence. [989C] What may yet happen which has not already occurred or been done among human beings? What new thing never before experienced, which is still worthy of our attention? In my opinion, there is nothing which one might term "brand new," reckoning it newly discovered, nor anything unknown to people in the past. But just as earlier things have been hidden in forgetfulness, so also, to future generations, what now exists will be dimmed by time.[3]

(5) These things I am now preaching are not just my ramblings; on the contrary, they have all been thought through in a way which befits me, to whom the kingship of the Hebrews in Jerusalem was entrusted. I have investigated with great care, and wisely penetrated the whole nature of the earth, and I know that it is most complicated, so that human beings are assigned to toil upon the earth, constantly carried away with some new rationalization for the drudgery, which comes to nothing.

(6) All [989D] things here below are filled with an alien, hateful spirit, so that they can never be the same again, but neither does the whole thing go up in smoke: so great is the absurdity which overwhelms human affairs.

(7) [Eccles 2] Once as I reflected I supposed that I might be wiser than all those who had lived before me up to my time;[4] [992A] I knew how to understand both proverbs and the natures of things.[5] But it dawned on me that it was useless to progress so far, that knowledge follows upon wisdom, and with knowledge comes a lot of work. [Eccles 2] Having judged this to be the case, I thought to change to another plan of life, and to give myself over to luxury and try out all kinds of pleasures.

(8) But now I understood how foolish all such things are, and I stopped pursuing aimless amusement, and chastened pleas-

---

3. This paraphrase of Eccles 1.11 may have a double meaning, in view of the Platonic doctrine of the pre-existence of souls.
4. Gregory here seems to be drawing from 1 Kings 4.29–31.
5. See 1 Kings 4.32–33. A clear and attractive presentation of how a knowledge of the natures of things is connected to true wisdom can be found in Charlotte Stough, "Stoic Determinism and Moral Responsibility," in *The Stoics*, ed. John M. Rist (Berkeley: University of California Press, 1978), 203–31.

ure[6] into temperance by punishing it sharply. [992B] I concluded that the soul is able to stop the nature of the body from becoming intoxicated and flowing like wine,[7] and that continence makes desire[8] its servant. That made me want to investigate what serious pursuit does face human beings, and what genuine good they can achieve during this present life.

(9) I tried all the other things which are considered worthwhile: building great mansions and planting vineyards, laying out parks, obtaining and cultivating all kinds of fruitbearing trees, where also huge cisterns to catch water were built to supply plenty of irrigation for the plants. I also acquired a great number of workers, male and female servants, getting some of them from elsewhere but enjoying the use of others born in my own household. [992C] Herds of four-footed beasts, many of cattle, others of sheep, came under my power, more than anyone in the past. Treasures of gold and silver flowed to me, since I had made the kings of every nation bring me gifts[9] and tribute. Great concerts were organized for my enjoyment, with men's and women's voices together achieving a most harmonious sound. I arranged parties, and for this part of my pleasure appointed cupbearers of either sex, nor could I number them, so far did I outstrip in these regards those who ruled before me in Jerusalem.

(10) Then it began to transpire that I had less of the fruits of wisdom as I filled with those of lust against the good. For having yielded to everything which caught my eye [992D] and to the unbridled impulses of the heart which beset me from every side, I had given myself over to the pursuit of pleasure; thus I enslaved my power of choice to all the wretched luxuries. For my longings were so inclined to wrongdoing that I thought some of these things were noble, and the rest were all right for me to do.

---

6. "Pleasure" (ἡδονή) is an irrational and disordered reaction to something good.
7. This is more than merely metaphor in Gregory's psychology; the vital tension (τόνος) of the body becomes too relaxed when one reacts in a disordered way to something good.
8. Specifically, disordered desire (ἐπιθυμία), an irrational reaction to prospective good.
9. Reading δωρυφόρους with Billius, rather than Migne's δορυφόρους. Cf. 1 Kings 10.23–25.

(11) When I woke up and opened my eyes, I discovered that the things [993A] I was doing were despicable and dangerous, the works of no good spirit. For now nothing whatsoever that people fancy seems worthwhile to me, or worth pursuing if rightly considered. When I compared the good things of wisdom with the evils associated with folly, what wonder that I am properly amazed at such a man as behaves irrationally: surely when he gets hold of himself he will turn back to what is right! For the chasm between prudence and folly is huge, like the difference between day and night. The person who has chosen virtue, therefore, resembles one who sees each thing clearly, even things above, and makes his journey while the light is brightest; but the one entangled in wickedness and all kinds of error seems like a person lost on a moonless night, blind to what is in front of him and cut off from the real world by the darkness. [993B]

(12) But when I looked for a different end to each of these lives, I found none,[10] and having made myself as it were a fellow to fools I expect to receive the wages of folly. For what good comes of those elaborate arguments, or what profit of so many words, where the floods of nonsense gush up as from the fount of folly? But the wise and the foolish have nothing in common, not in human memory, not in divine reward.[11] All the affairs of human beings are already overtaken by their end, even as they seem to be just beginning. But the wise will never share the same end as the foolish.

(13) Therefore I even came to hate this entire life of mine,

---

10. This is in agreement with Eccles 2.14b–15a, but Salmond takes it as, "And when I considered the end of each of these modes of life, I found there was no profit in the latter . . ." That fits better with what follows in Gregory, but it requires him to go directly against the clear sense of Ecclesiastes. John Jarick, *Gregory Thaumaturgos' Paraphrase of Ecclesiastes*, Septuagint and Cognate Studies, vol. 29 (Atlanta: Scholars Press, 1990), 41, says, "Gregory will move quickly in the next verses to assure his readers that this does not mean that there **is** no difference between the results of these two sorts of living; it just means that there was a time when Solomon was not as wise as he later became." For the elements of dialogue internal to this work (which become explicit in 45–46 and 56), see the introduction, section 40.

11. The presence of a notion of divine reward shows the extent to which Gregory is reinterpreting Ecclesiastes for Christian purposes, not merely trying to give it an exegesis.

wasted on meaningless things, which I passed enmeshed in the cares of this world. For to put it in a nutshell, [993C] all that I had accomplished with so much grief were works sprung from irrational impulse; and someone else—wise or foolish, who knows? —will inherit them, the cold leftovers of my labors. Rebelling against these conclusions and rejecting them, I saw clearly the genuine goods which face a person:[12] the knowledge of wisdom and the possession of fortitude.[13] If someone failed to realize the importance of these things but was captivated by others, such a person would prefer bad things to good, pursue wickedness rather than decency and frantic activity rather than peace and quiet, and would be beset by many crises, constantly preoccupied, night and day—the body with heavy labors, the soul with ceaseless worries, the heart pounding—under the pressure of conflicting situations.

(14) For the perfect good does not reside in food [993D] and drink,[14] even if it is ultimately from God that people get fed, since none of what has been given us for our preservation lies outside his providence. But the good man who obtains wisdom from God has obtained heavenly happiness; the wicked, however, beset by heaven-sent woes and sick with greed, strives to amass a lot, and in the face of the Ruler of all things seeks to put to shame the one whom God has honored, thus presenting unfit gifts, since he has made deceitful and vacuous objects the pursuits of his own wretched soul.[15] [996A]

(15) [Eccles 3] The present time is packed with contraries: births, then deaths; plants' blossoming, then their withering away; healings and killings; putting up houses, and tearing them down; lamentations and laughter, dirges and dancing. First people collect things from the earth, then they toss them away. At one moment a person is madly in love with a woman, and next

12. Here Gregory offers a contrast with the "serious pursuit" that faces people, which he mentioned in (8).
13. The Greek word here, ἀνδρείας, can be translated as "fortitude" or "manliness"; the modern English equivalent may be something like "maturity."
14. Cf. Rom 14.17.
15. While this is possibly an allusion to Abel and Cain (Gen 4), it would be interesting to know if Gregory has a more contemporary reference in mind for "the one whom God has honored"—Jesus Christ? The martyrs?

moment he hates her with a passion. Now one finds something, now one loses it; now one holds on to something, now one gives it away; one day someone killed, on another he was slain; he spoke, then kept silent; loved, then hated. Human affairs are sometimes a battleground, other times at peace, since things which appeared to be good change to acknowledged evils in no time. So let us cease from aimless thrashing about. [996B] For all these things, it seems to me, are calculated to drive people mad with poisoned darts. Some wicked opportunist has this age in his grip, striving mightily to destroy God's handiwork, deliberately making war upon it from start to finish.

(16) I am convinced that the greatest goods for a human being are cheerfulness and kindness, and one receives even this transitory blessing from God only if justice directs one's actions. But one can neither subtract from nor add to those eternal and incorruptible matters which God has definitively decreed. Is there anyone, then, who does not regard them with both fear and wonder? For what has happened is settled, while what is to come already exists in foreknowledge. But one who has been unjustly treated has a helper in God. [996C] In the regions down below I have seen a pit of punishment which awaits the impious, but there is another place reserved for the good.

(17) I reflected that all things alike are under God's government and judgment; it is the same for just and unjust, rational and irrational. For to all in like fashion a span of time is allotted, and death awaits, and the animal and human races are alike before God, differing from each other only in the ability to speak articulately.[16] But all the same things befall them, and death envelops them, the other animals no differently than human beings. For breath[17] is alike for all, and nothing greater is in human beings, but all are of little moment for the same reason: they are constructed from the same earth and are destined to be dissolved

---

16. For this way of distinguishing animal and human by the power of articulate speech, see the Stoic Diogenes of Babylon (c. 240–152 B.C.) as quoted in Diogenes Laertius, 7.55 in H. F. Arnim, ed., *Stoicorum veterum fragmenta* (Leipzig: B. G. Teubner, 1924), 3:212. A development of this idea is also found later in Nemesius of Emesa, *De natura hominis* 1, in *Nemesii Emeseni De natura hominis*, ed. Moreno Morani (Leipzig: B. G. Teubner, 1987), 4, ll. 16–24.

17. πνεῦμα.

into the same earth. For it is unclear, in regard to human souls, whether they will soar on high, [997A] and in regard to the others, those which belong to irrational animals, whether they will drain away. And it seems to me that no other good exists besides comfort and living in the here and now. For I do not suppose that it will be possible to return again to the enjoyment of these things, once a person has tasted death.

(18) [Eccles 4] Turning my back on all these considerations, I carefully examined—and rejected—all the forms of viciousness which flourish among people. Some are made to weep and mourn when they are unjustly treated, struck down inescapably, [997B] since obstruction on every side cuts them off from their defenders, indeed from any help at all. Meanwhile, the men of violence are exalted on high, from which they too will fall; of the wicked and the reckless, those who have died have fared better than those who are still alive. But much better off than either is the one who will be like them, but has not yet been born, because he has not yet encountered human wickedness.

(19) It also became clear to me how much his neighbors' envy pursues a man, a virus from an evil spirit, and that whoever catches it, and as it were gets it in his system, is reduced to consuming his own soul, chewing and swallowing an inconsolable grief with his own body, at the thought of how well others are doing. [997C] A reasonable person might prefer to fill one hand simply and modestly, rather than both with difficulty and the entanglement of a deceitful spirit.

(20) And there is something else which I know turns out badly, because a man has made a bad choice. Take someone completely alone, who has neither brother nor son, and although abounding in many possessions has his avarice for company, and is unwilling to devote himself to good works to any degree whatsoever. I would gladly ask him for what purpose he toils so hard, desperate to avoid doing anything good, but obsessed by his manifold desires to make deals. Are not those much better off than he, who set up a community of life together, from which they derive the very best of fruits? For when two men confront the same situation uprightly, [997D] even if something should befall one of them he has no small protection in his companion.

The very greatest calamity for a person in trouble is not to have anyone to put him right again. Furthermore, those who live together both double their prosperity and blunt the winds of adversity; as a result, they dazzle us by day with their mutual openness, and by night they glow with quiet dignity.[18] But the one [1000A] who pursues life without sharing undergoes his life as threatening, since he has not realized that, when people stand together, even if someone thought to attack them his plan would be reckless and unsafe, and that a rope of three strands is not easily snapped. (21) I think more highly of a youth who is poor but wise than of a witless old king, to whom it never occurred that some convict could be taken and made emperor, and later fall deservedly from his undeserved sovereignty. For it turns out that those who live under the young man, since they are subject to someone intelligent, are free from grief, [at least][19] so many as are older. For relative newcomers cannot praise this man, since they have never experienced anyone else, and are apt to follow irrational opinion and the impulse of a contrary spirit.

(22) [1000B] If you are going to preach, concentrate on directing your own life uprightly, and praying for the foolish, so that by achieving understanding they may know enough to turn away from doing wicked deeds. [Eccles 5] It is good to speak sparingly, and to keep a tranquil heart in the heat of arguments. No need to blurt out one's thoughts heedlessly, even when they are out of place or just came into one's head; on the contrary, [1000C] we should keep in mind that, even if we are a great distance from heaven, we must realize that we speak in God's hearing, and it is to our advantage to speak circumspectly.[20]

(23) But just as the bizarre imagery in dreams corresponds to the manifold concerns of the soul, so also babbling goes hand in hand with foolishness. If a promise is made in prayer, let it be fulfilled in action. It is typical for fools to be quitters; you, however, be true, knowing it is much better to avoid making a vow or

---

18. This evocation of a common life should be compared to his admiring description of the companions of Origen, and may also reflect his own reputed preference for devout companionship. See *Address* 16.196.

19. There is something missing here in the Greek.

20. The Greek word ἀπεριπτώτως is characteristically Stoic.

METAPHRASE ON ECCLESIASTES   135

undertaking to do something than to default on a vow. One must completely avoid [1001A] the spouting of unseemly words, since God is listening. For the one intent on such things, the only result is that he gets to watch his own works being destroyed by God. For as most dreams amount to nothing, so also do most things which people say.[21] But the fear of God, rare though it is, is mankind's salvation.

(24) Whence there is no need to wonder when you behold the oppression of the poor and the corruption of judges. But one does need to avoid appearing to be superior to the very powerful. For even if this were allowed, wickedness alone would not save you from the fearsome things which would happen to you.[22]

(25) But just as the possession got by theft is most harmful and most unholy, so also to the man who sets his heart on possessions will accrue neither the plenty he seeks nor his neighbors' favor, especially should they acquire extraordinary wealth. For this is worthless. [1001B] Goodness, on the other hand, when she fills her companions with joy, makes them strong by endowing them with the power to see everything in perspective. It is also a great thing not to get too engrossed in such concerns. The poor man, though he be a slave, and though his belly not be full, enjoys the gentle release which comes with sleep; but the craving for wealth is accompanied by sleepless nights and distress of soul.

(26) What could make less sense than this: the fact that the one who stores up wealth and holds onto it with much effort and care is also cherishing for himself the seeds of innumerable evils? That wealth too must some day perish and rot away, whether the owner has children or not; willy-nilly, that man must fall back into the earth and vanish, just as he once came to be what he now is. [1001C] Though he will leave with empty hands, he will make it worse for himself, as if it had not occurred to him that the end of life which awaits him is just like its beginning, and that he is toiling at meaningless things, yielding to some puff of wind rather than to concern for himself, consuming his entire

21. A theory of dreams is implied here, according to which they (like what we say) are the spontaneous product of the soul's discipline or lack of it.
22. The obscurity of this sentence is a puzzle which neither I nor earlier translators have been able to solve.

life in the most unholy lusts and irrational impulses, to say nothing of griefs and infirmities. In a nutshell, such a man's days are darkness, and his life is sorrow.

(27) But that is good and not to be despised; for it is a gift from God for someone to be able to rest happily from his labors since he has received his possessions from God, not from theft. This man will not sicken with grief, nor in general be a slave to evil inclinations; he counts his days in good works, with goodwill toward all [1001D] and rejoicing in the bounty of God.

(28) [Eccles 6] Now I shall tell you the misfortune which is most [1004A] prevalent among people. Suppose that God, in fulfilling all their desires, would deprive someone of absolutely none of those things which appeal to passionate desire—plenty of money, widespread fame, or the other things people pant after—but that the one who has everything will turn it all over to someone else, as if afflicted by heaven with this one evil, that he does not get to enjoy it, falling without having borne fruit for himself or for his neighbors. I present this as a great proof and a clear demonstration of exceeding wickedness: when that man who has honestly earned the name of father of a great many children and has lived a long time has still not been filled with goodness in his soul to such a point as not to have the experience of death. I would envy him neither his large progeny nor his length of days; and I even think that a fetus miscarried from its mother's womb is better off than that man. [1004B] For as it came forth to no purpose, so it departs just as secretly into oblivion, not having encountered evils or seen the sun. This is easier to take than the wicked man who, though he measure his life in thousands of years, does not know goodness. Death is the end for both.

(29) While the thoughtless one is refuted especially by the fact that he has not managed to satisfy any of his cravings, the prudent person does not get entangled in these passions. More often than not, uprightness of life leads a person by way of poverty. What wanton eyes behold drive many mad, exciting their souls, pushing them to mindless effort, in the futile craving to be noticed. For those things which now have come to be were known ahead of time, and it is clear that no person can manage to withstand the forces which control him. [1004C] Nevertheless,

idiocies are epidemic in the human race, increasing the madness of those who engage in them.

(30) [Eccles 7] For though it is not at all more helpful for someone to know that what he wants will befall him during his life—let us take this as given—likewise it is vain human curiosity to pry methodically into (and even pretend to know) how things will be for each one after death. [1004D] But a happy memory is more soothing to a soul than oil is to a body, and life's leaving better than its beginning; better to lament than to party, and to associate with mourners than with revelers. For thus it is when someone is facing the end of life without having taken care about those things which concern him.

(31) A prudent temper is preferable to laughter, for a sober expression on the face helps keep the soul steady. The souls of the wise have a sad and reserved look, while those of the thoughtless gush with excitement. The rebuke of a single wise person is much more to be sought than [1005A] hearing a whole chorus of vulgar, wretched folk singing our praises. For the laughter of mindless people is like the sound made by a big bundle of thorns burning in a fierce fire. And this is pitiful enough, but the greatest evil is the spreading of lies; this lays snares for the souls of the wise, and threatens to break down the noble resistance of the good. It is proper to praise when talk ceases, not when it starts; and to approve a moderate disposition, not an unstable[23] and confused one. By all means, one should keep one's irascible appetite in check and not easily be carried away by anger, to which the foolish are enslaved.

(32) But they sin who say that earlier generations were given a better life, and they fail to understand that wisdom is completely different from abundance of possessions, and that it is as much more conspicuous as silver outshines its own shadow. [1005B] Real life, for a human being, comes not from the precarious possession of wealth, but from wisdom. And who, pray tell, will be able to declare God's providence, so great and so beneficent? Or to summon back what seems really and truly to have been consigned to oblivion by God?

---

23. Gregory puns on μέτριον (moderate) and μετεωριζόμενον (unstable, up in the air).

(33) Although earlier I did what was not right, I have considered all things, both the just man who remained in righteousness and did not stray from it until death, but was even plotted against on its account,[24] and the impious who perished along with his own wickedness. The truly righteous ought not at all to appear as such, or to overplay a reputation for wisdom, lest in stumbling at one thing he sin again and again. And do not be reckless and rash, lest death snatch you away early. [1005C] But the greatest good is to lay hold of God, and when in this condition to refrain from sin. For to finger pure things with a guilty hand is odious. But the one who obeys, in the fear of God, escapes from all that is opposite.

(34) Wisdom can be of greater assistance than a company of the strongest men in town, and it also usually knows when to excuse those who fail to do their duty. For there is not one person who has not stumbled. But to the words of the impious one should pay no attention at all, lest, having heard with your own ears what was said against yourself (such as the grumbling of a disaffected servant), then you too, stung to the heart, may in your subsequent dealings be provoked into reviling him in return. (35) But though I knew all these things, and received wisdom from God, when I later threw her away[25] I could no longer be the same. For wisdom deserted me [1005D] for a limitless time, to an immeasurable distance, as if she could never again be mine. Finally I completely stopped seeking her, nor was I concerned any longer to evaluate the folly and the empty desires of the impious, and their life of distraction.

(36) Once in that frame of mind, I was carried into the same mistakes, and driven by a deadly lust, I knew Woman, who is a kind of net[26] or what amounts to the same thing. [1008A] For her heart ensnares the passers-by, and with the simple touch of her hand to theirs she detains them as if[27] she had tied them up

---

24. Cf. Wis 2.12–20.
25. Cf. Sir 47.14–21.
26. Greek, γῆν, but early editors suggest the emendation to πάγην or σαγήνην, both of which are words for nets.
27. S. D. F Salmond, trans., *The Works of Gregory Thaumaturgus, Dionysius of Alexandria, and Archelaus*, Ante-Nicene Christian Library 20 (Edinburgh: T. & T.

and dragged them off. One may be rescued from her, but only if he has the gracious God watching over him, whereas someone who is enslaved to sin would not escape. I searched through all women, looking for their self-control, but in not one did I find it. One may in a thousand men find one who is self-controlled, but not a woman.

(37) One thing became very clear to me, that people, though their souls came from God's hands as simple, draw to themselves quite disparate notions and interminable inquiries, and while claiming to seek wisdom, they waste their time on trivia.

(38) [1008B Eccles 8] But wisdom is discernable in a person, and shows in the face, lighting up the one who possesses it, and correspondingly a shameless look immediately marks the one in whom it dwells as worthy of contempt.

(39) One must always pay close attention to the words of the king, but by all means avoid an oath, especially one made in the name of God. Likewise one may listen to wicked speech, but should avoid every blasphemy against the Ruler.[28] For one cannot complain at what he sends us, nor contradict the views of the sole Ruler and King. It is better, as well as more profitable, for one who continues in the holy commandments, to stay far from the words of the wicked. For the wise man understands and foresees that the judgment when it comes will be just. For all the things that happen in this human life may expect retribution from above.

(40) The wicked, in contrast, does not seem at all to realize that since a great providence hangs over him, nothing whatsoever will be hidden in the hereafter. For he knows not the things to come, since no one will be able to tell about them adequately: that nobody will be strong enough to prevent the angel from bearing his soul away,[29] [1008C] nor may any procedure at all be

---

Clark, 1871), 14, n. 8, says, "This use of ἢ εἰ is characteristic of Gregory Thaumaturgus. We find it again in his *Panegyr. ad Orig.* 6, ἢ εἰ καὶ παρὰ πάντας, etc. It may be added, therefore, to the proofs in support of the common authorship for these two writings."

28. Δεσπότης was a common word for God, even in early Christian writings.

29. A common image of death in antiquity. Cf. the *Acts of Perpetua and Felicitas* 11, and for a frightening account of the sinner's death, the *Life of Pachomius* 82 in

found to renegotiate the moment of death; but it is like when one is surrounded in the midst of battle, one can see no escape in any direction, and all a person's impiety utterly collapses.

(41) And I am shocked when I observe how numerous and serious are the things which people plot to their neighbors' harm. But I understand that the impious are snatched away early and vanish from our midst, because they [1009A] gave themselves over to frivolity. For since God's providence does not deal quickly with everyone, on account of his great forbearance, nor does it immediately punish offenses, on that account the wicked man thinks he can go on sinning and get off scot-free. He does not realize that even after a long time his misdeeds will not be forgotten. Truly, to fear God is the greatest good. If the impious person falls from that, he will not practice his folly for long.

(42) The most deplorable, misguided opinion often persists among people concerning the just and the unjust: they mistake each group for their opposites. When someone is just he is not thought to be so, and correspondingly the impious person is regarded as prudent. This, I propose, is the hardest error of all to endure.

(43) There was a time when I thought food and drink the greatest of good things, [1009B] and that the person most favored by God was the one who enjoyed these things to the greatest extent all his life. I considered such well-being to be the only consolation of life. And so I paid no attention to anything other than this view: neither night nor day would I abstain from what people consider delicacies. I found out that whoever wallows in

---

Pachomian Koinonia 1, trans. Armand Veilleux (Kalamazoo: Cistercian Publications, 1980), 108–9: "If it is a soul with an evil way of life, two merciless angels come to fetch it at the time it is to be visited. When the man is at the point of death, when he no longer recognizes anyone, one of the merciless angels is placed near his head, the other at his feet; and thus they begin to thrash him until his wretched soul is on the point of going up. Then they thrust into his mouth a hooked object, a sort of fish-hook, and they yank that wretched soul out of his body; it is dark and shady. Then they tie it to the tail of a spirit-horse—for [the soul] also is a spirit—and thus they take it away and pitch it into torments or else to the bottom of hell, according to its works' deserts." Veilleux in a note refers the reader to F. Cumont, "Les Vents et les Anges psychopompes," in *Pisciculi. Studien zur Religion und Kultur des Altertums* (Münster: Aschendorff, 1939), 70–75.

such things will never be able to find the truly good, hard as he tries.

(44) [1009C Eccles 9] For at that point I thought that all human beings earned the same deserts. So if a wise person was absorbed with righteousness, turned away from wickedness, and avoided enmity by being decent towards everyone, as is pleasing to God, that person appeared to be laboring in vain. The just and the impious, good and wicked, pure and impure, the one who reverenced God and the one who did not, both seemed to meet the same end. For when the unjust and the good, the one who commits perjury and the one who completely avoids an oath, could hope to reach the same end, the false impression may arise that all are treated alike when they die. But now I know that these were fools' opinions, both erroneous and misleading.

(45) People say many things, such as, "A person who dies is gone forever," and, "A live man is better off than a dead one, even if he lies in darkness, even if he lives his life like a dog, [1009D] while the dead man was like a lion." "For this much the living know very well, that they will die; but the dead don't know anything at all." "There are no rewards for anyone, when duty has been done." As far as the dead are concerned, both hatred and love come to an end. As for their ambition, it has departed, and their life has vanished. No further claim on anything remains for the one who has departed this life once and for all.

(46) As error goes on chanting these themes, it also offers such counsels as these: "You there! What are you accomplishing if you don't enjoy yourself, if you don't eat your fill of goodies, and top it off with wine? Do you not see that these were given by God for our unrestricted enjoyment? Put on clean [1012A] clothes, anoint your head with oil, give this woman and that one the eye, and pass your empty life foolishly. For nothing else is left for you, not here, nor after death. Do whatever you fancy, for no one will trouble you for these things with so much as a twinge of conscience, nor does anyone outside the human race take any note of what takes place among us. And Hades, whatever that might be, to which we are said to depart, is devoid of wisdom or sensation." These things are what the foolish say.

(47) But I know well that those who seem lightest on their

feet will not finish that great race, nor will those who in people's opinion are strong and fearsome win the fearsome battle. Sound thinking is not determined by the surfeit of food, nor does understanding usually keep company with wealth. I do not share the rejoicing of those who [1012B] imagine that everyone will receive the same. Those who cherish such illusions seem to be fast asleep, and not to reflect that when they are carried off suddenly like fish and birds, they will languish amidst evils, shocked to get the penalty they deserve.

(48) But wisdom I consider such a great thing, that I consider even a little town, with few inhabitants and besieged by the forces of a great king, to be great and mighty if it have even one poor citizen who is a wise man. For he might be able to save his city both from the enemy warriors and from the siegeworks. And others do not acknowledge that wise man, since he is poor; but I rate his strength in wisdom far higher than this popular prestige. [1012C] But for the moment wisdom is scorned if it is accompanied by poverty; later on it will be heard drowning out the rulers and tyrants who set their heart on wicked deeds. For wisdom is stronger even than iron; while one person's folly puts everyone in danger, even if they disregard it.[30]

(49) [Eccles 10] For when flies fall in the balsam oil and drown, they make that [1012D] fragrant ointment unattractive both to look at and to use. But wisdom and folly do not deserve to be remembered in the same breath.[31] The wise man directs himself along the right road in human affairs, but the fool has turned to the worse,[32] nor will there ever come a time when he can use folly as the guide to good deeds.[33] [1013A] Even the thoughts of his heart are empty, since they are filled with folly.

(50) Friend, even if a hostile spirit should come upon you,

---

30. This last phrase represents either of the two Greek texts, κἂν πολλοῖς καταφρόνητος ᾖ (PG 10.1012C) or κἂν πολὺ εὐκαταφρόνητος ᾖ (Maurist edition of Gregory Nazianzen, 1.888B).
31. The point seems to be that folly taints wisdom as the flies do myrrh.
32. "Right" and "left" carried the evaluative sense of "good" and "bad" in Greek; see Geoffrey Lloyd, "Right and Left in Greek Philosophy," in *Right and Left: Essays on Dual Symbolic Classification* ed. Rodney Needham (Chicago: University of Chicago Press, 1973), 167–86.
33. Or, "when the guide of good deeds indulges in folly."

continue to be of good cheer, knowing how God can forgive even a great multitude of sins. But the works of a tyrant, and of the father of all wickedness are these: the fool is exalted on high, while the one rich in good sense is humbled; and one sees slaves to sin riding horseback, but priestly men walking in lowliness, to the gratification of the wicked.

(51) But if someone plots against someone else, he has without knowing it set an ambush first and only for himself. Whoever takes away another's security will fall victim to the serpent's bite. But the one who removes stones submits to no small burden, and the wood-cutter carries danger in his own tool, [1013B] if the axe-blade should happen to fly off the handle; the one who does these things will be thrown into confusion, since he is not gathering in a good cause, and is increasing his own wrong-headed and short-lived effort.[34] The serpent's bite is hidden; those who chant spells will bring no relief, for they are empty.

(52) The good man, on the contrary, does good for himself as well as for his neighbors, but the fool falls into ruin through his imbecility. From the moment he opens his mouth he begins foolishly and breaks off abruptly, displaying his brainlessness throughout.

(53) It is impossible for a person to know, or to learn from a human source, what has always been or what is yet to come. For who will disclose it? A person who does not know how to reach the good city sustains damage in his eyes and in his entire face. [1013C] I predict bad things for that city whose king is young and whose rulers are gluttons. But I bless the good land which is ruled by the son of one who is free. Here they will enjoy good things in their season, who have been deemed worthy to rule there.[35] But the irresolute and the lazy diminish their inheritance because they are contemptuous; and misusing everything for their own greed, they are easily led by money, and willing to do anything shamefully and poorly for a little profit.

(54) But it is fitting to obey the king, and the rulers or lords,

---

34. I take this admittedly difficult passage as reflecting on the one who takes away another's security: whether he does so by removing stones or by chopping away at wooden supports, he is himself vulnerable.

35. There may be an allusion here to Gal 6.9.

and not to incur their hatred or ever to direct any offensive word at them. Be afraid that whatever it is, even though said in private, will somehow come to light. For to the rich, great, and only King, speedy and all-seeing messengers[36] relay everything, as they carry out their spiritual and [1013D] rational service.

(55) [Eccles 11] To share one's bread and the necessities of human life is just. For even if in the short term some think you have lost, as if you had thrown your bread in the water, still, in time to come, your human kindness will not seem unintelligent. Give unstintingly, and share what you have with many, for you do not know what tomorrow will bring. The clouds do not withhold their abundant dew, [1016A] but let their rain fall upon the earth; and the tree does not stand forever, but even if men spare it the wind will blow it down. Many people would like to know in advance what heaven will send, and even after surveying the clouds or testing the wind someone may refrain from harvesting or from winnowing, since he is certain of nothing and does not know what will come from God—any more than what sort of child the pregnant woman will bring forth. But having sown in due season, harvest the fruits when the time for that arrives, for it is unclear how much better the plants will get. But would that all things would come out well!

(56) Someone who thinks, "The sun is fair. Life is sweet, and how good it is to celebrate ceaselessly on all occasions," and, "Death is fearsome, eternity is bad, and comes to nothing"— such a one supposes it necessary to enjoy all the present apparent pleasures. [1016B] And he counsels the young to spend the best years of their lives in surrendering their souls to every pleasure, and to gratify their lusts and do whatever appeals to them, and to feast their eyes on pleasant sights and turn away from everything else. To such a one I will say, "You are out of your mind, sir, not looking ahead to the judgment of God on all these things." Licentiousness and dissipation are evil, and our bodies' vile excitability is destructive. Youth's close attendant is stupidity, and stupidity leads to destruction.

(57) [1016C Eccles 12] So one ought to fear God while one is

36. Greek ἄγγελοι, here transposed quite out of the context of earthly kings.

still young, before giving oneself over to wicked deeds, before God's great and fearsome day comes, when the sun will no longer shine, nor the moon, nor the other stars; when the powers above, the angels who protect the world, will be shaken in that storm and tumult of the universe. At that the powerful men will stop, the women at work will stop, fleeing into the dark recesses of their houses and shutting all the doors. And a woman whose fear stops her from grinding will speak in a squeaky voice like a tiny bird. But all unclean women will fall back into the earth, and cities and their blood-stained rulers, while they await the punishment from on high, when that most bitter and bloody time comes [1016D] (like a blossoming almond tree),[37] and continuous punishments beset (like a great multitude of swarming locusts), and the lawless are hurled far away (like a blackened and good-for-nothing caper plant). And the good man will go rejoicing into his eternal home, but the heedless fulfill their destiny in grief, and neither the silver they saved up nor their fine gold is any further use to them.

(58) For a great calamity will befall all things, [1017A] even to a pitcher standing by a well, and a wagon wheel which has been abandoned in a ditch, when the course of the ages[38] comes to an end along with this water-fed life, when this water-bearing[39] age has passed. But while people still remain on the earth there is one salvation, if their souls should recognize it and fly up to the one who gave them birth. I say once again, as I said before, that people are in a condition of futility, nor can the futility of the things they propose be exaggerated. My labor would be superfluous if I were preaching like a wise man, because I am trying to teach this people characterized by ignorance and incorrigibility. It takes a man of lofty character to be able to penetrate the meaning of words of wisdom. But now since I am old, and have come through a long span of life, I have labored to discover

---

37. In this and the two following expressions, Gregory seems to me elaborating an allegorical interpretation of the key terms in Eccles 12.5b.

38. The Maurist edition assures us that the correct reading is χρόνων.

39. The λουτροφόρος was an unmarried relative of the bridegroom, who brought water for washing to the couple about to be married. Gregory uses this metaphor to relate the present age to the age to come.

the excellent things of God [1017B] by way of the mysteries of the truth. I understand how he awakens souls, and how the admonitions of the wise stimulate them no less than bodies are controlled with a goad or pinned with a nail.[40] Some will provide those wise teachings, accepting them from a single good shepherd and teacher, all explaining most abundantly, in unison with each other as from a single mouth, what is believed.[41]

(62) But there is no profit in multiplying words, nor do I advise you, friend, to write down meaningless things about what it is proper to do—an area where there is no further need for aimless labor. But let me make one last plea. O people, behold I proclaim to you clearly and concisely: Fear God, the ruler and observer of all things, and keep his instructions, too. Be assured that everyone will be judged later on, and all will receive as they deserve the recompense for their works, the good and likewise the evil.

---

40. Cf. *Address of Thanksgiving* 6.78, 81.
41. This may be Gregory's way of saying that the Preacher foresaw the gospel writings. Jarick, 304, points out that in the New Testament Christ is designated both Shepherd and Teacher.

CANONICAL EPISTLE

MOST HOLY FATHER, [1020A] the food will not weigh us down, if the captives ate what their captors set before them, for this one reason above all the others, that the barbarians who have overrun our territories did not sacrifice to idols. The Apostle says, "Food is for the belly, and the belly for food. God will abolish the one and the other."[1] But our Savior, too, when he made all things clean, said, "It is not what enters that defiles someone, but what comes out."[2] And likewise the captive women who were befouled when the barbarians violated their bodies—except if someone had even earlier been convicted of the life of "following after their own wanton eyes," as the Bible says,[3] [1020B] that is, their lewd demeanor was suspect even at the time of their capture; and with such women one should not readily [1021A] share the prayers.[4] But if a woman who has lived in complete chastity and has exhibited an earlier life pure and above all suspicion has fallen into lewdness from force and constraint, we have a precedent in Deuteronomy in the case of the young woman whom someone found in the open country and seized her, and lay with her. It says, "You shall do nothing to the young woman, for she has no fault worthy of death; this case is just as if someone rose up against his neighbor and took his life. The young woman cried for help, but no one came to her aid."[5] The present circumstances are identical.

2. [1025D] Greed is terrible, and it would take more than one letter to list the holy Scriptures where not only robbery is denounced as horrible and to be shunned, but all greed and seizing

---

1. 1 Cor 6.13.
2. Matt 15.11.
3. The phrase comes from Num 15.39.
4. If this seems unusually harsh, one should recognize that "to share in the prayers" is probably a reference to eucharistic Communion.
5. See Deut 22.25–27.

others' possessions out of base covetousness. And everyone of this kind is publicly banished from the Church of God. Only impious people who hate God and whose error has no bounds[6] would dare to think, at the time of the raid, amid such wailing and lamentations, that a moment which brought ruin to everyone else was for them an opportunity for profit. For that reason such persons should be [1028A] publicly banished, lest wrath be visited upon the entire people, and especially upon the leaders who did not flush these men out. For I fear, as Scripture says, lest the wicked and the just perish together.[7] The Bible says it is because of whoring and greed "that the wrath of God comes upon the sons of disobedience. Therefore do not associate with them, for once you were darkness, but now you are light in the Lord. Walk as children of the light (for the fruit of light is found in all that is good and true), and try to learn what is pleasing to the Lord. Take no part in the unfruitful works of darkness, but instead expose them. For it is a shame even to speak of the things that they do in secret; but when anything is exposed by the light it becomes visible."[8] That is what the [1028B] Apostle says. But if, though people have paid the penalty for earlier covetousness which took place during the peace, they return to their grasping ways as soon as the wrath arrives, profiting from the blood and misery of people who have been driven from their homes or taken captive, what else should they expect than that by contending for greed they have heaped up wrath both for themselves and for the whole people?

3. [1029D] Look, did not Achan the son of Zerah dishonestly [1032A] steal from the devoted things,[9] and wrath came upon the whole people of Israel?[10] And he alone sinned, but he was

---

6. This last relative clause is not in the *editio princeps* of Voss.
7. The reference is to Gen 18.23. A similar sentiment, though with a different scriptural warrant (Gen 19.17), is expressed in Basil of Caesarea, *ep.* 217, canon 84.
8. Eph 5.5–13. The *editio princeps* of 1604 omits this quotation; Dräseke and Pitra, like critical editions of the Greek New Testament, have "and right" between "good" and "and true" in Eph 5.9.
9. I.e., those things set aside for God.
10. Josh 7.1. In Josh 7.20–21, Achan confesses, "... this is what I did: when I saw among the spoil a beautiful mantle from Shinar, and two hundred shekels of

not the only one to die in his sin. Now to us, in the present circumstance every asset which does not belong to us but to someone else should be regarded as "the devoted things." For he, Achan, took as spoil, and these men now have taken "as spoil"; but he took what belonged to the enemy, while these now have taken what belonged to their brothers, making for themselves a deadly profit.

4. [1033B] Let no one deceive himself, as if he had "found" things, for not even a finder is permitted to profit. "If you see your brother's ox and his sheep straying on the road, do not ignore them, but turn them around and take them back to your brother. But if your brother is not nearby, or you do not know him, gather them together, and they will be with you until your brother comes looking for them, and you will give them back. And do the same regarding his ass, the same with his garment, the same [1033C] with every lost item belonging to your brother—whatever he may have lost, and you find."[11] So says Deuteronomy. But in Exodus, even if someone finds what belongs to his enemy, not just his brother, it says, "Turn and take them back to their owner's house."[12] But if it is not permitted to take advantage when someone is lazy and taking it easy and careless of his own property, be he brother or enemy, how much more so if he is in straits, and fleeing from the enemy, and had to leave his possessions behind?

5. [1037B] Other people deceive themselves that it is merely as replacements for their own lost possessions that they appropriate others' belongings that they find; since the Borades[13] and Goths made war on them, so they may be Borades and Goths toward others. For that reason we sent our brother and fellow-elder [1037C] Euphrosynos to you, so that following the rule communicated herein he might both accept the right accusations and banish the right people from the prayers.

---

silver, and a bar of gold weighing fifty shekels, then I coveted them, and took them."

11. Deut 22.1–3.
12. Exod 23.4.
13. The historian Zosimus seems to be referring to the same people when he speaks of "Borani."

6. [1040A] [Concerning those who detain by force prisoners from the barbarians.][14] We have been told that something incredible has been going on in your region, which must be the work of unbelievers and ungodly people who do not even know the name of the Lord, because some of them have sunk so far into savagery and inhumanity as to detain forcibly some escaped prisoners. Send [1040B] some people out there, lest thunderbolts come down and strike those who are doing such things.

7. [1040C] [Concerning those who joined up with the barbarians, and dared to wrong the members of their own people.] As for those who joined up with the barbarians and came along with them as captives, forgetting that they were people of Pontus and Christians, and even sank so far into barbarity as to kill members of their own people by beating[15] or strangling, and to point out roads and houses to barbarians who did not know them: [1040D] these must be excluded even from the audience[16] until a general agreement regarding them occurs to the assembled saints, and before them, to the Holy Spirit.[17]

8. [1041D] [Concerning those who shamelessly broke into others' houses during the barbarian invasion.] Those who shamelessly broke into others' houses, if they are convicted of the charge, are not even to be deemed worthy of the audience; but if they declare themselves and make restitution, they should prostrate themselves among the penitents.

9. [1044D] [Concerning those who have found, either in the open field or in their own houses, things left behind by the barbarians.] Those who have found something left behind by the barbarians, either in the open field or in their own houses, should likewise prostrate themselves; but if they declare them-

---

14. This opening phrase and those which open sections seven, eight, and nine look like additions to the text; J. Dräseke, "Der kanonische Brief des Gregorios von Neocäsarea." *Jahrbücher für protestantische Theologie* 7 (1881): 735–36, characterizes them as headings which stood in the margins of several of the codices.

15. I.e., with a club; or by crucifixion, though other forms of execution were known by the term ξύλον. Peter Heather and John Matthews, *The Goths in the Fourth Century* (Liverpool: Liverpool University Press, 1991), 9, translate it "gibbet."

16. See canon 11 below, where this term is explained.

17. This last is a fairly conventional reference to Acts 15.22, 28.

selves and make restitution, they are to be deemed worthy of the prayer.

10. [1045C] But those who carry out the commandment[18] must carry it out without any dishonorable gain, not asking for any reward or bounty or finder's fee, whatever name they call these things.

11.[19] [1048A] The "weeping"[20] takes place outside the door of the worship space; there the sinner has to entreat the faithful who are entering to pray for him. The "audience"[21] is inside the gate in the vestibule area, where one who has sinned has to stand until "the catechumens," and then leave. "For when one has heard [1048B] the Scripture and the instruction," it says, "let him be put out, and not deemed worthy of the prayer." The "submission"[22] is when someone, after standing within the church door, leaves with the catechumens. "Standing with"[23] is when one stands along with the faithful, and does not leave with the catechumens. Finally comes "participation"[24] in the Holy Communion.

---

18. This appears to refer to those who are in charge of putting things right after the Goths' departure, whether local leaders, an emissary like Euphrosynos, or those sent out in section 6 to set detained captives free. Ἐντολή in this instance would refer to the rule laid down by Gregory.

19. This canon has long been recognized as an addition based on Basil of Caesarea, whose function was probably to elucidate the categories used by Gregory.

20. In Greek, πρόσκλαυσις, which suggests that the weeping is intended to communicate to the faithful the intensity with which the sinner wishes to enter the process of penitence.

21. Greek, ἀκρόασις. 22. Greek, ὑπόπτωσις.
23. Greek, σύστασις. 24. Greek, μέθεξις.

TO THEOPOMPUS, ON THE IMPASSIBILITY AND PASSIBILITY OF GOD

ONE DAY, as I was about to come to the place where I usually stayed, a certain man whose name was Theopompus asked me whether God was impassible. After a brief delay I answered him with some distaste, "How can we not say that God does not fall under passion, O Theopompus?" And when he took pains to follow my response with another question, I increased my pace to get away and arrive at the place where friends used to gather. And when I had sat down with those who happened to be there, extending my hand to them, I was on the point of asking them about what I had said the previous day, when Theopompus arrived; coming right up to me he began to speak thus: "The uneducated and those unfamiliar with doctrine, O Gregory, should be eager to learn from teachers and those with wide experience. But because I have decided to occupy myself intensely with this question which lies before us, I beg you to propose a remedy for these conflicting thoughts, which are constantly in my mind and leave me no rest. I beg you to help me by your clear and competent explanations relative to this question which is addressed to us."

2.[1] But when this petition was followed by deep silence, I resumed speaking as follows: "Our dear Theopompus has conferred a great and unusual favor on us by wishing to reopen that question which I think demands investigation and is of concern to everyone, 'Whether God is impassible?'" To this question my immediate response was, "How could we all possibly not confess, O Theopompus, that God is impassible?" When this gave rise to a buzz of discussion among those present, I in turn asked

---

1. The numbered text divisions correspond to the divisions in Johannes Baptista Pitra, *Analecta sacra spicilegio Solesmensi* (Paris: Ex publico Galliarum typographeo, 1883), 4:103–20, 363–76.

Theopompus what he had thought about my reply. He answered thus: "If God is impassible by nature, it follows that he can never suffer even if he should wish to, because then his nature would be doing something that was contrary to his will." To that I gave the following response. "Do not blaspheme, O Theopompus, nor bring God under a constraint of necessity by opposing the constraint of his nature to his will. If God cannot accomplish what he wills, then he is subject to a very great passion, because then we would be saying that his will was subject to the constraint of his nature. God forbid that this should be! That is the view of those people who have received just a small whiff of education and place God under the constraint of necessity. But truly, O Theopompus, we must never think that any powerful constraint of necessity ever hampers God from doing what he wills, because we must say that God is above everything whatsoever and is not subject to anything. Do you not know, dear friend, that God alone is free, superior to all things and having authority over all things, and is in no respect subject to the constraint of necessity? Therefore it is an effrontery to deprive God of authoritative freedom of action."

3. In answer to these things Theopompus replied, "Let us accept what you said, that God is free, for we do not dare deprive God of freedom. But your response does not solve my question, O skilled teacher Gregory. For I asked you whether God was impassible. Now in your response you acknowledged that God is impassible. Then I came back to you with the question whether he is not prevented by his impassible nature from bearing human passions, since his nature is perfect and incorruptible. If God is not of his own accord prevented from undergoing passion, because he always is what he is, given the impassibility of his nature, then I would like to reach a clear explanation of the matter from your love of God and to learn accurately from your charity. For I am unsure in my thinking whether the impassible God can undergo anything unbecoming to him—since as we said he is impassible. It has also occurred to me that, as some people thoughtfully point out, if God's nature stands in the way of his will, the whole question would be pointless. But if God's impassibility is not capable of human passions, why should I not

answer you forthrightly, saying that the nature of God is opposed to his will—just as I said before, as the impassible nature of God is more powerful than his will, even though he is God."

4. Then, since many of those who were present were waiting to see what I would respond to this question, I straightaway answered him then and there: "My dear Theopompus, a human being, whose nature consists of body and soul, cannot do everything that comes into his head, as we can easily see and understand—since the fashioning of his nature and the constitution of his body are bound by the ordinance of his Creator. On account of this constraint of necessity which is stronger than we are, the human will's impetus towards action is far from being able to carry out unhindered all that it proposes, because each of the two[2] favors its own interests. Hence a human being is in all things inferior to its Maker. For whatever is subject to generation and corruption is prevented from being omnipotent. Now it is fitting for us to consider the divine nature, which is ineffable and inexpressible, unlike any other thing whatsoever, subjected to no law, no necessity, no habit, no intractableness, no fear, no development and no sickness. By a power which overcomes everything and is overcome by nothing, it is able to do anything. But never, O Theopompus, may we think of God as coming in conflict with his own will because he submitted himself to passion even though God is by nature impassible. For we do not sever the will of the divinity from that most excellent essence which always is as it is, continuing essentially one and the same, in one form, one act of being, one immutable will; which takes its orders from itself, and governs itself. It itself can do all things, from itself and in itself and through itself, so that nowhere is its will hindered by its impassible nature, which remains always what it is, from doing what it wills. For I have said that God is one, and it is precisely this same God who is not prevented by any constraint from doing what he wills, since its own essence does not consist of different, mutually opposed, substances. We affirm that the nature and substance of human beings consists of dissimilar natures,

---

2. Body and soul, according to Ryssel; nature and will, according to Martin; Brock inclines to the latter interpretation (personal communication).

namely, soul and body. And insofar as the will of the one does not agree with the will of the other, consequently those things which people wish to do are not always accomplished, because the nature of one part, going against the other part, hinders one from doing whatever he wills. But he who alone is infinite perfection and beauty, who contains all things by his goodness, who has all things under him which either have existed or are, who is high above everything, since his understanding is incorrupt, a complete stranger to and exalted above every evil, as I said before, that one alone is simple and uncomposite, is unmingled with evils thanks to the unity of its essence, with one good will, indivisible, never provoked, perturbed, or undermined, not penetrated, conquered or harnessed. It is exalted above all passions, and agrees in itself in everything which it plans to do, because it suffers no hindrance from its nature, since it is remote from all distress, nor does anything war or fight against it, or put up resistance to it. Thus he is free and his will has authority over all things, and by his all-surpassing power he can do all things. So do not think, dear friend, that the almighty power, which is absolutely never subjected to any passion, is hindered by anything from carrying out the expression of its will."

5. But Theopompus answered and said to me, "Even I was well aware, O teacher Gregory, that God enjoys the most efficacious will, full of freedom and power over all, and that no one should dispute about the things you have said. But what I am doubtful about is this, whether the nature of divinity, the being that is without passion, is not intrinsically impeded from suffering; but rather is opposed to any willingness on its part to endure suffering, which is something alien and unbecoming to it, as has been more than adequately shown by your clear points on the matter. In fact, if anyone would resist these explanations, he would not only be found unlearned but also rash and a thorough villain, for it is fitting to ascribe to God dominion and power over all things. But because I prefer to choose good and reject evil[3] I

---

3. L. Abramowski, "Die Schrift Gregors des Lehrers 'Ad Theopompum' und Philoxenus von Mabbug." *Zeitschrift für Kirchengeschichte* 89 (1978): 286, sees an allusion to Isa 7.15–16 here.

have wanted to investigate and examine whether God ever contemplated suffering human passions, because his impassible nature is always what it is."[4]

6. I, however, answered him: "O Theopompus, do you seriously intend to depart from the opinions of Isocrates and distance yourself greatly from them, so that you may arrive at the healthy and true views which I have set forth to you with clear arguments? Listen, therefore, listen, O Theopompus, and consider clearly in your mind, as you give him credence in your heart to what I say to you: Passion would truly be passion if God proposed something of no benefit or fittingness to himself. But when the will of God is aroused to heal and remedy the evil thoughts of human beings, we cannot then call it a passion of God that this God, by his humility and extraordinary abasement, serves the human race. Since now the human heart has turned away from true worship and in the pride of living beings has honored matter more than God,[5] and from the growth of this has been without exception trapped in its lusts, so when God wanted to draw it back from them, those passions which occurred at his will for the common benefit are not considered passions for God. For his blessed and impassible nature manifested its impassibility precisely in its passion. For whatever suffers is subject to passion when destructive passion prevails over it against the will of the one who suffers. But when someone voluntarily—being by nature impassible—is involved in the passions so as to defeat them, we do not say that he has been subjected to passion, even though he shared in passions by his own will. For we can see the way even doctors, when they want to cure those who are afflicted with grave illnesses, gladly take upon themselves hardships in their ministry to the sick, for they already look forward to the joy which will be theirs from the recovery. Choosing the good news of the cure of

---

4. Ryssel, 77n., explains, "Theopompus would have it that it is impossible for the Godhead to suffer, since the substance of God, because of his impassibility—which proceeds from the omnipotence just mentioned—can still not experience any suffering; that is, on account of the very omnipotence of God espoused by Gregory, Theopompus contests the possibility of divine suffering, because this is as such excluded by his omnipotence."

5. Abramowski, 286, sees an allusion to Rom 1.23ff.

the sick removes the doctor's indignity and toil,[6] when he puts aside his authority temporarily and subordinates his will, being found in the form of a servant,[7] while he serves the sick and exchanges the honor of his profession for servitude. And this indignity we do not say is an indignity to the doctor, on account of the healing which follows from it, nor do we deny him the honor of his profession, when we see him voluntarily carrying out the duty of a servant. For when all those things have been carried out which medical art has convinced him should be done, then joyfully he resumes his earlier dignity, and the healing of the sick is more preferable to him and gives him more joy than the honor of his profession in which he was standing. For the rest, he was in no way diminished during the brief time in which he debased himself[8] and carried out the duty of service needed to heal the body. For he knew that, by means of the temporary indignity he would briefly incur, he would obtain healing for the sick, from which he would receive glory far in excess of the indignity. So how could we deny that he who alone is good[9] and who is above all vainglory, untouched by indignity, impassible in passions, most excellent of all, in his impassibility reigned over the passions, when by his Passion passion itself suffered? For the impassible one became the suffering of the passions, inflicting suffering on them by the fact that impassibility manifested itself as his impassibility in his Passion. For what the passions do to those who are passible, that same thing he, the impassible one, did to the passions by his Passion, in that by his impassibility suffering occurred to the passions. Therefore since we say that the effectiveness of the passions was overcome by his participating in them, what else can we say that he is than the cause of suffering for the passions? For if a piece of

---

6. Abramowski, 286, sees here a reminiscence of the play on "joy" and "shame" in Heb 12.2.

7. Reminiscence of Phil 2.6–7, as Abramowski points out, 286, n. 52; it is also, she thinks, the only real point of contact with Origen in this work. The text she offers for comparison is *Cels.* 4.14.

8. Abramowski, 286, finds the phrase "for a brief time" typically Johannine (cf. John 7.33, 12.35) and, in connection with Phil 2, "eine wichtige Hilfe zum Verständnis dessen, was man im uneigentlichen Sinn Gregors Christologie nennen kann, was aber besser *theologia* in ihrer irdischen Phase heißen würde."

9. Abramowski, 286, sees this as an allusion to Matt 19.17. I think it is so general a remark as not to need a source.

adamant struck with iron does not suffer by the impact, but on the contrary remains impassible as it was, to such an extent that the force of the impact returns upon the smiter, since adamant shows itself impassible by nature and does not yield to the impact of the passions, why should we not say that the impassible one became a cause of suffering for the passions? For when someone does not cringe at a blow and is not terrified by fear,[10] how could we say that the passions are not made to suffer, even though he of his own will enters into relation with them? Or how would he not be impassible who received no harm from the passions in his own Passion? Or how would he not be immortal who, passing through death, was not held fast by death?[11] When God arrived at death, that was the death of death, since he was not held by it, and likewise the impassibility of God was the cause of suffering of the passions, when he entered into the passions. For if earthly things truly show their power and impassible nature when they are mixed with things which are their contraries, how much more ought we to understand that the Passion of God was the cause of suffering of the passions! Similarly iron, by striking adamant, meets its match and is itself damaged due to the hardness of the adamant on which it strikes. Likewise God, who is strong by his will and impassible in his essence, continued in his impassibility when he took upon himself the passions, even while he was tested by iron and fire, for the nature of Godhead is stronger than anything, even when it is in passions. For it was the true argument for God's impassibility and immortality when, in the midst of the things which cause suffering, he himself appeared to be the cause of the sufferings, since the testing teaches us what really was being accomplished. For we would not have known the impassible to be impassible if he had not participated in the passions and undergone the force of the passions. For impassibility eagerly rushed upon the passions like a passion, so that by his own Passion he might show himself to be the cause of suffering of the passions. For the passions were not entirely able to stand against the weight of the power of impassibility. Nor ought we to

---

10. Compare Ignatius of Antioch, *Polyc.* 3.1: "Stand firm as an anvil when you are struck, for a great athlete can be beaten and win."

11. Abramowski, 277, sees an allusion to Acts 2.24 here.

be astonished, O learned Theopompus, that the impassibility of God thwarted the passions, since we see that the eyes, when we gaze intently and try to see in the rays of the sun, suffer passion from the rays.

7. "What we are trying to say is this: God, who is above the possibility of corruption and passion, above the possibility of death and injury, and who is, as we can say, insensible to any suffering, truly made the passions suffer, since the passions were not strong enough to withstand his impassibility. Thus he is truly impassible and surely the thwarter of death, since by his death he confirms his immortality and by his Passion demonstrates his impassibility. When the crown is bestowed on athletes and combatants competing in the contest, and when the prizes of victory are granted to those held worthy because of their triumph, it is not right to give these out before the athletes, tested in competition and struggle, have first of all merited the crown of victory.[12] It is likewise with passibility and impassibility. Impassibility is not exalted over the passions unless it first shows its power through suffering. Therefore passion does not, as many would have it, make for shame and weakness in God, for the surpassing nature of God has shown its unchangeableness by being tested by the passions. For he who was within the gates of death,[13] and who thanks to his immortality as God vanquished death by his impassibility, can surely be hailed as God, since he is subjected to no authority, held captive by no power, he does not give way to corruption, is not shaken by pain, and not held fast by death.[14]

"This is the almighty God, this is true dominion, this is sovereign authority, which when it encounters death suffers no injury from death.

8. "But those who want to find fault with this supreme wisdom and this will, hidden in its majesty from everyone; who deny the surpassing power of that God by whose death impassibility was extended to all men; who mock[15] God's arrival at death, and do

---

12. Abramowski, 286, sees allusions to 1 Cor 9.24–26 and 2 Tim 4.7–8.
13. Martin, in a note, refers here to Job 38.17.
14. Abramowski, 286–87, refers again to Acts 2.24 and 27.
15. Abramowski notes that this word in the Syriac Peshitta is used at Luke 23.35, in connection with the mocking of the crucified Jesus.

not understand that the surpassing brightness of his coming must be contemplated with the eye of their mind; and who therefore suppose that this incomprehensible and inconceivable arrival of God at death, without corruption, is a foolish story—these are stuck in darkness in their erroneous understanding, destined to death and corruption. When a king or official enters a prison in order to deliver a sentence against the evildoers who were held there, to each according to his works, and puts up with the vile stenches and violent words there at the entrance of the prison, it would not be fitting to call the king himself one of the evildoers, seeing that he went of his own volition to the imprisoned malefactors. Thus must we think of God. For on account of his impassibility he has no part in mortality, and because of his immortality he can fearlessly tread death underfoot, and because of the power of his Godhead, he is without suffering, impervious to death; and it is in name only that he participated in the visible resemblance of mortal beings. When therefore we hear that God suffered by his coming to death, we should realize that he did not take on any of the sufferings of death, but met death immortally and impassibly, by the power of his authority, and came back from death as God who can do everything. For the incomprehensible coming of God to death truly manifested the powerfulness of his divinity and the impassibility of his nature together.[16] For what mortal was ever able to despise death? Or what human being could ever escape the strength of its power? But if this be impossible, as it is, then we must concede authority over death to God alone. Therefore, God enters the gates of death without knowing death.[17] But those who are condemned to death for breaking the commandment[18] will have an everlasting abode with death. So on what basis do many mock God's wise encounter with death as a humiliating imputation and a despicable shame, and dismiss those who so preach as childish and stupid?[19]

---

16. Sebastian Brock suggests reading *hwyt* for *hwy* (Paul de Lagarde, *Analecta syriaca* [Leipzig: G. B. Teubner, 1858], 53, l. 19), yielding this sense.
17. Abramowski, 287, thinks this should be "without knowing corruption," with reference to Acts 2.31 and 13.37.
18. Abramowski, 287, sees an allusion to Rom 7.10.
19. Abramowski, 287, sees an allusion to 1 Cor 1.23.

9. "On account of the impassibility of God, who through death and shame appeared the victor, don't suppose, O dear Theopompus of ours, that it was impossible for God to arrive at death and bear the marks of death without deception. For if the story of the wise people of old talks about an animal, which despite its weakness could overcome the nature of fire—for when it finds itself in an all-consuming blaze of fire and runs to and fro in its midst, it suffers no harm from the hot coals—why should we not call it superior to the all-consuming fire, because this animal is not subject to the action of the flame and, on account of the great amount of coolness it possesses, cools the fury of the flame, suffering nothing from the action of the fire which destroys everything? If then the salamander, a mortal animal subject to corruption, renders the burning quality of a flame ineffectual because of its great amount of coolness, how should we deny that God, who is superior to death and corruption, possessed impassibility when he encountered death? Likewise the animal, though subject to corruption, was able to bear the contact with the fire. If things contrary to each other, by their natural power, can hold firm and not perish when they are involved with other harmful things, why should we be astonished that the Being who is superior to matter and impassible in every circumstance, by being involved with death, showed the impassibility of his nature and was the thwarter of the passions and of death by his death? In this then consists the immutability of God's impassibility. For how can that most blessed one be harmed by coming into this wicked world[20] who, insofar as it would be helpful to souls, shared in the visible appearance of mortal human beings,[21] while nothing of the powerfulness of his divinity was left behind, but from eternity he is as he is. How could the most blessed one not remain always the same, since his own Being can suffer no harm nor his will be violated or be constrained by chastisement? How may that one, who is never diminished by anything we could think of, not be called impassible, always remaining what he is: through his own all-powerful will, he partakes of and distributes his own gifts, took on for a short time the form of

20. According to Abramowski, 287, this is Johannine language (e.g., 1 John 5.19).
21. Once again, says Abramowski, 288, alluding to Phil 2.7.

mortal human beings[22] because, by his own most wise counsel, he worked whatever he wanted and by his powerful will accomplished what he set out to do, maintaining his divine power, remaining what he was, and suffering nothing in his sufferings, because in his sufferings his impassible nature continued as it is. For if, by his will, the essence of that most blessed one is severed, he is not at all diminished, for his essence is the same, because his nature was manifesting the immutability of his divinity, while the beating, cutting, hurting and sickness were never able to harm God at all. For those things which are worsted by passions and changed by corruption we should name 'passions'; but those things which happen by the surpassing wisdom of God and the economy of the admirable craftsmanship of God we must not speak of as passions of God, since it is known that not even one thing effected passions in him, on account of the impassibility of his nature. No matter how often a sword passes through a flame of fire, it never severs it in two by its passage, even though body passes through body. If therefore the severing of bodies which are subject to corruption happens in an imperceptible way, because the substance of fire always remains the same and never sustains a severance because of its uninterrupted coherence, despite the slashing of the sword (for the subtlety of fire does not permit anything loose to persist in it, even when it is cut off by a sword, since its intensity binds it together on all sides, and despite the passage of the sword cutting it, the flame everywhere adheres to itself, never being severed at all)—so if the cutting of a tangible body, namely fire, is past explanation and demonstration, how much more is it right to say concerning the most blessed being, which is remote from corruption, surpassing passible bodies, beings, and natures, beyond all concepts, that it remains always the same, even in its sufferings, especially since its impassible nature, when it is involved with the passions, is in no way confined by them. Since it is not touched by or subordinated to the passions, it thwarts them by its impassibility, in that by undergoing the trial of the sword it then altogether manifests

---

22. Abramowski, 288, sees a combination of Phil 2 and the Johannine "for a short time."

its power when it continues unharmed by it. For the purity of the Godhead, its foreknowledge, and its incomprehensible subtlety not only remain unsevered by the insignificant bodies which set upon it to pierce it through, because he is supreme and higher than all bodies; but we also affirm that those same bodies undergo severance of the will which would seek to sever the divinity, which is not severed thanks to the subtlety of its nature and purity of its knowledge. Rather it passes through all bodies and as it were makes cuts in them, because to sever all bodies is easy for God.

10. "Since these things are so, therefore, it is right for us to conclude namely that the divinity has manifested its impassibility by means of its suffering, and, even if it involves itself in the passions, it has manifested the wisdom of its power in every way. Do not suppose, dearest Theopompus, that the power of the most blessed one is unable to penetrate these bodies which inflict sufferings. Similarly we see that the sun's rays pass right through clear glass: light from the sun passes through, and bodies are in no way hindered from subtly passing through other bodies of a dissimilar nature. And if one kind of matter does not prevent the force of another kind of matter from passing through it, on account of its subtlety, must we not concede that the substance of God, which is higher and stronger than everything, passes without hindrance through all other bodies which encounter it, thanks to its subtlety, so that not in any way does divinity suffer from the passions, since the nature of the most blessed and incorruptible one is known to remain always in the same condition. In that comparison which we drew with the rays of the sun, the light itself remains the same, in no way diminished, even if it bestows from its splendor on the needy. How much more the most blessed one, being higher than all things and God rich in mercy,[23] in bestowing his benefits on the needy, continues the same and loses nothing thereby. So the unsearchable and unexplainable descent of God to human beings ought not, as some say in their silly fables, to be called "a passion of the impossible." These surely did not stop to think that God is not at all search-

---

23. Eph 2.4.

able nor can be restricted, neither by his nature, nor by any other being, from carrying out his will. We affirm that he alone is supreme and free who is not oppressed by the law of his own nature, who does not experience coercion through contradiction to his power, who is not held fast in the grip of his riches, who is not concerned for the majesty of his divinity and is not terrified by death. But if he feared the fire, if he were frightened by the sword, trembled at the abyss and refused to risk himself with wild animals, how could we call such a one God, who thus panicked in the face of the sufferings which cause harm to human beings? But if the most blessed and incorruptible God should come to the fire, not fearing the fire because he always continues the same, and should despise the greedy flames, since the fire is not always the same—for how can we say that fire, whose activity dies down, is itself always the same?—is not that God alone impassible, despising the sword, scorning the fire, not fearing death? For he in his sufferings continues as he is, voluntarily taking human sufferings upon himself, and does not suffer the pains which arise from human passions. For God is the one who is unharmed by every suffering, and it is his property always to remain the same. But the one who suffers harm from the passions, is overthrown by pains, is hindered by the force of necessity from carrying out good things, this one is not worthy of mention, even if he be called God. The one who indeed is not subject to death, who shows his impassibility by his suffering, let him come and do what it is fitting for God the helper[24] to do, and let what belongs to me be transformed, while he continues in his immutability, and let him be everything, though being outside everything. For this will is impossible which is not hindered by the chains of the force of necessity from coming to those human beings who yearn for a divine manner of life.

"But that one who contemplates absolutely everything by the majesty of his divinity, and in his lofty blessedness chooses stillness for himself; and who takes delight only in his own blessed state, disdaining everything else because of the excellence of the rule of stillness that he has chosen: must we not say that the race

24. Abramowski, 288, sees this as representing the βοηθός of Ps 27.7 LXX.

of mortals is far superior to such a 'blessed one,'[25] especially those who, for the sake of their cities and out of love for their friends, did not spare their own lives who by their own will proved superior to sufferings and, by their extraordinary fortitude, did not think of their sufferings as sufferings? Of old, a man whose name was Theseus[26] chose death for himself, so that they might not become the slaves of the Lacedaemonians. Epaminondas also was immolated, lest the Athenians be made subjects. Lykiskos[27] allowed himself to be killed lest the Aetolians be led into captivity. Theodore cut his tongue out lest he betray his friends. Phison was crucified, lest he abuse the freedom of speech which he held; Anaxarchus was dismembered, lest by deceit he disturb Nicocreon; Diogoras was sent into exile by the Athenians; Socrates was immolated; Philoxenus was ordered to break rocks.[28] We ought not only to praise but even to wonder at Callimachus and at Cynegirus, for although his whole body was pitted with many arrows and one might describe him as a living corpse, he was a terror to his enemies and a helper and protection to his fellow citizens.[29] Chiron, not sparing himself, handed over his head to his enemies joyfully. How should we not also wonder at Ammonius[30] who, ignoring the pain of his wound, ran to his city to announce their victory over the enemies, and who when he had arrived at the city, while saying to all the assembled citizens, "Rejoice, we are victors," died on the spot. But again Eurytas, while he lay sick in bed, hearing that war at that time against the Macedonians was growing more violent for his own people, carried away with love for his own people ordered his

---

25. Irenaeus, *haer.* 3.18.6, makes a similar point.

26. Friedrich Baethgen, review of *Gregorius Thaumaturgus* by Victor Ryssel, *Göttingische gelehrte Anzeigen*, pt. 44 (1880): 1400, proposes this in place of the MS *t'yws* or Ryssel's conjecture of "Codros."

27. This also from Baethgen, 1400, instead of "Leucippus," which is the name represented in the Syriac text. He cites Polybius 32.20a.1, 3; and Livy 42.38 and 45.28.

28. Plutarch, *Moralia* Loeb 6.206–7.

29. On the heroics of Callimachus and Cynegirus at the battle of Marathon, see Herodotus 6.114.

30. Herodotus does not tell of this incident. Gregory's version most closely matches that in Plutarch, 347C, where the hero is the aptly named Eukleas (=Famous). The Syriac *'wmnys*, according to Brock, may represent "Eumenius."

servants only to bewail and bear him into the battle, where he could fall with his fellow citizens. But Aristodemus, declining war and fleeing to Sparta, is considered by everyone as low and abject.[31]

11. "So regard, dear friend, how great a contempt for death mortals have shown for the sake of their cities and friends, manifesting excellence, wisdom and bravery. Sometimes, because of their solidarity with their friends they have scorned life, not mindful of their wives,[32] and for the sake of their cities they have unhesitatingly chosen the end of their lives. These, thanks to their unfettered free will and pursuit of virtue, decided joyfully not only to let themselves be sawn apart by tyrants but did not even shrink from being nailed with nails to the wood, purchasing the freedom to express their thoughts by their death.

12. "But God, who does not need praise and is far superior to passions, came of his own volition to death, without fear or trembling disturbing him in the least. But if, since he is God, we consider as glorious the indignity that occurred to him in his Passion, are we, out of our concern for his honor, withholding his assistance from humanity?[33] But what shame could God sustain in his Passion, who in his immortality thwarted death by his death? But God did not experience the passion of embarrassment, so that he would be ashamed to suffer, since pride is always far from him. But what weakness, embarrassment or contempt could have affected God, since he entered death in order to cut off death from human beings? For he who covets vainglory and fears lest he lose it will never be willing to undergo the suffering of death. Far from God's being afraid lest glory be taken from him and he lose it entirely, he would sooner have the passion of iron or fire than the suspicion of vainglory. For if God suffered from the desire for vainglory, this would be a passion of which he could not be cured. But if God does not crave glory, since he is

---

31. Herodotus 7.229–31 tells of Aristodemus and Eurytus, who were sick at the time of the battle of Thermopylae. The latter went to fight anyway, while the former did not. For "Macedonians" we should understand "Persians," of course.

32. Eberhard Nestle, review of *Gregorius Thaumaturgus* by Victor Ryssel, *Zeitschrift der deutschen morgenländischen Gesellschaft* 35 (1881): 786, thinks that "wives" is a scribal error in Syriac for "life," but Brock thinks this would make the text very repetitive.

33. Brock prefers taking *nsb* as *nessab*, rather than *nsab*.

above all passions, then he, who is life and is superior to death, can enter death, inasmuch as he would not receive sufferings from death and would free mortals from death, because he himself is God who remains always in his impassibility, even when he is in the midst of suffering. For when someone in his impassibility both sustains passion and puts it far from himself, why should this one not hasten to come to death, so as to cut off death? For the life of those who fear that they will die in death is not life, but if Life is not subject to death, by his very death he challenges death to demonstrate that he is life. For look, we see in the case of light, when it is associated with darkness,[34] that its rays do not participate in the latter nor become dim, even though they are poured out into darkness. For the admixture of darkness with light does not dim the light, but rather the light by its radiance illumines the darkness which, as something weaker, is swallowed up by something bigger, more excellent, and stronger than it. But with the departure of the light the darkness remains in its obscurity. It is also this way with God: when he voluntarily entered into death, he was not so contemptible as to flaunt his omnipotence when it was struck by the obstinate resistance of the power of death, but he emptied himself of the dominion which he had over all things, while the nature of God remained, even in death, without corruption, and by the powerfulness of his impassibility he subordinated the passions, in the manner of light when it is associated with darkness. For passions are then deemed truly strong when they remain what they are even when they are associated with their contraries. And this mingling ought not to be supposed to be in imagination or pretense, but truly carry the confirmation of the fusion, even though they are entities opposed to one another which, by the powerfulness of their nature, can remain without corruption and without suffering, in the intermingling with other entities. For example the salamander, the animal which can despise the flame, and adamant when it is struck by iron (not in imagination and pretense, as we said) remain impassible.[35] Asbestos, too, remains whole if it takes fire

---

34. Abramowski, 282, sees here a reminiscence of 2 Cor 6.14.
35. Abramowski, 282, thinks the repeated use of "not . . . in imagination and

upon itself, suffering no harm from its association with fire. If we can observe entities involving matter suffering no change to their nature when they are associated with other entities which cause corruption, remaining quite whole and incorrupt, and losing nothing of their substance, why is it repugnant or difficult for us to speak of that incorruptible essence of God which also remains in the state of impassibility, even when it meets up with things which cause sufferings?

13. "Do not suppose, my dear Theopompus, as by some it is craftily maintained, that the most blessed and incorrupt one is he who neither acts nor grants to another to act. For one who is like that labors under weakness. For what reason declares that in the case of him who does not manifest virtue, who does not give knowledge to human beings or instruct others in wisdom, who does not understand what is good, who does not provide for the healing of souls, who is unable to promote the good, we should describe such a one as blessed and beneficent? For what kind of blessed and immutable God can it be who is unwilling to cut out the growing root of evil thoughts or, by the abundant goodness innate in him, to take deadly impulses away from souls, as if by cauterizing? Rather, the incorruptible and blessed one is he who kills the passions, who makes people wise, implants divine knowledge, and manifests virtue. But we say that in God it would be a great passion not to care for human beings, to be unwilling to see good done, and to neglect the welfare of the human race. But he who drives out the corrupting passions at the very root from which they spring in the human mind, and takes pains to produce excellent human beings out of rejected ones, how will he not be called impassible, since he drives passions out of human beings and brings death to the passions?

14. "You, therefore, O Theopompus, in your heart as in a court of law, give judgment as one who has closely followed the footprints of wisdom; regard, and with an unprejudiced mind and open understanding consider: when is it proper to understand that passion occurs in the incorrupt and most blessed one?

---

pretense" is the contribution of the Syriac translator in the circle of Philoxenus of Mabbug, who is concerned to underline a Christological point.

When he shows himself helpful, merciful, and sharing his grace? Or when he shows himself hard-hearted, harsh, and devoid of pardon or any compassion? But on the contrary, we recognize the impassible God especially as the one who is the author of good works and who makes foolish people wise.[36] For there is no law by which we must call him 'most blessed and incorrupt' who takes no care at all of the human race. For if we recognize the wise and intelligent man only through the works which he accomplishes by his skill, no one is called an expert craftsman until he has shown that he can take crude and unpromising materials and produce a work by the craft which he possesses. For a work of art, when it has taken shape, clearly indicates the silent thought of the artist. How much more clearly, therefore, ought we to understand and call the most blessed one 'most blessed,' when the blessed nature which he has and always belongs to him has come into the light, when we see the deeds which really teach us about him. But those who take the view that the most blessed one spends all his time in his mansions, turns in on himself and looks at himself, despises all things alike, prefers leisure for himself rather than the care of all things, and is complacent in himself, and who regard as passions for him his zealous efforts on behalf of the human race—I do not know what to say of them. How can we properly call a being most blessed and incorruptible who gives human nature no evidence of himself? If then these things are so, give up the idea that this is the true nature of God, since you are still utterly ignorant of God, when you say that forever and from eternity he remains in stillness in his Being. For how can he whom you cannot know be most blessed and incorruptible, or how can he be wise and generous with his gifts, who did not come into your experience? But I say this: is he the most blessed and the distributor of benefits who shows himself to be the helper of human beings and aider of those who are without hope?[37] For as we cannot in our mind understand the wickedness of evil people unless we first see their wicked deeds—for we

---

36. Abramowski, 289, sees here an allusion to 1 Cor 3.18.
37. 1 Thess 4.13 (Ryssel, Martin) added to Ps 27.7 LXX (Abramowski, 289). Brock suggests Eph 2.12.

cannot accurately perceive the full implications of deeds hidden in someone's mind unless they come into the light—so in similar fashion we call the most blessed and incorruptible being 'most blessed' when it does works appropriate to its blessedness, carefully uncovering the good works which are manifested by it. The sight of what is visible gives testimony to what is hidden. For a wise and gracious man's genuine disposition is not recognized until he joyfully presents the completion of actions which correspond to his virtue. But how can we speak to human beings of the noble disposition of the most blessed one if not a single opportunity to encounter the most blessed one has furnished us with what we should say? For the one who does not stir us by his good works or who does not draw us by repute, how can we attribute blessedness to him if the state of his blessedness and his abundant goodness in everything are altogether hidden from us?

15. "But if you have this opinion about God, this is your affair, not God's, since he is most blessed and generous in his gifts. You are quite far from recognizing them, because he has not shown you his incorruptible nature, higher than all things, since he is revelling in that luxurious ease which befits God, as you have in your view maintained: because this in your judgment properly befits God, that God is turned towards himself and wallows in himself, with the result that he does nothing and allows others to do nothing. For whoever is thus occupied is weak. Tell us, O wise one, what passion or what infirmity the most blessed and incorruptible God contracted by bringing assistance perceptible by human beings, especially to those who from ignorance are far removed from his goodness, are driven toward the abyss by the violence of the chastisement of the passions, and are not able by their own efforts to attain virtue. But, if it is right at all to speak boldly but truly, the being is not blessed and incorruptible who does not call or try to draw to himself[38] those who have as it were fallen overboard from the ship and are drowning because they do not know his goodness, especially those who, caught in the ocean of the world, cannot attain to virtue and have become

---

38. Abramowski, 289, proposes here a combined allusion to Isa 43.1 and Jer 38.2–3 LXX.

alien from God. Therefore what kind of blessed God is it, lavish with gifts, outstanding by the generosity of his goodness, who has neither benevolence nor involvement nor liberality nor any of those deeds which befit virtue and which are aids from God who is generous in his assistance?

16. "If therefore, you are seized by a vivid imagination and want to compose and depict for yourself a God who loves himself, wallowing amid his riches, enjoying his glory, and will not let himself be moved to assist anyone else, everyone being utterly rejected and outcast, far removed from the assistance of the most blessed one, how great is the cruelty when they die in droves from ignorance of virtue! Even suppose this most blessed being, lavish with its gifts, is God, let us leave him for the moment and come to wise human beings to learn from them the teaching of true philosophy, because they have summoned those who have fallen and gone astray in this natural world, calling out to them with great urgency. If the philosophers had remained silent while droves of human beings were perishing, Critias would have died for the love of power, because he kept silent; Alcibiades would have died for the sake of lavish gift-giving, despite his speech. The Persians and Medes of Susa would have had a great advantage, being unarmed, as they came to Macedonia. Why therefore are you silent, O blessed one, while all these are perishing, when the wise, that they may help them, chose not to remain quiet? This is the essence of virtue, O blessed one, this is the fruit of philosophy, namely, that those alone ought to be described as blessed and munificent whose concern is directed not only toward caring for themselves but also toward their neighbors, especially those who are subjected to passions of the soul. Even Diogenes the Cynic himself,[39] when he was one day upbraided by a young man from Attica in these words, 'Why, since you praise the Lacedaemonians and belittle the Athenians, do you not go to live

---

39. Brock notes that this is "close to Stobaeus, *Floril.* 3.13.43 (=Wachsmuth, vol. III, p. 462; Gaisford, vol. I, p. 324), who alone attributes it to Diogenes (and mentions Attic youth). Other variants in Plutarch, *Mor.* 230F (attributed to Pausanias, son of Pleistonax) and Diogenes Laertius, II.70 (attributed to Aristippus). Gregory Thaumaturgus is thus the earliest witness to the attribution to Diogenes."

in Sparta?' responded thus, 'Doctors also usually go to the sick, not to the healthy.' So human philosophy itself shows those who are yearning for excellence how to heal the illnesses of soul, and does not allow them to reject or despise even one passion of a single soul of a single human being, but instead they assiduously hasten and run to restore those who have fallen away from virtue in their way of life. Should we not say that God, who is the teacher of all philosophy and who is truly most blessed and munificent, of his own accord came here, where the hordes of passions have made their nest, to visit those who are taken captive by the passions? Would we not indeed call it a passion of the soul, if someone does nothing which befits a virtuous life? Look, even Hippocrates[40] from Cos, writing to the Abderites, said that 'the love of money is a sickness of the soul.' He also added, 'The habitation of human beings is poor because everywhere the love of money has penetrated like a winter wind, which no one can withstand,' and, 'Would that all the physicians would gather together and come and heal the torment of the madness its evil inflicts, since they have called love of money blessed when it only makes them sick and torments them. I, too, believe that all the sicknesses of the soul are rooted in the stubborn delusion which is created by the enticement and imagination of the thoughts. Only when the soul is cleansed of this by virtue can it recover.' 'Would that it were possible to cut out the bitter root of the love of money,[41] so that no trace of it remained; then you would recognize that human beings, with their bodies and sick souls, were purified and cleansed.' But since so much wickedness in the world besets the human race, the most blessed one can be called 'most blessed and munificent' first when, by means of the impassibility of his nature, he is seen in the blessed state that is from himself, which is appropriate to God, with the gratitude for the gifts which are distributed by him to everyone. For Plato himself said, 'Envy is beyond the limits of the divine being.'[42]

17. "He came therefore, O happy one, Jesus came, who is king

40. The Syriac has "Isocrates."
41. Abramowski, 289, sees an allusion to 1 Tim 6.10.
42. *Phaedrus* 247a. Brock notes that the Syriac implies a variant *horou* for *chorou*.

over all things, that he might heal the difficult passions of human beings, being the most blessed and generous one. But yet he remained what he is, and the passions were destroyed by his impassibility, as darkness is destroyed by light. He came therefore, he came in haste,[43] to make people blessed and rich in good things, immortals instead of mortals, and has renewed and recreated them blessed forever. To him who is the glorious king be glory forever. Amen."

43. Abramowski would see this as reflecting the *speuson* in the Cod. Alex. of Ps 39.14 LXX, and Cod. Sin. of Ps 69.2 LXX: "Make haste to help me!"

TO PHILAGRIUS [EVAGRIUS],[1]
ON CONSUBSTANTIALITY

AM FULL OF WONDER [1101A[2]] and exceedingly amazed at the forthright way in which you raise such problems and such great inquiries by your precise questions, making it so that we are forced to speak and to undertake the hard work of demonstration, because you bring us questions which are both unavoidable and useful. Clearly there is every need, after your inquiries, for us to make clear responses. And right at this moment, the question you have proposed went like this and concerned this matter: in what way might the Father and Son and Holy Spirit have a nature (which one might properly call substance[3] rather than nature)—would it be simple, or compound? For if simple, how does it allow of the number "three" of those just named? For what is simple is single in form and without number. [1101B] But what is in the category of numbers must be divisible, even if it is not numerable;[4] but what is divided is liable to passion, for division is a passion. So if the nature of the Most Great[5] is simple, the attribution of names is superfluous; but if the attribution of names is true, and one must rely on the names, suddenly the "single in form" and "simple" goes by the boards. So what kind of nature belongs to it?

(2)[6] That is what you asked us. The doctrine of the truth will

---

1. On the original name of the addressee, see the Introduction (47)-(52).
2. These are references to PG 46, where our text is printed among the letters of Gregory of Nyssa.
3. For a thorough (though perhaps not conclusive) discussion of this term in the Fathers, see Christopher Stead, *Divine Substance* (Oxford: Oxford University Press, 1977).
4. The point seems to be that what is in the category of number may not in fact be numbered, e.g., singularity.
5. τοῦ κρείττονος, as God is often termed in the other works attributed to Gregory.
6. This paragraph is not translated by Michel van Esbroeck, "Sur quatre traités

furnish the demonstrations of these things with exactitude, not by irrationally proposing the fantasy of an unprovable faith, from the difficulty of providing a proof; nor by trying to hide the unsoundness of its conviction with the testimonies of ancient myths; but, with discernment based on exact investigation and straight thinking, by setting forth the confirmation of the proposition until it is clear.

(3) [1101C] So come, let the doctrine commence our initiation here, and let it say how the divine ought to be conceived, whether simple, or threefold. For thus the triplicity of the names forces us to speak and likewise to believe. Some, contented with these things, have contrived unsound and totally outdated teachings, [1104A] thinking that the substance undergoes a passion of division corresponding to the application of the names. Granted, as you say, that they uphold the teaching of their hypothesis without a sound basis; but let us turn our own mind to the right conception of what is known. First we shall put forward what God is, and then in this way we shall come with exactitude to the demonstrations.

(4) It is an entirely simple and undivided substance, since it is what is simple and bodiless by nature. But perhaps the doctrine of the difference of names tells against me, abolishing the singleness of form of the Most Great by the number "three." So on account of the singleness of form must we abandon the confession of Father, Son, and [1104B] Holy Spirit? Heaven forbid! For the attribution of names will not damage the undivided unity of the Greatest. Objects of intelligence,[7] though they bear countless names (since they are called by lots of different names in different nations), are yet beyond all designation, since nothing is a proper name[8] of intelligibles and incorporeals. For how might

---

attribuées à Grégoire, et leur contexte marcellien (CPG 3222, 1781 et 1787)," in *Studien zu Gregor von Nyssa und der christlichen Spätantike*, ed. Hubertus R. Drobner and Christopher Klock (Leiden: E. J. Brill, 1990), 3–15; van Esbroeck's French translation based on his own collation of twelve MSS begins on page 8. He does not have a note to the considerable difference in text at this point.

7. Τὰ νοητά: in contrast to sense-objects.

8. This distinction between what we call something and its *proper* name comes into play in Justin, 2 *Apol* 4(5).6–5(6).4, where the point is made that the one

these things be designated properly, which are neither subject to our vision, nor capable of being caught by human senses at all? But let our soul be taken as the humblest member of the intelligibles, for the exact understanding of the All.

(5) [1104C] For soul is designated by a feminine name, but has nothing to do with female nature, since it is neither male nor female in essence. And likewise word, brought forth by it, has a masculine name but it too, as we say, is totally distinct from masculo-feminine bodiliness. But if the least of the intelligibles, soul and word, do not have a proper name, how shall we say that the first intelligibles, beyond all the intelligibles, are called by proper names? But the nomenclature is useful, necessary for leading us to an understanding of the intelligibles. But some, obtusely thinking that the substance is divided right along with the epithets, think entirely [1105A] unworthy things of the divine with their notions.

(6) But as a consequence we know, as people who have the truth, that the divine and indivisible substance of God is undivided and single in form; but for the usefulness of our souls' salvation it seems both to be divided in designations and to submit to the force of division, as we said. For just as the soul, which is a kind of intelligible, gives birth to a multitude of infinite thoughts but is not thereby divided by the passion of thought, nor does the soul get a multitude of thoughts poorer by having had them, but becomes richer rather than poorer; and just as the uttered word is [1105B] likewise common to us all, since it is undivided on the one hand from the soul which has declared it, yet nothing less is hereby furnished to the souls of the hearers (since it is gained by the latter without being separated from the former, working unification rather than division between their souls and ours); thus it is I think that the Son is never divided from the Father, nor the Holy Spirit again from the latter, similarly to the idea in the mind.

(7) For as no division or cleft is conceived of between mind and

---

who gives a name must be senior to what is named; thus even "God" is not God's real name, but an opinion which naturally arises in the human heart.

idea and soul, so neither is cleft or division conceived of between the Holy Spirit and the Savior and the Father; [1105C] since, as we said before, the nature of intelligibles is indivisible, so is that of divine things. Or again, just as the relation between sun and ray is not such that division is found, because it is impassible and bodiless, simple and undivided; but the ray is joined to the sun while on its side the sun, like a kind of eye,[9] pours out a river of rays onto the universe, making as it were floods of light for us, and making an ocean for the cosmos generally; in just such a way a kind of "rays" of the Father have been sent upon us, the resplendent Jesus and the Holy Spirit. For as the rays of light are naturally related to each other without division, neither separated from the light nor cut off from each other, and transmit the grace of the light even unto us [1105D]—in the same manner too, our Savior and the Holy Spirit, the twofold ray of the Father, ministers even unto us the light of the truth and also is united to the Father.

(8) But also just as from a certain spring of waters which ungrudgingly wells forth water like nectar, it happens that an abundant stream and unchanneled flood is carved into rivers which may be two as regards their stream, but have a single flow from [1108A] the beginning, from one eye of the well. Though it is double in its flowing due to the forms of the channeled rivers, yet there is no damage to its substance from the division, for while the stream is divided by the arrangement of the rivers, yet it possesses one and the same quality of the fluid: even if each of the aforesaid rivers should seem to be defined for a long way, and to be very remote from the spring, at least it has its beginning united to its origin[10] for the continuity of the spring. In very much the same way also, therefore, the God of all good things, the Lord of the truth and the Father of the Savior, the first cause of life and the tree of immortality, the spring of life unending, though he sent us as intelligible grace a certain double flow of the Son and the Holy Spirit, did not himself suffer anything as if

---

9. In some ancient theories of vision, the eye reached out to objects of vision with a stream of light.
10. Literally, "mother."

damaged in substance, for he did not undergo diminution [1108B] owing to their coming to us. And they both extend all the way to us and have remained no less undivided from the Father. For as we said from the start, the nature of the Greatest Ones is indivisible.

(9) It would have been possible to find much, O most reverend sir, even more than what has been said, in rigorous demonstration of the complete necessity of the union of Father, Son, and Holy Spirit, as one must needs accept it. But since it is easy for you and your companions to figure out much from little, for this reason I have thought it right to bring the discussion concerning this question to a close here.

APPENDIX
OTHER WORKS ASSOCIATED WITH ST. GREGORY THAUMATURGUS

TO TATIAN, ON THE SOUL

YOU HAVE DIRECTED ME, [1137A] O worthy Tatian, to send you the discourse on the soul, set forth with effective proofs, and you have asked me to do this without using the testimonies of Scripture, although that is, for those who wish to think piously, true teaching which is more convincing than any human reasoning. For you say that you do not seek this for your own benefit, already having been taught to depend upon the holy Scriptures and traditions and not to confuse your mind with the twists and turns of human arguments. [You seek it] to refute the opinion of the heterodox, who are unwilling to believe the Scriptures, and use their expertise to try to upset [1137B] those who are unused to such arguments. Therefore I readily accede to your request, not pretending to be inexperienced in constructing such discourses, but glad that you have such a high opinion of me. You know enough to publish those things which you deem well said, but to keep confidential and refrain from repeating those things which fall short of what they ought to be. Either way, you show your favor and friendship towards me. Knowing that, I have with every confidence set eagerly to the work of exposition. I shall use a certain order and sequence as I present the argument, of the sort that experts use with people who wish to study something scientifically.

(2) First of all, I shall lay out the criterion [1140A] by which it is the soul's nature to be comprehended, then the grounds on which it is shown to exist; then whether it is substantial or is an accident. Following on these, whether it is a body or incorporeal, then whether it is simple or composite, then in turn whether it is mortal or immortal, and finally, whether it is endowed with reason or not.

(3) These are the matters which usually come up in the doctrine on the soul, since they are the most important and can de-

fine it by its properties. As proofs to establish the soundness of my conclusions I shall appeal to the common notions on which it is natural to rely as evidence for the facts in question. For the sake of brevity and ease of use, I shall use only the arguments which relate to the necessity of the issue, in this case [1140B] syllogisms, so that when the ideas are clear and easily admitted they may produce in us a kind of readiness to stand up to our opponents. So we shall begin our discourse at that point.

By what criterion the soul can be comprehended.

1. All existing things are either recognized by the power of sense or comprehended by the power of mind. What falls in the range of the power of sense properly appeals to sense for proof, for, as soon as we encounter it, it generates in us the phantasm of the object. What is grasped by the power of mind, on the other hand, is recognized not from itself but from its operations. So since the soul is unknown from itself, it will properly be known from all that it has done. [1140C]

Whether the soul exists.

2. Since our body is moved, it is moved either from without or from within. That it is not moved from without is manifest from the fact that it is not being moved by pushing or by pulling, like things which lack soul. And again, though it is moved from within, it is not moved by nature, like fire. For the latter never stops moving as long as the fire is alight, while when a body has become dead it ceases to move, though it is still a body. So if it is not moved from without, like things which lack soul, and not by nature like fire, it clearly is moved by the soul which gives it life as well. So if the soul is shown to be what gives life to our body, [1140D] it will patently follow that the soul is known by its operations.

Whether the soul is a substance.

3. That the soul is a substance is shown in this way: first note that the definition of substance can fittingly be applied to it [i.e.,

the soul]. Here it is: "substance" is being identical with itself and one in number, which can support contraries alternately. But it is obvious that the soul itself, while it does not change its own nature, supports contraries alternately, for righteousness and wickedness, fortitude and cowardice, self-control and wantonness can all be found in it, though they are contrary to each other. So if the property of substance is to be able to support contraries alternately, it is shown that, since the soul also fits under this definition, [1141A] then the soul is a substance. Then also, since the body is a substance, the soul must also be a substance, for it could not be that what receives life is a substance but what gives life is not. Otherwise what does not exist could also be said to be the cause of what does; or again, one would have to be mad enough to say that that which has its origin in something and cannot exist without it causes the being of that in which it exists.

Whether the soul is incorporeal.

4. That the soul is in our body was shown above; now we need to ask *how* it is in the body. On the one hand, if it lies alongside the body like a pebble next to another pebble, the soul will itself be a body, but the body will not be entirely [1141B] ensouled, for it will touch only on one side. But if they were mixed together or thoroughly blended, the soul would be multifarious and not simple, inconsistent with the proper definition of the soul. For what is multifarious can be both divided and taken apart, and what can come apart is composite. What is composite, however, is three-dimensional. When body is added to body, it increases in mass, but when the soul is in the body, it does not increase its mass, but rather makes it live. So the soul will not be a body, but incorporeal.

(2) Another argument: if the soul is a body, it is moved from without or from within. But it is not moved from without, for it is neither pushed nor pulled, like soulless things. Neither is it moved from within, like ensouled things, for it would be ridiculous to speak of "a soul's soul." Therefore it will not be a body; so it is incorporeal. [1141C]

(3) Another: if the soul is a body, it has sensory qualities, and

is nourished. But it is not nourished. And if it is nourished, it is nourished not in a corporeal way like the body, but incorporeally, for it grows in reason. Nor does it have sensory qualities, for justice is not seen, nor fortitude, nor any of such things—yet these are the qualities of the soul. Therefore it is not a body; so it is incorporeal.

(4) Another: since all corporeal substance is divisible into ensouled and soulless, let those who say that the soul is a body declare whether the soul must be said to be soulless [1141D] or ensouled.

(5) Another: if every body has color and quantity and shape, but none of these is to be seen in the soul, then the soul is not a body.[1]

Whether the soul is simple or composite.

5. Now it is shown whether the soul is simple, which would be strong proof of its incorporeality. For if it is not a body, and every composite is a body, but what is compounded is compounded of parts, then it would be multifarious. But since it is incorporeal, it is simple; whence it is uncomposite and without parts.

Whether our soul is immortal.

6. I think that being immortal must follow upon being simple. [1144A] Here is why: nothing that exists is perishable of itself, since it would not then have come into being in the first place. The things that perish are destroyed by their contraries. Therefore everything which is perishable comes apart, and what can come apart is composite; what is composite is multifarious; but it is clear that what is compounded of parts is compounded of different parts. What is different is not the same. Therefore the soul, since it is simple and not compounded of different parts, and is uncomposite and cannot come apart, for that very reason is imperishable and immortal.

---

1. These last three arguments are not found in the version of the treatise which is preserved in PG 91.357 under the name of Maximus.

(2) Another argument: everything which is moved by something else, since it does not have living power from itself but from what moves it, lasts as long as it is under the sway of the power acting [1144B] within it. But when the active power ceases, that which takes its movement from it also ceases. But since the soul is self-moved, it never ceases to be. A consequence of being self-moved is eternal movement; what always moves, never rests; what never rests, never comes to an end; what never comes to an end, never perishes; what does not perish is immortal. So if the soul is self-moved, as has been proved above, it will be imperishable and immortal, according to the foregoing syllogism.

(3) Another: everything which does not perish from its own badness is imperishable. Evil is opposite to good, which is why it causes it to perish. For nothing else is [1144C] bad for the body but suffering, disease, and death; just as its goods are beauty, life, health and vigor. Now if the soul does not perish from its own badness—what is bad for the soul being cowardice, wantonness, envy and the like, but all these things do not deprive it of life and movement—then it must be immortal.

Whether the soul is reasonable.

7. There are many ways to show that our soul is reasonable. First, from the fact that it has discovered the arts which are helpful to life; for one would not say that the arts just came into being, as it were by chance, nor will he show them to be useless or unprofitable for life. [1144D] Now if the arts contribute to what is helpful to life, and the helpful is worthy of praise, and what is worthy of praise is devised by reason, and these are the discovery of soul—then our soul must be reasonable.

(2) Another argument: our soul is shown to be reasonable from the fact that our senses are not capable of comprehending facts. For we cannot arrive at the knowledge of existing things by sensory contact, if we want not to be misled[2] concerning them. When things are the same size and color but are different in kind, our sense power is too weak to distinguish between them,

---

2. Reading ἀπατᾶσθαι with the version printed in PG 91.360C1.

since it lacks reason. Now if our senses, as long as they are without reason, impart to us a false image of existing things, [1145A] we need to think whether we have truly comprehended things or not; and if they are comprehended, it is a different power, one superior to the senses, which attains to these things. But if they are not comprehended, we will not be able to tell what we see[3] from what is. But it is clear that things are comprehended, from the fact that we use each of them appropriately for our benefit, and again fashion them into what we want. Therefore if it has been shown that we comprehend existing things, but the senses, since they lack reason, reach misleading conclusions, we will have a mind which distinguishes all things by reason, and recognizes existing things for what they are. But mind is the reasonable part of soul; therefore the soul is reasonable.

(3) [1145B] Another: we never do anything without envisaging it beforehand, and this is nothing other than the soul's proper quality; for the knowledge of existing things does not come to it from without, but it itself paints reality as it were with its own notions. Therefore, when it has sketched the action ahead of time in itself, it then moves thus to action. The soul's proper quality, however, is none other than to do everything by reason, for in this it differs from the senses. So it has been shown that the soul is reasonable.

---

3. Taking θεωρούμενα here in its general sense, not in the sense of noetic contemplation, since that involves comprehension.

GLOSSARY ON EZEKIEL

WE UNDERSTAND that "the human being" [1.10¹] is the rational; "the lion," the irascible; "the young cow," the passionately desiring; "the eagle," the conscience over the others,² which Paul calls "spirit of the human being."³ The one seated is the Father; the wind [1.4], the Holy Spirit; the cloud, the Son.⁴ "Out of the north" means from the introductory, leading to the greater things; "brightness," on account of being illuminated;⁵ "fire," because of the instruction; the "flashing with fire," since from the gaps come the chastisements. The purified part of the soul is called "electrum," which must mean that "the likeness of the human being" [1.5] is presupposed. But every rational nature is "winged" [1.6–7] with spiritual wings.⁶ But they are bound closely together with each other by what is common and through likemindedness. The "human hand underneath" [1.8] is so-called

---

1. LXX reference.
2. The first few lines of the *Glossary* match a passage from the very end of Origen's first Homily on Ezekiel, where Jerome translates, "Quae est tripartitio animae? Per hominem rationale ejus indicatur, per leonem iracundia, per vitulum concupiscentia . . . ut per aquilam spiritum praesidentem animae significet. Spiritum autem hominis dico quae in eo est" (PG 13.681B). To this passage of Jerome's translation there exists a corresponding passage in Greek from a catena, and it is not unreasonable to suppose that it represents the Greek of the homily.
3. 1 Cor 2.11. Origen speaks of this "spirit of the human being" in his *Comm. in Mt.* 13.2 (PG 13.1093B), where he distinguishes it from the Spirit of God, and likewise in his comment on Ps 30.6 (PG 12.1300B), where he points out that Scripture uses "pneuma" in three senses, for mind (διάνοια), soul, and the συνειδός which is joined to the soul.
4. The only parallel I have found to this trinitarian interpretation is in Jerome, *Comm. in Ezek.* 1.1 (PL 25.20AB), where he cites the view of some unspecified commentators: "Qui autem in contrariam partem sentiunt, hoc est, bonam, spiritum auferentem, sive extollentem, Spiritum sanctum intelligunt, qui auferat ab hominibus vitia atque peccata, sive jacentes attolat ad sublimia, faciatque recedere ab Aquilone vento frigidissimo . . . Nubem quoque magnam ad personam Christi referunt."
5. Possibly a reference to baptism?
6. The winged soul: Plato, *Phaedrus* 246C.

on account of good order, but the "firmament" [1.22] on account of what is solid; the "rainbow" [1.4 Hebrew and 30.24], on account of the peace and covenant [given] us by God.[7] "Sapphire" [1.26] means the ineffable things; "crystal" [1.22], the clean and undeceitful.[8] Their feet are "straight" [1.7] on account of what is fixed and stable. "Fire in the midst" was "concentrated" [1.13], not loose and running away. But "brightness" [1.4, 13] is so-called on account of the end of the refreshment.[9] But the footprint of the feet Symmachus says belongs to a calf because it tills the ground, but Aquila says it is round[10] on account of the beauty of their shapes. But the form of the wheels, as Symmachus says, is hyacinth.[11] But it is bent back, like the likeness of the Bezek,[12] as if hard-toothed, not having the whole of the light, but like the form of the Bezek, that is, of the lightning-flash. If on the one hand he should complete the form of the human being, he rules other men; but if not, he undergoes the contrary. The lion has something, haughtiness, energy, so that we might enjoy him well. The young cow, so that we might suitably desire strongly. Isaiah says, "You[13] will hallow him in a burning fire."[14] "From the loins, and upwards, electrum" [1.27] is said, for what are above do not need chastisement. "From the loins down, fire" [1.27] signifies the deeds of generation, but these need chastisement. The Spirit first exalts what is clean; then those who have not been cleansed from this, the fire cleanses.[15] "Brightness" [is] a good end. For such are the chastisements. A Demiurge has one rule:[16] to make the under-

---

7. Textual comment on the rainbow in Origen's Hexapla (PG 16.2399). Jerome, *Comm. in Ezek.* 1.1 (PL 25.31C), connects the Ezekiel passage with the end of the Flood.
8. The cleanness of crystal is mentioned by Jerome, *Comm. in Ezek.* 1.1 (PL 25.29B).
9. This term was often used for spiritual perfection or eternal bliss.
10. 1.7, Aquila.
11. 1.16, Symmachus.
12. On this *hapax legomenon* in the Hebrew, which has been transliterated into the Greek, see Josua Blau, "Zum Hebräisch der Übersetzer des AT," *Vetus Testamentum* 6 (1956): 97–99. According to Origen's Hexapla (PG 16.2406), Theodotion transliterated the word in his version.
13. *Sic*; LXX has the third person here.
14. Isa 10.17.   15. Cf. 1 Cor 3.15.
16. ὅρος.

lying matter as he wishes and as is allowed to his skill. As God is good and wise, so also is a demiurge, but not like us, since he is simple and uncomposite, while we, existing as composite beings, are not thus. "Wisdom was justified by her children,"[17] calling the wise her children. And again the Savior himself spoke to them in the verse, "The sons of this age are wiser than the sons of light, in their generation,"[18] calling "sons of light" those enlightened by gnosis.[19] And "we are by nature children of wrath"[20] says not what is according to nature, but that those who sin become truly responsible for wrath. And concerning Judas it was written that he was "son of perdition,"[21] but it calls him son of perdition because he did the works of perdition. Isaiah went about three years naked and unshod.[22] Moses, they say, after he heard the oracles of God, never touched a woman again, nor begot a child.[23] "The abomination of desolation which stood in the holy place,"[24] they say, because the temple which is in Jerusalem will be built later on, when the Antichrist will have been believed by the Jews to be the Christ, and will have been enthroned, and will appear to be the king of the whole world. It will come at the desolation of the world, for he is the abomination of desolation. The three children who were in Babylon and in the furnace are said to be children of Hezekiah,[25] and Ezekiel to have been earlier the servant of Jeremiah.[26]

17. Luke 7.35.
18. Luke 16.8.
19. The reader should remember that "gnosis" had a perfectly good positive meaning, especially with writers like Clement of Alexandria.
20. Eph 2.3.
21. John 17.12.
22. The *Martyrdom of Isaiah* 2.10–11 speaks of a two-year period in which Isaiah and others went to the mountains, lived on herbs, and wore sackcloth; see *The Old Testament Pseudepigrapha*, ed. James H. Charlesworth (Garden City: Doubleday, 1985), 2.158.
23. This is a widely known legend. See Louis Ginzberg, *The Legends of the Jews* (Philadelphia: Jewish Publication Society of America, various dates), 2:316, 4:419, n. 122, and the literature there cited, including Philo, *Life of Moses* 2.3.2.
24. Matt 24.15.
25. See Ginzberg, *Legends* 6:368, and two patristic passages commenting on Isa 39.7: Origen, *Comm. in Mt.* 15.5 (PG 13.1264C–65A) and Jerome, *Comm. in Is.* 39.7 (PL 24.399B).
26. S. Fisch, *Ezekiel* (London: Soncino Press, 1950), x, says, "... according to Targum Yerushalmi quoted by Kimchi on i.3, Buzi his father was identical with Jeremiah."

LETTER OF ORIGEN TO GREGORY

"How and to whom the investigations of philosophy are helpful for the interpretation of the sacred Scriptures, with scriptural testimony."

GREETINGS IN GOD, my most devoted and venerable son Gregory, from Origen.

(2) As you know, the pursuit of understanding, since it calls for asceticism, can involve exertion, which leads as much as possible (if I may put it that way) toward the goal of that for which a person wishes to train. Thus your pursuit can have made you an expert Roman lawyer and a Greek philosopher of those schools which are deemed significant. But I would wish you to employ the full power of your pursuit ultimately for Christianity; therefore as a means I would beseech you to extract from the philosophy of the Greeks all those general lessons and instructions which can serve Christianity, and whatever from geometry and astronomy will be useful for interpreting the holy Scriptures. Thus, what the children of the philosophers say about geometry and music, grammar, rhetoric, and astronomy, as handmaids to philosophy, we also may say concerning philosophy itself in relation to Christianity.

2. And precisely this point is hinted at by the passage in Exodus written from the person of God, when the children of Israel are told to ask their neighbors and acquaintances for gold and silver vessels and for clothing, so that having despoiled the Egyptians they might find material to fashion from what they acquired for the worship of God.[1] For from the goods of which they despoiled the Egyptians, the children of Israel fashioned the contents of the Holy of Holies, the Ark with the covering, and the Cherubim, and the mercy-seat and the golden jar in which

---

1. Exod 11.2.

was put the manna, the bread of angels. These were probably made from the finest gold of the Egyptians; from the next best to that were made the lampstand of solid gold by the inner veil, and the lamps on it, and the golden table on which the shewbread rested, and between the two the golden incense-pot. If there were gold of third and fourth quality, from it was made the sacred vessels. And other things were made of the silver of Egypt, for when they dwelt in Egypt the children of Israel gained this from their stay there, to make good use of such precious material for the worship of God. From the clothing of the Egyptians would have come what needed the work of embroiderers, as Scripture calls them, since the embroiderers stitch together one kind of fabric to another with the wisdom of God, so that there might be the veils and the hangings without and within.

3. And what should I fashion with this untimely digression, on how the things they got from the Egyptians were so useful to the children of Israel, on what the Egyptians were unable to make proper use of, but the Hebrews through the wisdom of God could employ for pious purposes? Holy Scripture knew that some would take the descent into Egypt from their own land by the children of Israel badly; indicating in mysterious fashion that dwelling among the Egyptians, that is, the lessons of the world, would be bad for some, after they had been brought up on the law of God and the Israelite service to him. Hadad the Edomite did not fashion idols,[2] as long as he stayed in the land of Israel, since he did not eat the food of the Egyptians; but when he left Solomon the wise and went down to Egypt, he left the wisdom of God and became a member of Pharaoh's family, marrying his sister-in-law and having a child who was raised among the children of Pharaoh. Therefore, even if he went back up to the land of Israel he went back to divide the people of God, and to make them say to the golden calf, "These are your gods, O Israel, who brought you out of the land of Egypt." So I, having learned by experience, would say to you that it is a rare person who takes what is useful from Egypt and when he has left there makes things for the worship of God; Hadad the Edomite has many brethren.

2. 1 Kings 11.14–22.

They are the people who after "living Greek" produce heretical ideas, and as it were fashion golden calves in Bethel, which means "house of God."[3] It also seems to me that in this way the Logos is mysteriously indicating that they have installed their own fabrications for the holy Scriptures in which the Word of God lives and which are figuratively "Bethel." The Logos says that the other statue was installed at Dan, and the boundaries of Dan are the outermost, close to the boundaries of the Gentiles, as is clear from what was written in the book of Joshua.[4] So too some of the fabrications constructed by those I have termed "brothers of Hadad" are close to the boundaries of the Gentiles.

4. You therefore, my true son, devote yourself first and foremost to reading the holy Scriptures; but devote yourself. For when we read holy things we need much attentiveness, lest we say or think something hasty about them. And when you are devoting yourself to reading the sacred texts with faith and an attitude pleasing to God, knock on its closed doors, and it will be opened to you[5] by the gatekeeper of whom Jesus spoke: "The gatekeeper opens to him."[6] And when you devote yourself to the divine reading, uprightly and with a faith fixed firmly on God seek the meaning of the divine words which is hidden from most people. Do not stop at knocking and seeking, for the most necessary element is praying to understand the divine words. Calling us to this, the Savior not only said, "Knock and it will be opened to you," and, "Seek and you shall find," but also, "Ask, and it will be given to you."[7] These have been ventured from my paternal love toward you. Whether what I have dared seems good or not, God knows and his Christ and the One who shares the spirit of God and the spirit of Christ. Would that you may share it, and always increase your participation, so that you may say not only, "We have become sharers of Christ,"[8] but also, "We have become sharers of God."

---

3. Gen 28.17–19.
4. Josh 19.40–48 talks of the land allotted to Dan, but does not mention its remoteness; that is reflected in the frequent biblical phrase for the whole land of Israel, "from Dan to Beersheba," Judg 20.1, etc.
5. Matt 7.7. 6. John 10.3.
7. Matt 7.7. 8. Heb 3.14.

INDICES

GENERAL INDEX

Abraham, 46
Abramowski, L., 8, 15, 27, 54-55, 60, 155-73 *passim*
Alcinous, 109
Alexander (of Comana), 70-72
Angel, good spirit, 97-98, 100, 102, 125, 126, 144
Athanasius, 110
Athenagoras, 96
Athenodorus, 1, 14, 17, 18, 19, 92

Baethgen, F., 29, 165
Baptism, 47
Bardy, G., 3
Basil of Caesarea, 4, 10, 19, 26, 30, 37, 148, 151
Bernardi, J., 14
Berytus (Beirut), 2, 101, 102
Bienert, W., 9, 36
Bigg, C., 19
Blau, J., 188
Böhlig, A., 20
Bosnia, 13
Brakmann, H., 6, 83
Brock, S., 28, 160, 166, 169, 171

Caesarea in Cappadocia, 14, 18-19
Caesarea in Palestine, 2, 5, 10, 16, 17, 19, 20, 50
Caspari, C. P., 31
Chadwick, H. 12, 114, 116
Clement of Alexandria, 114
Comana, 69
Creel, R., 27
Crouzel, H., 2-6, 8, 12, 16-17, 20-21, 23, 27-28, 31, 36, 101, 105, 108-9, 115, 120, 125
Cyprian of Carthage, 78

Decius, persecution of, 2, 4, 76, 78
Demons, evil spirits, 48, 56-59, 61, 75, 80-82, 85-86, 132, 140
Devos, P., 74
Dillon, J., 110, 115
Dionysius of Alexandria, 6, 9, 23, 78
Dräseke, J., 2, 25-26, 29, 33, 36, 150
Ducaeus (Fronton du Duc), 7-8

Elijah, 68
Elisha, 68
Esbroeck, M. van, 1, 6, 31, 174
Eusebius of Caesarea, 1, 14, 16-18, 105
Evagrius Ponticus, 30, 32

Firmilian of Caesarea, 4, 14, 18-19, 50
Fisch, S., 189
Fouskas, K., 1-5, 16, 26, 36
Frend, W., 76
Frohnhofen, H. 27

Gallandius (Andreas Galland), 8
Gallay, P., 29
Gebhardt, E., 32
Ginzberg, L., 189
Gnostics, 20-21
God, 54, 57, 80-81, 83, 93, 96, 103, 109, 116, 120, 122, 126, 131-32, 134-36, 138-39, 144, 146, 152, 192; as creator, 43, 58-59, 67, 127; transcendence, 47, 58, 153-55, 162, 175-76; Father, 97
Goths, invasion by, 2, 12-13, 26-27, 149
Gregory Nazianzen, 6, 14, 22, 29-30, 32, 34, 37
Gregory of Nyssa, 1, 3-4, 8, 10, 12, 29, 30, 32, 35, 43, 55; his *Life of Gregory the Wonderworker*, 13-16, 28, 41-87

GENERAL INDEX

Gregory Thaumaturgus: Bible, use of, 9–10, 12–13, 21; "Creed," 5, 8, 10, 15, 54; death and burial, 3, 84; *Lives*, 3–4; moral ideas, 10–13; ordination, 2, 52; preference for solitude, 11, 51; "the Teacher," 28, 60, 63, 71, 75, 81–82, 153, 155; *Address of Thanksgiving*, 16–21, 91–126; *Metaphrase on Ecclesiastes*, 22–25, 127–46; *Canonical Epistle*, 25–27, 147–51; *To Theopompus*, 27–28, 152–75; *To Philagrius*, 29–32, 174–78
Gregory Thaumaturgus (?): *To Tatian*, 32–34, 181–86; *Glossary on Ezekiel*, 34–36, 187–89
Guyot, P., 2

Hallman, J., 27
Heather, P., 26, 150
Heil, G., 16, 41, 48, 54–55, 70

Ignatius of Antioch, 158
Irenaeus, 165

Jarick, J., 23, 130, 146
Jerome, 22–23, 187–88
Jesus Christ, 9, 13, 15, 21, 37, 56, 67, 76, 79, 82, 84, 86, 147, 172–78, 187, 192; incarnation, 58, 158–59, 161; *see also* Logos
Jews, 73
John the Evangelist, 53–54
Joseph (the patriarch), 49–50
Josephus, 46
Joshua, 65
Junod, E., 36–37
Justin Martyr, 33, 43, 98–99, 117, 121, 125, 175

Kennedy, G., 42
Klein, R., 2, 17, 20
Knauber, A., 2, 19–20, 106
Kobusch, T., 27
Koetschau, P., 4, 17, 84, 105, 125

Lane Fox, R., 3, 14, 64
Leanza, S., 22–23
Le Boulluec, A., 19
Lebreton, J., 33
Lechler, G., 29

Lloyd, G., 142
Logos, Word, 46, 54, 95–99, 104, 125, 192; *see also* Jesus Christ
Long, A., 114
Lucian of Samosata, 94
Lycus river, 66, 68

MacMullen, R., 14
Macrina, 4, 19
Marcellus of Ancyra, 30
Marotta, E., 92, 96, 99–100
Mary, mother of the Lord, 53–54
Mateo-Seco, L., 43
Maximus the Confessor, 32–34
Metcalfe, W., 100
Millar, F., 2
Modrzejewski, J., 92, 101
Montfaucon, B., 35
Moses, 51, 64, 80, 189
Mossay, J., 35
Mozley, J., 27
Musonius of Neocaesarea, 4, 61
Muyldermans, J., 6, 35

Nautin, P., 12, 16, 18, 21, 23, 37, 101
Nemesius of Emesa, 33, 132
Neocaesarea, 1–2, 8, 10, 15, 19, 45, 59
Nicholas of Methone, 33
Noakes, K. W., 24–25

Origen, 2, 8–9, 11, 13–14, 16–17, 19, 21, 23, 34–35, 50, 108, 113, 116, 122, 187–88; *Letter to Gregory*, 36–37, 190–92

Papadopoulos, K., 52
Pasquali, G., 29
Paul of Samosata, 3, 14, 29
Perry, T., 25
Peter (apostle), 74–75
Phaidimos of Amaseia, 2, 4, 51–52
Philo, 122
Philosophy, 11–12, 19–21, 46–47, 103, 108–20
Pitra, J.-B., 26, 28–29
Platonism, 20, 33, 107, 109–10, 112–13, 122, 172, 187
Plutarch, 112, 114, 165
Pontus, 1, 8, 14–15, 18–19, 44–45, 150

GENERAL INDEX

Procopius of Gaza, 22

Refoulé, F., 30
Rist, J., 110–11
Rondeau, M.-J., 25
Rufinus of Aquileia, 3, 22
Ryssel, 5, 28–29

Salmond, S., 130, 138
Samuel, 69
Schönfeld, M., 2
Sextus, Sentences of, 12, 116
Simonetti, M., 21–22, 30
Sinko, T., 29, 34
Slusser, M., 11, 25, 31
Solomon, 24, 63–64, 127
Soloviev, A., 13
Spirit, Holy, 9–10, 41, 52, 54, 61–62, 75, 121, 150, 174–78, 187, 192
Stead, C., 174

Stoicism, 12, 99, 106, 110–12, 125, 128–29, 132, 134
Stough, C., 128

Telfer, W., 3, 15
Theodosian Code, 8
Theophilus of Antioch, 96, 110
Trinity, 10, 15, 29–30, 54, 174–78, 187
Troadios, 81

Uthemann, K.-H., 31

Valantasis, R., 18, 104
Van Dam, R., 14–16
Veilleux, A., 139–40
Vinel, F., 23
Vossius (Gerard De Vos), 3, 6–7

Weijenborg, R., 30
Whealey, A., 33

INDEX OF HOLY SCRIPTURE
Books of the Old Testament

Genesis
1.9: 67
2.15: 122
3.13-18: 123
3.18: 107
3.23: 122
8.1: 127
18.23: 148
28.17-19: 192
39.6-23: 49
48.15: 98

Exodus
2.15: 51
11.2: 190
14.21-29: 65
17.8-13: 80
23.4: 149
24.12-15: 55

Numbers
15.39: 147

Deuteronomy
22.1-3: 149
22.25-27: 147
34.6: 3

Joshua
3.14-4.18: 65
7.1: 148
19.40-48: 192

1 Samuel
16.7: 69
18.1: 104-6

1 Kings
3.16-28: 63
4.29-33: 128
10.23-25: 129
11.14-22: 191

2 Kings
2.6,14: 68

Job
38.17: 159

Psalms
17.4: 124
27.7: 164, 169
92.12: 46
104.9: 67
121.4: 125
124.6: 80
126.6: 125
137: 124-25

Ecclesiastes
passim: 127-46
4.7-12: 12
7.12: 12

Wisdom
2.12-20: 138

Sirach
47.14-21: 138

Isaiah
7.15-16: 155
9.5: 98
10.17: 188
43.1: 170

Jeremiah
38.2-3: 170

Ezekiel
1.1-27: 187-89

Books of the New Testament

Matthew
7.7: 192
15.11: 147
24.15: 189

Mark
4.3-8: 106
12.41-44: 95

Luke
7.35: 189
10.30-37: 125
15.11-32: 123-24
16.8: 189
23.35: 159

John
1.12: 43
10.3: 192
17.12: 189

Acts
2.24: 158, 159
2.31: 160
3.8: 74

5.1-11: 74
5.15: 74
7.22: 47
9.15: 72
13.37: 160
15.22,28: 150
17.28: 60

Romans
  1.14: 108
  1.23-25: 156
  7.10: 160
  11.17-24: 106
  14.17: 131

1 Corinthians
  1.23: 160
  2.9: 43
  2.11: 187
  3.15: 188
  3.18: 169
  6.13: 147
  9.22: 62
  9.24-26: 159

2 Corinthians
  6.14: 167

Galatians
  1.16: 53

Ephesians
  2.3: 189
  2.4: 163
  2.12: 169
  5.5-13: 148

Philippians
  2.6-7: 157, 161

1 Thessalonians
  4.13: 169

1 Timothy
  6.10: 172

2 Timothy
  4.7-8: 159

Hebrews
  1.3: 54
  3.14: 192
  12.2: 157

Revelation
  22.5: 125

www.ingramcontent.com/pod-product-compliance
Lightning Source LLC
Chambersburg PA
CBHW032034290426
44110CB00012B/806